D1474123

Fair Governance

Fair Governance

Paternalism and Perfectionism

F.H. BUCKLEY

OXFORD
UNIVERSITY PRESS

OXFORD
UNIVERSITY PRESS

Oxford University Press, Inc., publishes works that further Oxford University's objective of excellence in research, scholarship, and education.

Oxford   New York
Auckland   Cape Town   Dar es Salaam   Hong Kong   Karachi   Kuala Lumpur   Madrid   Melbourne
Mexico City   Nairobi   New Delhi   Shanghai   Taipei   Toronto

With offices in
Argentina   Austria   Brazil   Chile   Czech Republic   France   Greece   Guatemala   Hungary   Italy
Japan   Poland   Portugal   Singapore   South Korea   Switzerland   Thailand   Turkey   Ukraine
Vietnam

Copyright © 2009 by Oxford University Press, Inc.

Published by Oxford University Press, Inc.
198 Madison Avenue, New York, New York 10016

Oxford is a registered trademark of Oxford University Press
Oxford University Press is a registered trademark of Oxford University Press, Inc.

Library of Congress Cataloging-in-Publication Data

Buckley, F. H. (Francis H.), 1948-
    Fair governance : paternalism and perfectionism / Francis H. Buckley.
      p. cm.
    Includes bibliographical references and index.
    ISBN 978-0-19-534126-3 ((hardback) : alk. paper)
1. Paternalism. 2. Akrasia. 3. Perfectionism (Personality trait)
I. Title.
    JC571.B763 2009
    172—dc22

                                               2008037360

1 2 3 4 5 6 7 8 9

Printed in the United States of America on acid-free paper

Note to Readers
This publication is designed to provide accurate and authoritative information in regard to the subject matter covered. It is based upon sources believed to be accurate and reliable and is intended to be current as of the time it was written. It is sold with the understanding that the publisher is not engaged in rendering legal, accounting, or other professional services. If legal advice or other expert assistance is required, the services of a competent professional person should be sought. Also, to confirm that the information has not been affected or changed by recent developments, traditional legal research techniques should be used, including checking primary sources where appropriate.

(Based on the Declaration of Principles jointly adopted by a Committee of the American Bar Association and a Committee of Publishers and Associations.)

You may order this or any other Oxford University Press publication by visiting the Oxford University Press website at www.oup.com

For Esther and Sarah

Contents

Preface

Till through wise handling and fair governance, I him recured to
a better will.
Edmund Spenser, The Faerie Queene II.i.54

THE FAERIE QUEENE, one of the longest and least read poems in the English language, is an allegory of the contest between virtue and vice. Virtue wins, but not before vice's charms are laid bare, and Spenser's tribute to self-restraint, temperance, and chastity remains one of the most sensual poems in the English canon. This serves Spenser's dramatic purposes since the struggle to be virtuous would not be heroic unless the hero were severely tempted, nor would the virtuous lesson beguile the reader were vice's smiling face obscured.

Spenser's Las Vegas is the Bower of Bliss, a garden of every sexual delight, ruled by the enchantress Acrasia, whose name means "Unruled." Acrasia is a temptress, beautiful and passionate, who enthralls men with her charms. "Her bliss is all in pleasure, and delight, wherewith she makes her lovers drunken mad" (II.i.51).

To her Bower comes Guyon, the knight of temperance. Guyon is tempted, as any of us would be. He is torn between good and evil counselors—really two parts of himself. The good counselor is a palmer or pilgrim, who represents Guyon's conscience; while the evil counselor is Genius, the tempter within each of us. Between these two, Guyon must struggle (his name means "wrestler"). He rejects Genius' offer of wine, an offer which is repeated by the lovely Excess, who is clad in revealing, disordered robes.

In her left hand a cup of gold she held,
And with her right, the riper fruit did reach,
Whose sappy liquor, that with fullness swelled,
Into her cup she squeezed
That so fair winepress made the wine more sweet. (II.xii.56)

Guyon presses on, past naked ladies gamboling in a stream and singing an intensely erotic song:

> *Ah! see the virgin rose, how sweetly she*
> *Doth first peep forth with bashful modesty,*
> *That fairer seems the less ye see her may!*
> *Lo! see, soon after how more bold and free*
> *Her bare bosom she doth broad display;*
> *Lo! See soon after how she fades and falls away! (II.xii.74)*

Not surprisingly, Guyon falters for a moment, "and somewhat began [to] relent his earnest pace, His stubborn breast began secret pleasures to embrace" (II.xii.65). But Guyon fights off the temptation, finds Acrasia on her bed of roses, and casts a net over her. He destroys the Bower and releases her lovers, who had been transformed into beasts.

That's all very well, but are we really quite sure we want to see all our Bowers of Bliss destroyed? Not every lover is happy to be released from Acrasia's captivity. One of them, Grille, steps forward to complain that he would rather remain a hog and indulge in his animal appetites. A bad choice, but let him be, Spenser tells us. "Let Grille be Grille, and have his hoggish mind" (II.xii.87).

Spenser described the battle for self-control to which each of us is called. Like Guyon, we are asked to rise heroically above our passions. We do not do so by hiding from the world, like a monk. Instead, we must go forth into the world and encounter temptations. Like the knight, we should arm ourselves with good counsel and the good habits which, when accumulated, make up a good character. We will encounter Bowers of Bliss but must break them down only after we land on them, not before.

This book describes a further way in which we might fend off temptations by removing them from our path through legal means. We might ban the Bowers of Bliss and proscribe the beds of roses. Occasions of sin might be made criminal, and those who succumb to temptation fined. This is the strategy of *paternalism*, which supplants the self-control devices the subject might employ on his own. The paternalist restricts our choices, not to harm us but to make us better off.

We are apt to regard the paternalist as an officious Puritan who sees himself as commanding the moral heights and legislating for weak and foolish subjects beneath him. Such suspicions are justified when the paternalist's expression of sympathy for the weak-willed masks the voyeur's lascivious interest in vice or the hypocrite's desire for personal advantage. Were we to imagine that the paternalist's motives are always pure and his rules well chosen, we would commit what economist Harold Demsetz called the "Nirvana fallacy" of comparing fallible real world people with infallible idealized paternalists.[1]

We are not so naïve as that. Nevertheless, to give the paternalist his due, we should ask whether his subjects might willingly embrace the fetters themselves, in their own self-interest. We might want to encourage ourselves to stop drinking by making alcohol more expensive. Or we might want to ensure that we won't touch hard drugs by making them illegal. If every person wanted the fetters imposed on him, then the case for paternalism would seem compelling.

Part I of this book examines the justifications offered for paternalistic fetters on individual choice. Older versions of paternalism drew a distinction between the paternalist and an inferior class of subjects whose choices he circumscribed, such as children and the mentally incapable. A newer paternalism, which draws its support from empirical studies of cognitive errors and weakness of the will, would restrict everyone's choices. Examples of this kind of paternalism include mandatory pension laws which force us to save and which address our bias for present over future pleasures. We might remove bad choices by outlawing them or by strengthening the incentives to resist them. Other possible justifications for restrictions on choice are based on informational handicaps or the ways in which laws might shape what we desire.

Part II then discusses *perfectionism*, which would fetter our choices when these are immoral. (There's a certain amount of jargon here, which we'll try to keep to a minimum.) Perfectionism partially overlaps with paternalism, but the two are quite different. While paternalism overrules individual choices because they are inconsistent with the subject's deep preferences, perfectionism restricts choices because they are simply bad. The paternalist would nudge the subject toward choices which reflect his true desires, while the perfectionist would ban immoral choices, whatever the subject's preferences might be. I distinguish further between a *private perfectionism* that seeks to reform the subject himself from a *social perfectionism* that seeks to protect people whom the subject might influence by his behavior.

Some of the arguments in this book were also made in Just Exchange (Abington: Routledge, 2005); and portions of the book were adapted in part from several of my articles: *When the Medium is the Message: Corporate Buybacks as Signals*, 65 Indiana L.J. 493 (1990); *Three Theories of Substantive*

Fairness, 19 Hofstra L. Rev. 33 (1991); *The American Stay*, 3 S. Calif. Interdisciplinary L.J. 733 (1993); *The American Fresh Start*, 4 S. Calif. Interdisciplinary L.J. 67 (1994); *Culture and Liberty*, 19 Quinnipiac L. Rev. 665 (2000); and *Liberal Nationalism*, 48 U.C.L.A. L. Rev. 221 (2000). (All Internet searches were performed in June 2008.)

For their comments and assistance, I am indebted to Tyler Cowen, Gerd Gigerenzer, Charles Goetz, Christophe Jamin, Alan Charles Kors, Bertrand Lemennicier, Jeremy Rabkin, Ilya Somin, Todd Zywicki, and James Q. Wilson. The book was written with the assistance of the George Mason Law & Economics Center, to which I am grateful, the more so as I am its director. I am thankful to its staff, to Pamela Ryon Entsminger, Jeff Smith, and John Giacomini. I am also grateful to Dean Dan Polsby, and to Deborah Keene and Rae Best at the George Mason University Law Library. For their useful comments, I am indebted to workshop participants at Aix-Marseille, Paris-II and the American Enterprise Association, and to students at George Mason University School of Law and Sciences Po. It was a delight to work with the very helpful people at Oxford University Press, and I owe special thanks to Chris Collins, Isel Pizarro, Sarah Bloxham, and Viswanath Prasanna.

Finally, Esther Goldberg read each draft of the book closely and gave invaluable comments and editorial assistance, and I owe her more than I can say.

PART I

Voluntary Servitude

WHAT VICE, OR RATHER what unhappy vice, to see an infinite number of people, not merely obeying but serving . . . a single person. . . . Should we call this cowardice? When a thousand, a million men, a thousand cities, fail to protect themselves against the domination of one man, this cannot be called cowardly, for cowardice does not sink to such a depth. . . . What monstrous vice, then, is this which does not even deserve to be called cowardice, and for which no name is vile enough.

Étienne de la Boétie, De la servitude volontaire ou contr'un

ONE

Paternalism and Perfectionism

There is nothing so very blessed in merely doing as one likes.

Matthew Arnold, Culture and Anarchy

LARRY FLYNT IS A MAN with a mission. The publisher of *Hustler* magazine, with its explicit photographs of people having sex, sees himself as a defender of liberty. When prosecuted for obscenity, Flynt saw the broader implications of the case.

> Though many view him only as a purveyor of porn, Flynt says he cares passionately about the Constitution and particularly the First Amendment. "I first became involved with the First Amendment when I was sentenced to 25 years in prison for conveying sexual expression."[1]

Antiporn laws went the way of the dodo even before the rise of Internet porn. However, there are still a great many activities that are banned or regulated by the government. There's yet another set of activities which, while not banned, are made more costly by government disincentives or made more attractive by government subsidies. Here's a very partial list or things banned, regulated or subsidized, all of which raise questions about the proper scope of government and the legitimate right of individual choice and self-expression.

- Smoking marijuana
- Drinking alcohol when one is under 21
- Driving a car when intoxicated
- Being nude in public
- Getting married
- Saving money in a pension plan

What all these have in common is that the state interferes with our choices, and that is the subject of this book.

For liberals, the perennial problem of political philosophy is when state interference with our choices is justified. Liberals start with a presumption in favor of liberty, of letting people choose for themselves.[2] Ordinary preferences or desires are deemed to be clothed with moral dignity, just because they are *our* choices. Those who deny this, who think our preferences unworthy of respect, might be called antiliberals. For them, restrictions on choice are untroubling. What people want doesn't much matter.

So defined, Larry Flynt is a liberal. But so too are a great many of us. Indeed, I'd suggest that nearly everyone is a liberal. If I want to distinguish between liberals and antiliberals, it's only to describe what just about all of us believe in.

Notice that I use the term "liberal" in a special way here. What I don't mean are left-liberals, the Move-On activist and the academic progressive. And I'm not necessarily referring to conservatives when I speak of antiliberals. As I use the terms, liberalism and antiliberalism don't connect with current political labels. Liberals might be right-wing libertarians such as Grover Norquist, who want to shrink the state down to a size where you can drown it in the bathtub. But they might also be left-wing progressives who want to expand the role of the state. And while antiliberals might be social conservatives who seek to promote a single idea of the good, they might also be Marxists who believe that our preferences are based on a "false consciousness" that does not reflect our true interests and that the dictatorship of the proletariat might legislate for them whether they like it or not.

The term "liberal" has also been appropriated by political philosophers to describe their own, not uncontentious, theories. For example, Ronald Dworkin's liberalism is founded on equality rights that demand prima facie equal respect for all preferences. Dworkin argues that, for liberals, the state should be neutral as between different conceptions of the good life because it would not treat people as equals if it preferred one person's conception of the good over that of another.[3] We'll look more closely at Dworkin's views in Chapter 9. For the moment, I note only that I use the term in a different and older sense, to refer to the respect to be accorded to individual choices.

As liberals, we don't make a fetish of choosing. We are not asked to shop till we drop. The shopaholic might in fact enjoy shopping, but people like me who hate shopping will do so as little as possible, and there's nothing wrong with that. What matters is not whether we shop, but whether shopping makes us better off. So there's something more basic than exercising a right to choose, and that is satisfying our desires or preferences. And while there might be an occasional mismatch between what we prefer and what we choose, we are nevertheless best able to satisfy our preferences when we are free to choose for ourselves. This is the distinctive claim of modern liberalism.

Premoderns saw things differently. For Thomas Aquinas, freedom was not about satisfying preferences, which might be good, bad or indifferent. Instead, freedom was the freedom to do good. People who did evil were not exercising their freedom but instead revealing a character defect. So long as moral choices are not fettered, a person is free. We are free when we are permitted to attend church and not free when we are prevented from doing so. We are also free when hard drugs are made illegal. That's not how we moderns tend to think of freedom. For us, freedom means the right to make either good or bad choices, so long as no one is harmed except ourselves.

Some see themselves as more up-to-date still than the moderns, and call themselves postmoderns. Like the premoderns, postmoderns discount the value of people's preferences. For postmoderns, what matters is not whether something is preferred, but *what* is preferred. The simple fact that something is desired doesn't cut it. And it's not just that preferences don't count. It's that political theories built upon preference satisfaction—economics, "consumerism," political liberalism—are built ignobly upon a base foundation. Free contracting permits people to satisfy their preferences? What's so good about that?

What distinguishes liberalism from antiliberalism is that, for liberals, preferences deserve prima facie respect whatever their content might be. When asked whether a person should be permitted to do x, liberals think it a sufficient answer that he prefers to do x, unless it can be shown that the option deserves to be banned. By contrast, antiliberals deny that preferences have moral status in themselves. First you see what the person wants, then you decide if this counts.

In more technical language, liberals regard preferences as prima facie content independent, while antiliberals see them as content dependent.[4] If content dependent, the value of a preference depends solely upon its content, upon what is preferred; if content independent, the preference is accorded respect without regard to what is preferred because of the positive value which attaches to personal autonomy. For antiliberals, my preference for x has moral significance only because x was all along a good thing to do. The fact that I chose it doesn't do anything in itself. At best, it certifies the existence of a prior duty. I should be permitted to give to charity not because my choice should be respected but because that is what I ought to do. This assumes a deeply illiberal world, thick with background duties, where everything that is not required might be prohibited.

If antiliberalism might be all duty, liberalism is not the absence of duties. Liberalism should not be confused with an ethical nihilism that denies the possibility of moral discourse. Instead, liberalism is an explicitly moral doctrine because it condemns unjustified restrictions on free choice as wrongful. Liberalism must also be distinguished from a moral hedonism that would permit a person to satisfy all his preferences. Some of the things we want are harmful to others and might be legally banned. What liberals do assert is that, as a prima facie matter, preferences deserve our respect. Where they don't, where we should restrict people's choices, is the subject of this book.

All this might seem like a distinction without a difference. Liberals and antiliberals would both ban certain choices. Both would subscribe to some degree of *paternalism*, under which the state is permitted to interfere with a person's choices with the goal of making him better off. But the important difference between them is that liberals would resist a thick paternalism that restricts all choices; while antiliberals would deny any moral status to personal preferences and, therefore, could not object to the most extensive paternalism. Only liberals may participate in the debate about the proper scope of paternalism.

To be sure, real antiliberals are few in number, and just about everyone wants some kind of paternalism. Paternalists of the right might ban sexually immoral contracts, while paternalists of the left might concentrate their ire on transgender inequality. We are, nearly all of us, paternalists on some issues and not others. That is, we are nearly all liberals, which in turn means that we believe that people should be permitted to do what they like unless there are supervening reasons for paternalism. The presumption is always in favor of liberty, and it is the paternalist who must justify the interference.

I want to sidestep a number of vexing problems of moral philosophy. This is a book about politics, not moral theory, and I don't want to claim that morality is simply about preference satisfaction. In particular, life is more than just maximizing pleasures. In a famous thought-experiment, Robert Nozick asked us to imagine an "experience machine" to which we're hooked up and which gives us more pleasure than we could ever have without it.[5] The catch is that we'll be unconscious the whole time, and that once hooked up, we can't escape from the machine. We'd think we were making a friend or reading a great book. We wouldn't have a life, but we'd be tricked into thinking we were living one. Given the choice, then, would we be willing to be hooked up? The question answers itself. Life is more than about pleasure.

Because none of us would prefer to be hooked up to the experience machine, Nozick's thought-experiment is not a telling objection to the idea of preference satisfaction. We prefer to live our own lives, and don't need a paternalist to ban experience machines. However, other objections are more troubling. Preference satisfaction is a subjective standard: it's about what each individual wants. But perhaps some goods should be pursued whether a person desires them or not. This is an objective, not a subjective, standard. The basic goods will include such things as family life, close friends, a sense of accomplishment, laughter, play, and good health. We'll look at this question more closely in Chapter 6, but at the risk of giving away the ending, I don't think that objective standards make a strong case for overruling people's choices.

🎢 Interfering with Individual Choice

This part of the book takes its title from Montaigne's friend, Étienne de la Boétie, and his essay on human bondage. Both men knew something about how one person might surrender himself to another. When Montaigne asked himself why he loved la Boétie, he answered "because it was him; because it was me." That's more than understandable. What did not make sense to la Boétie was the voluntary surrender of oneself to one's political masters. There were so few of the king's men in France, so few musketeers. And yet they held an entire country in subjection. And so, la Boétie concluded, the king's subjects had to be complicit in their subjection. But why would they accept this?

Paternalism suggests an answer to la Boétie's question: the paternalist restricts choices to make the subject better off, and because of this, the subject might willingly accept the paternalist's guidance. Suppose I knew that for decisions made at home on Thursday afternoon (or at a bar on Saturday night), I would inevitably go wrong and regret my choice. My freedom to choose would then be self-defeating. And where I will systematically make poor choices as compared with those the paternalist would make for me, I might willingly surrender a portion of my freedom in the tainted class where I would choose unwisely, even as the king's subjects might yield up their liberties to him if pure freedom came down to mere anarchy.

Not every restriction on individual choice constitutes paternalism or aims to make the subject better off. There are at least six nonpaternalistic arguments for fetters on choice, based on (a) distributional concerns, (b) egalitarian rights, (c) positional theories, (d) collective choice concerns, (e) externalities, and (f) perfectionism. We will spend some time on (d), a good deal of time on (e) and (f), and list (a) through (c) simply to dispose of them here.

Distributional Concerns

The distributional case for restrictions on personal liberty proposes mandatory transfers of wealth to a deserving class of recipients, generally from rich to poor, and typically through taxation and welfare benefits. More broadly, theories of distributional justice would evaluate legal rules according to their effect on the favored class ("Is it good for the Belgians?"). Most people agree that the state should distribute resources from the rich to the poor, which provides a reason to impose a tax burden on the former. This is generally not regarded as a fetter on free choice—but try to tell that to people who pay their taxes and can't buy what they would in a world without taxes.

It is sometimes thought that the liberal assumes that the background distribution of assets is fair and that readjusting for differences in wealth is not needed. That might be true for a certain kind of (libertarian) liberal, but most liberals would reject this. They would recognize that the set of existing property rights might be unfair and would agree to a reshuffling of assets, through tax and welfare laws. But apart from that, the liberal might resist fetters on choice. He might concede the point about distributional justice without yielding anything else to the paternalist. He might draw a sharp distinction between the public law of taxes and welfare benefits on the one hand, and the private law of free contracting on the other.

Egalitarian Rights

The 1964 Civil Rights Act banned discrimination in hotels, apartments, and even boarding homes. At the time, some thought this an unwarranted restriction on free choice, especially when it came to Mrs. Murphy's desire for all-Hibernian boarders. Since then, however, most people have come to accept these restrictions as reasonable limits on bargaining freedom because of the egalitarian ends they serve. By banning discrimination, even private discrimination in housing, they promote racial justice, that all citizens are to be treated with equal respect. How far such restrictions might extend, beyond racial, religious, and gender discrimination, remains a matter of controversy, but the broad principle that our choices might legitimately be fettered to promote a more egalitarian society is generally conceded.

Positional Theories

On positional theories, duties are imposed through birth or some characteristic not of one's choosing. A Frenchwoman might owe duties to *la patrie*, a son to his family, and a Catholic to his birth religion; and these qualities restrict his freedom of choice. What fetters our freedom is the position we occupy, whether we chose it or not.

Positional theories suffer from their association with Sir Robert Filmer and his patriarchal theory of how we owe allegiance to kings. Filmer argued that kings are the direct descendents of Adam and are thus the fathers of their people. Patriarchalism is easily ridiculed and did not survive the drubbing it took from John Locke. "Glib nonsense" was how Locke described Filmer's divine right of kings. However, positional theories are not so easily dismissed. The claim by environmentalists that we owe duties to the earth is, in its most plausible form, an assertion of positional duties owed to future generations. Those who are alive today are caretakers, with a duty to those who come after us not to despoil the environment. The same is true of our duties to God, through whom we owe duties to the earth. "The earth is the Lord's, and the fulness thereof" (Psalms 24:1). We are born into such duties. We are tangled up in them, whether we like it or not, and are not entirely free to cast them off.

Nonvoluntary positional duties must be distinguished from duties which attach to freely chosen positions. No one is forced to be president of the United States; but to become president, a person must swear an oath to perform certain duties. This is not a fetter on his freedom, as the obligations are freely assumed. Similarly, a person who enlists in an army has surrendered a portion of her liberty; but, as she chose to do so, she is not made less free by enlisting. Just the opposite. Barriers to enlistment or to long-term commitments would represent a restriction on his liberty. I am less free when I am not permitted to join the army.

Collective Choice Concerns

What remains are the three nonpaternalist explanations for interfering with personal preferences that we'll examine in detail. The collective choice argument for fetters on choice is based on a divergence between the self-interest of individuals and the interests of the same people when in groups. The classic example of this is the well-known prisoners' dilemma game, where the parties are collectively best off when they cooperate with each other but are individually better off when they don't do so. For example, bargainers are collectively better off when they all cooperate by performing their promises. What this means is that, if you add up the gains of the two parties together, they'll do better if both perform than they would if one performs and the other doesn't. However, an individual bargainer will do best if he performs and the other doesn't—if he gets the goods and doesn't pay for them, or if he gets the purchase price and doesn't give up the goods. The problem is that when everyone expects the other party to breach, no one will perform and the benefit of the bargain will be lost to both parties. The buyer won't buy and the seller won't sell. So both parties will be better off if they can bind themselves to perform through contracts enforceable in a court of law, as we'll see in Chapter 5.

Externalities

The economist's externalities are the spillover effects that personal choices have on third parties. These might be positive (where we confer a benefit) or negative (where we impose a burden) on the third party. Positive externalities—the inventor who patents a new drug that saves the lives of others—quite obviously should be encouraged and not fettered. However, the costs that negative externalities impose on third parties might supply a reason to restrict individual choices. I should not be permitted to emit pollution that harms my neighbors, nor should I be allowed to rob and kill to get my way.

This supplied John Stuart Mill with what he thought was the only justification for fetters on choice, in his 1859 *On Liberty*. "The sole end for which mankind are warranted, individually or collectively, in interfering with the liberty of action of any of their number is self-protection," said Mill. We might interfere with your choices to protect others, not to protect you. Harm-to-others is what matters, not harm to oneself. "The only purpose for which power can be rightfully exercised over any member of a civilized community, against his will, is harm to others. His own good, either physical or moral, is not a sufficient warrant."[6]

When Mill spoke of harm-to-others, what he had in mind was physical harm. Making contract killings illegal is not a restriction on liberty and instead preserves the intended victim's liberty. What Mill didn't mean by harm-to-others was the moral or social harm a person might impose on others through his bad example. When I transgress, I injure not only myself but also those whom I influence. For Mill, there was a bright line between the two kinds of harm, but as we'll see in Chapter 9, it's hard to draw a principled distinction between them.

Perfectionism

The perfectionist would overrule individual choices when these are immoral. Such theories, which are as old as Plato, assume that the state in its role as a perfectionist has a privileged view of the good and a duty to reform people, whether they want it or not. Perfectionism was the chief target of Mill's libertarianism, and though his views have largely triumphed, perfectionism is now enjoying a revival. Millian objections to state-enforced morality were more compelling during the Victorian era when societal restrictions on liberty were more extensive. When these restrictions are relaxed, in the liberal societies of today, a modest perfectionism is less offensive, and modern perfectionists such as George Sher who propose only minimal constraints on behavior are more persuasive.[7]

✹ Paternalism and Perfectionism

Paternalism and perfectionism often overlap (see Figure 1.1). When my deepest preferences are moral and my choices are immoral, restrictions on choice might amount to paternalism as well as perfectionism. The paternalist vindicates my deepest desires by shielding me from self-destructive behavior; and the perfectionist enforces morals by eliminating immoral choices. Criminalizing hard drugs might thus be an example of both paternalism and perfectionism. However, these are separate categories. Perfectionism does not overlap with paternalism where the restrictions on choice satisfy a person's deepest wishes without advancing a moral goal. For example, suppose that a cognitive error prevents me from taking out the amount of insurance I'd really like to have, and let's stipulate that this wouldn't advance a moral goal. Interfering with my choices would then amount to paternalism but not perfectionism.

I'll return below to differences between the two arguments for fettering choices. For now, I note that I define perfectionism broadly to include every

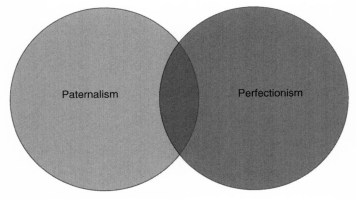

FIGURE 1.1 Paternalism and Perfectionism

moral injunction about how we ought to live. Moderns tend to define morality more narrowly, as concerned only with duties to others. We are immoral when we harm another, by hurting him or damaging his property. The older sense of morality was more expansive and referred to the ways in which an individual should act to extract happiness and joy from life. This might include appreciating good music and art, making close friends, worshiping God, or doing any of the countless things that make life worth living. Perhaps we have returned to that, with the current fetish about taking exercise, avoiding trans fats, and being slim.

John Stuart Mill captured the difference between the two senses of morality in his response to the mental breakdown he suffered when he was twenty. Mill had adopted his father's Benthamite moral code and supported the political reforms needed to promote the greatest happiness for the greatest number. That was all about other people, not oneself. Mill had assumed that were such reforms enacted he would be made happy. But then he realized, of a sudden, this was not so. "Suppose that all your objects in life were realized," he asked himself,

> that all the changes in institutions and opinions which you are looking forward to, could be completely effected at this very instant: would this be a great joy and happiness to you?" And an irrepressible self-consciousness distinctly answered, "No!" At this my heart sank within me: the whole foundation on which my life was constructed fell down.

In the end, Mill's depression lifted, but not through any political reform. Instead, it was the joy of music that brought him around (Carl Maria von

Weber's banal *Oberon*, of all things). Political reform could not satisfy Mill's desire for happiness, and a sterile Benthamite sense of duty to others could not suffice as a moral code. Mill needed something more, something that made life worth living, found in music and poetry. Some pleasures, he concluded, mattered more than others. Mill tried to express this difference in *Utilitarianism*, where he sought to reconcile Benthamite principles with his discovery of the qualitative difference in pleasures. I shall not pause to ask whether he succeeded. The deeper question is whether we ought to distinguish between different qualities of pleasure, between reading poetry and playing solitaire on the computer and, if so, whether this provides an argument for interference with individual choice. We'll take this up again in Chapter 9.

I evaluate arguments for paternalism and perfectionism by examining their consequences. Many libertarians argue that freedom or personal autonomy is an absolute and foundational good and that other goods are of instrumental value: they are not good in themselves except insofar as they promote freedom. For most of us, and particularly for consequentialists who weigh moral choices according to their consequences, this is exactly backward: the end state matters more than how we got there, what is chosen more than how we choose. For consequentialists, freedom is an instrumental good and valuable only insofar as it promotes desirable consequences. A bad choice is not made much better because it's a free choice.

This is not to say that consequentialists are indifferent to the quality of the choice. Our choices are means to an end, but as British philosopher Derek Parfit noted, "mattering as a means is a way of mattering."[8] The freely chosen ice-cream cone tastes better than the one forced on us, even if it's the same flavor. Free choices promote a sense of well-being by reducing the hostility and mistrust produced by coercion. In a medical setting, a requirement of informed consent promotes a patient's self-esteem and sense of responsibility for her own recovery. Nevertheless, the possibility of bad choices must be troubling to the consequentialist. And to the chooser as well. Could he do so, he might willingly surrender his freedom to choose to the paternalist, where doing so will make him better off overall.

Soft and Hard Paternalism

Paternalism involves two people—the paternalist and his subject—and implies a special relationship between them: the paternalist imposes his choices upon the subject and does so with the intention of benefiting him.

The paternalist might be mistaken. His choices might leave the subject worse off. Even then, he is still a paternalist, just a bad one. Crucially, he must intend to benefit the subject by taking choices away from him. If he does not seek to make the subject better off, and is animated solely by a selfish desire to benefit himself, he is not a paternalist but an oppressor. Or he might simply be self-interested and not care about the subject. The insurance company that offers cheap coverage to nonsmokers gives people an incentive to reduce the risk of cancer; but as the insurer cares only for its profits, it is not a paternalist.

So defined, paternalism is something other than a merely economic relationship. In the past, some employers hired people for the long haul, with an implicit promise that they would be cared for when they were too old to work. The employees traded a lower salary for the security of lifetime employment. This was the subject of Robert Frost's *The Death of the Hired Man*, where a shiftless worker returns to his employer to die. He does so because it was part of their bargain that this was his home. "Home is the place where, when you have to go there, they have to take you in." This might be seen as one kind of paternalism. For my purposes, however, Frost was not a paternalist because the bargain was purely economic. He took the hired man in from of a sense of duty and not to satisfy the man's deep preferences.

Some fetters might be welcomed by the subject, others not, and this suggests another distinction between different kinds of paternalism. Where the restrictions on choice are ones the subject would welcome, we may speak of *soft paternalism*; while those she would resist constitute *hard paternalism*.[9] The difference is not in the laws but in the way the subject regards them. Guyon, the heroic knight who wrestles with his passions, might seek the aid of soft paternalism; but only a hard paternalism could rescue the obdurate Grille.*

Soft paternalism second-guesses a person's choices with the goal of giving effect to his true desires. Mental biases or errors cloud his judgment. He seeks to do right but miscalculates. Alternatively, his judgment is clear, but weakness of the will prevents him from reaching the desired end. Acrasia beckons and he cannot resist. In either case, soft paternalism seeks to satisfy the subject's deepest wishes, ones he would choose for himself in the cold light of day. But when his deepest desires are corrupt, when, like Grille,

---

* The terms are sometimes defined differently, with hard paternalism refering to outright bans on proscribed activities and soft paternalism to advertising campaigns or economic incentives to influence behaviour.

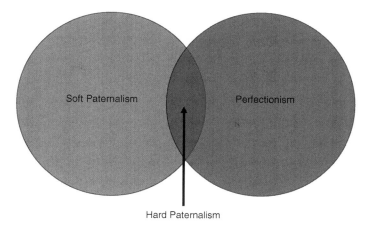

FIGURE 1.2 Soft and Hard Paternalism

he really pursues evil ends, soft paternalism is powerless against a clear-minded and resolute assertion of personal choice. In that case, only the hard paternalist might restrict a person's choices to enforce a vision of the good.

Hard paternalism is not as nice as soft paternalism and overrules a person's choices even when these represent her true wishes. For the hard paternalist, the problem is not that the subject is unable to identify and pursue her true preferences; instead, she has the wrong set of preferences and, like the swinish Grille, does not know what is good for him. In this kind of paternalism, the state enunciates a conception of the good life and frowns on choices that are inconsistent with it.

〽 Private and Social Perfectionism

As I use the term, perfectionism means the idea that the state should enforce morality.* Because he prescribes moral behavior, the hard paternalist is a perfectionist; and because he seeks to make the subject better off, he is a paternalist. The crucial distinction is therefore between soft paternalism

---

*   That's not the only way in which the term is used. Sometimes perfectionism is taken to refer to theories that define the good as the fulfillment of an idealized human nature. That's a theory of ethics, not political philosophy. It is concerned with how we should live, rather than whether the state should force us to live a particular way. In what follows, however, I see perfectionism as a political doctrine under which the state is entitled to promote its view of the good.

and perfectionism. The failure to distinguish between them has confused analysis and permitted the perfectionist to rely on appeals to deep preferences that only the soft paternalist may assert.

I refer to hard paternalism as *private perfectionism* to distinguish it from a different kind of perfectionism. Private perfectionism, as hard paternalism, seeks to correct the subject's corrupt choices and possibly to reform his character. By contrast, there is another kind of perfectionism, which I call *social perfectionism*. This does not constitute paternalism because its goal is not to reform the subject but to protect others from the spillover effects of his bad behavior.

What we do rubs off on other people. Good behavior provides a useful example for others and for this reason is celebrated and honored. The hero receives medals, the novelist acclaim, the inventor renown. Bad behavior also spills over and corrupts the innocent. The classroom bully invites us to share in his savage pleasures, the rake seduces his prey, the smoker offers us a cigarette. For these reasons, we should choose our companions carefully.

The social perfectionist gives up on the subject and seeks instead to protect those whom he might corrupt. We might be indifferent to Grille's fate but still seek to safeguard the moral welfare of third parties he might influence and society at large. In doing so, we must correct the subject's behavior, as he would otherwise continue to corrupt third parties. But that's only an instrumental goal. We're not really interested in Grille himself. And as the goal is not to rescue the subject, this is not a form of paternalism. However, as it seeks to enforce a theory of the good it is a form of perfectionism. To take an extreme example, when Socrates was condemned to death for corrupting the youth of Athens, the jury sought to protect the youth, not to reform Socrates.

Soft paternalism is enjoying a scholarly revival—less so hard paternalism and perfectionism. Arguments that the state should enforce morals would be laughed out of any law school workshop, but soft paternalism always gets a respectful hearing. The antiperfectionists who dominate the academy argue that the state should remain neutral as between competing theories of the good. Otherwise, we would privilege one person or group (or, worse still, one religion) over another, and this would be inconsistent with the duty to treat everyone equally.

Though perfectionism is regarded as an embarrassment in most academic circles, consistent antiperfectionists (called *neutralists*) are nevertheless rare. Conservatives have their perfectionist agenda, as do left-liberals. If the social conservative wants to enforce codes of sexual behavior, a very different set of

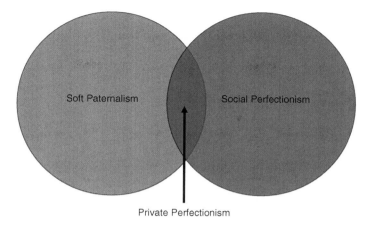

FIGURE 1.3 Private and Social Perfectionism

mores are enforced in the modern university, where "appeals to justice, prosperity, health and safety are clearly in, whereas appeals to high culture, salvation, and particular sexual moralities are out."[10] Just about everyone is a perfectionist on one issue or another.

In some cases, the state simply has to take sides. An individual might be personally agnostic on the subject of abortion. I don't have to have an opinion about it. But the state doesn't have the luxury of agnosticism here. It must either prohibit or permit abortion. Because it must protect human life, it must either treat the fetus as a person or not. And as the state can't be agnostic about abortion, neither can people who want the state to take sides on the issue. The conservative who wants to ban abortion and the left-liberal who wants to permit it must both be perfectionists, each with his own definition of life.

The case for neutralism is weaker than one might suppose. Neutralists sometimes suggest that those who would enforce morals seek to impose a Holy Fascism. "No one expects the Spanish Inquisition," said Monty Python; but some people expect it whenever they smell the brimstone of perfectionism. This is excessive, as not every theory is taken to the limit. The most prominent recent perfectionist, British jurist Patrick Devlin, argued for what he considered minimal restrictions on personal choice. Lord Devlin thought that legal intervention should respect the individual's privacy and should not be intrusive. It might in extreme cases ban private behavior that ordinary people would find shocking and that, if tolerated, would undermine the shared morality that holds society together. The goal is a commonsensical via media between illiberal moralizing and a strict neutralism.

Perfectionism should be reserved for the hardest cases; beyond that "[t]here must be toleration of the maximum individual freedom that is consistent with the integrity of society."[11] And this, thought Devlin, the common law did. We'll take up Devlin's perfectionism in Chapter 9.

The neutralist is most strongly opposed to perfectionism when it imposes criminal sanctions on immoral behavior. However, the perfectionist might prescribe a variety of lesser sanctions. These include administrative or civil sanctions that result in liability for monetary damages. We might not want to criminalize the expression of racial prejudice, but some of us might be willing to countenance civil actions by the victim in which moderate damages are awarded. There are still lesser remedies, such as the criminal or administrative sanction that has fallen into desuetude. In Virginia, for example, the Criminal Code makes adultery a misdemeanor. The provision is not enforced and would likely violate constitutional rights of privacy were prosecutors to do so. But it stands on the books, as a grim call to duty. Beyond this, some laws are merely hortatory, such as human rights codes to which no sanction for breach is attached. The neutralist might object that, toothless as they are, such laws nevertheless seek to influence behavior. To which the perfectionist will reply that that is the whole point. And so the issue is joined.

TWO

Hierarchic Paternalism

It is immensely moving when a mature man—no matter whether old or young in years—is aware of a responsibility for the consequences of his conduct and really feels such responsibility with heart and soul.

Max Weber, Politics as a Vocation

WHAT MOST OF US UNDERSTAND by paternalism is a special relation between two people, one of whom looks down on the other as incompetent to manage his affairs. The paternalist is the superior person who legislates for his less than capable subject. We'll call this kind of top-down relationship *hierarchic paternalism* because it divides people into different classes and assumes that the subject labors under a disability the paternalist does not share.

As his judgment is clouded, the wise subject would willingly surrender his will to the paternalist in such cases. With the benefit of full knowledge and calm deliberation, the subject would recognize that he is better off when he trades a miserable freedom for a happy servitude. Some defenders of slavery made just this argument before the Civil War; and not so long ago most men felt this way about restrictions on women's choices. No one would defend these today.

However, restrictions on children and the mentally incapable have persisted and with good reason. On reaching maturity, the child would welcome the fetters that prevented him from making disastrous choices at a time when she lacked the judgment to choose wisely for herself, and the same is true of the mentally incompetent whose competence returns.

I distinguish this kind of paternalism from one where we simply delegate choices to the expert. When I bring my car into the shop, I'll let the mechanic decide what to do, and provided it doesn't seem outrageous, I'll pay the bill at the end. The same is true when I visit my doctor. I might want to question him a little, but I am unlikely to second-guess him. This might turn into paternalism if the expert decides to keep a material fact from me "for my own good." The opinion of the expert would constitute paternalism, but I won't be dealing with this because the prevailing medical practice is that patients must be told the truth before they are asked to submit to any procedure.

%% Children

When I was fifteen, there was one thing that would make my happiness complete—a new Triumph TR-4 sports car in British Racing Green. The TR-4 was a real sports car, with all of the inconveniences of a Morgan and none of the conveniences. It didn't try to look snazzy, like a Lotus or an MGB, and it wasn't bulky like the subsequent TR-6 with its roll bar. Instead, the driver sat high in the car, seeing everything and visible to all. I had my mother halfway persuaded but my father vetoed the car. "Bloody Limey car," he said.

I still bear the psychic wounds of that episode. On the other hand, the wounds are merely psychic, unlike the physical wounds I might have suffered had I kept the car. Later, after I rolled the family car off a dirt road in the rain, and later still, when I drove it off a dead-end street, I had occasion to be thankful I wasn't driving a 2,000 pound sports car. Besides, by that time I had persuaded my parents that a Plymouth Sports Fury was a sensible family car.

To the extent that he wasn't motivated by his dislike of the English, my father had played the part of a paternalist. I'm glad he did, even if I resented it at the time. And at the time, many years ago, there were some adults who might have sympathized with me. They were called child liberationists, and they sought to empower children by opposing barriers to choice. I don't know how they felt about sports cars, but they weren't especially averse to risky behavior.

Child liberationism is a child of the 1960s, when the *New York Times* called children "the last minority" in the civil rights movement.[1] The demand for children's rights, fueled by a deep antipathy to paternalism, took its inspiration and rhetoric from anticolonialism, the struggle for racial equality, and feminism. Unless supervised by courts, parents might instill ill-informed and harmful beliefs about the shamefulness of nakedness and sexual touching. With girls, they might promote "feminine virtues."[2] The very idea of childhood was a social construct, founded not on mental incapacity but on a desire for subjugation by those in authority.[3] At the extreme, some child liberationists argued for a "right to alternate home environments," under which children could choose among a variety of arrangements, including twenty-four-hour child-care centers and children-operated residences. Others argued that children should be given full rights of sexual freedom and that the age of consent law be abolished.[4]

The children's rights movement received a boost from the 1959 United Nations Declaration of the Rights of the Child, which expanded the list of protected rights to include the right to education, housing, and playtime. A child should be raised "in a spirit of understanding, tolerance, friendship among peoples, peace and universal brotherhood, and in full consciousness that his energy and talents should be devoted to the service of his fellow men." These rights were expanded further by the 1989 U.N. Convention on the Rights of the Child, which included "the right of every child to a standard of living adequate for the child's physical, mental, spiritual, moral and social development."

From the start, the child liberation movement was beset with difficulties. First, children are manifestly less able to care for themselves than adults. They are ill informed about the choices open to them and, even if well informed, lack the capacity for long-range planning. Children also lack the self-control needed to invest in future opportunities by deferring present consumption. The problem with immediate gratification, my child used to think, is that it doesn't come fast enough. In addition, children's preferences are highly unstable, and today's future farmer might tomorrow become a future astronaut. Because their preferences are so capricious, children find it impossible to sustain the investments in education or training that long-range planning requires.

Second, many of the child liberationist's goals are simply too nebulous to count as rights. Parents should show love and warmth to their children and should raise them to become responsible, happy, moral adults.[5] These goods, of the greatest importance to children, cannot be specified with legal precision or made enforceable. It would be frightening to give a third party the power to take a child from its family because parents fail to satisfy vague standards of kindness and love. At best, children's rights might offer a minimal safety net when family bonds wholly fail, with children who are subjected to severe forms of abuse by their parents. However, this falls far short of the love and guidance that children need. What children need, more than rights, are loving parents, and this cannot be legislated.

A third difficulty is that the movement has served to shift control over children from parents to social workers, lawyers, and judges. As parental duties to children increased, so did the oversight by another set of paternal-ists. The modern children's rights movement is led by lawyers, serving as "children's advocates," and often in opposition to parents. A leading family law expert concludes that:

> Because so many children's advocates are distrustful of parent's treatment of their children, the judgments and decisions of parents are subject to an unprecedented degree of review by judges. As a result, the degree to which children's lives were subject to the control of the state because of the [early twentieth century] Progressives' efforts pales compared with what goes on today.[6]

Most child abuse cases don't involve real abuse but rather neglect, which is mostly a function of poverty. They frequently involve a poor single parent:

> Sometimes a child gets ill. . . . When a parent gets ill and a child gets ill, what does one do? You run out of food; it's cold out; you have to run to the store. But your child's got a fever and you can't bring your child with you. What do you do?[7]

The loss of parental control is troubling for a variety of reasons. Except in extreme cases, taking them from their parents is likely to leave children worse off. Too often, the real or imagined faults of parents are compared with an ideal world of super-competent social workers and lawyers who always know best. Judged by that standard, parents with traditional beliefs might lose their children to more progressive social workers, and the mother who spanks her child lightly could find herself hauled before a judge.

A Québec court recently provided an example of how an excessive con-cern for children's rights might weaken parental ties. A divorced father who had custody of his twelve-year-old daughter grounded her after she dis-obeyed his order that she stay off Internet chat rooms and after he discov-ered that she had posted inappropriate pictures of herself on an Internet dating site. The daughter ran off to her mother's house and successfully sued to be permitted to attend a three-day Grade VI field trip. The father reported that he was devastated by the ruling and refused to take his daughter back because he said he no longer had any control over her.[8]

As the likelihood of losing one's child increases, there comes a point where this weakens, not strengthens, family bonds, and further harms children. It is difficult enough to raise a child without worrying that a social worker might at any moment snatch her. The more that the relationship looks temporary, the less emotion parents will invest in it. An excessive concern for children's rights would also increase the cost of having children because parents would have to bear the emotional and legal costs associated with custody battles. This in turn would reduce family birth rates, which are already low.

A concern for parental rights also commends itself from a communitarian perspective. Communitarianism means several different things, but common to all is the idea that people live and thrive as members of a community and that communities deserve support for that reason. Now, communities are constituted by families, and family policies that impose across-the-board standards and ignore the real differences between diverse communities may greatly weaken them. Second-guessing the Amish who take their children from school at an early age would strike at the heart of a community that seeks to withdraw from the world.[9]

A final and related difficulty is that child liberationism suffers from an internal inconsistency: While employing the language of rights, child advocates often promote another form of paternalism. Children are to be accorded rights, but for the most part these are rights that children cannot waive and that might more accurately be described as duties. The movement is no less paternalistic when the child's "rights" cannot be exercised except by an agent on the child's behalf. Otherwise, married women who needed their husband's consent to buy and sell property had full contract and property rights before the Married Women' Property Act emancipated them, and one might be forgiven for wondering what the feminist movement was all about.

We are therefore presented with a choice between two kinds of paternalism: one where parents make choices on behalf of their children, and another where social workers, lawyers and judges make the choices. For my purposes, it is unnecessary to choose between them, as I wish only to insist that children cannot properly make such choices and that some form of paternalism is conceded.

One objection to paternalism, where children are concerned, is that the test of competence is arbitrary: has the person reached her eighteenth birthday? We assume that people under eighteen cannot govern themselves and that people over eighteen can do so. However, there are mature seventeen-year-olds and immature nineteen–year-olds. Like a sixty-five m.p.h. speed limit, the age of majority standard is both overinclusive and underinclusive. However, where the alternative is a case-by-case examination of dangerous driving or bargaining ability, a bright-line standard is the best we can do.

We settle on what the speed limit should be by determining when most people begin to drive safely; and we select the age to serve as the test of legal capacity by determining when most people are able to assume responsibility for their lives. Tailor-made rules that are fitted for each individual case would be costly to apply and subject to bureaucratic or judicial error, and these costs would be borne by people over eighteen. If a judge had to enquire into the competence of people over eighteen, some nineteen- and twenty-year-olds would be permitted to escape from contracts that, with the benefit of hindsight, turn out to be bad bargains. Because of this risk, they would find it difficult to find people to deal with them, and the imprecise standards would perversely fetter the freedom of true adults.

Child liberationism now seems a relic of the antinomian 1970s. We no longer hear calls for lowering the age of sexual consent. Instead, pedophiles are vigorously prosecuted for sex with minors and even for downloading child porn pictures off the Internet. We've also rolled back permissive drinking laws. Formerly, many states permitted eighteen-year-olds to drink, but a 1984 federal law increased the drinking age to twenty-one, in response to demands from Mothers Against Drunk Driving (MADD).

The cynic might note that child liberationism flourished at a time when my generation—the generation of vipers born just after World War II—remembered our own childhood and burned with resentment for the ills we suffered from parents and teachers. As we baby boomers approach retirement, our memories of childhood recede and new causes occupy our attention. The rights of the elderly, for example.

𝕸 The Mentally Incapable

The law of mental capacity has greatly changed over the last 100 years. Formerly, the test for capacity in criminal law was the very narrow *M'Naghten* standard: was the party "so deprived of his mental faculties as to be wholly, absolutely and completely unable to understand or comprehend the nature of the transaction."[10] If so, he might be acquitted of the crime by reason of insanity—and thereafter promptly locked up in a mental asylum. On that standard, very few people would be found insane. But when it came to involuntary committal in an asylum, it was relatively easy to lock someone up. The result was a narrow standard as a defense in criminal law and a broad standard for involuntary committal proceedings.

Today things are reversed. It is difficult to commit a person against his will to an asylum[11] but a lot easier for a person to set aside a contract or defend in a criminal case on grounds of mental capacity. In the twentieth century, the definition of incapacity in contract law expanded to reach the case of those who understood the nature of the transaction, but who labored under the compulsion of a mental disorder,[12] and even beyond this to cases of mental weakness or diminished mental capacity.[13]

However defined, there is no bright-line standard for mental capacity, as there is for children under eighteen. The merchant cannot card the mentally incapable, and might identify them only with difficulty or not at all. This will be especially problematical for merchants today because the modern definition of incapacity in contract law focuses upon the consumer's disability and not on the merchant's notice. As the possibility of honest mistake is greater, the merchant will be more reluctant to bargain with borderline cases. If he does, he can be expected to seek a premium price to compensate him for the greater risk that the contract won't be enforced. The expansion in protection never comes without a cost to its intended beneficiaries.

🦥 Slaves

When one passes from children and mentally incapable, a hierarchic paternalism that discriminates amongst classes of people according to race or sex is universally condemned. What is unjust, however, is not so much the paternalism but the invidious discrimination. Without paternalism, slavery would have been crueler still, which is not to say that the institution was anything other than monstrously unjust, or that southern planters treated their slaves kindly. However, the planters who really believed that slavery was a "providential trust,"[14] and that masters had moral duties to their slaves must have tempered their cruelty, unlike Harriet Beecher Stowe's race-hating overseer, Simon Legree. To view the slaveholder's paternalism as mere hypocrisy is to misunderstand his moral self image.

That doesn't make the paternalism much easier to swallow. The slaveholders' moral pretensions invite the ridicule they received in W.J. Cash's perceptive *The Mind of the South*:

To have heard them talk, indeed, you would have thought that the sole reason some of these planters held to slavery was love and duty to the black man, the earnest, devoted will not only to get him into heaven but also to make him happy in this world. He was a child whom somebody had to look after.[15]

The slaveholders are easy to condemn. However, they were not stupid, and in spokesmen such as George Fitzhugh they found intellectual champions of the first order. Fitzhugh is little remembered today, and was not a major figure even in his own time. He remains, however, one of the most articulate champions of antiliberalism. Current attacks on "neo-liberalism," on capitalism, free markets, free trade and globalization, whether from the right or left, largely repeat Fitzhugh's defense of the southern tradition at bay.

> Socialism proposes to do away with free competition; to afford protection and support at all times to the laboring class; to bring about, at least, a qualified community of property, and to associate labor. All these purposes, slavery fully and perfectly attains.[16]

What the slaveholder offered, said Fitzhugh, was a safety net that was wholly lacking in the industrialized north, where "wage slaves" worked harder, were paid less, and became destitute when they were too old to work.[17] Nor was there any element of fellowship and personal regard. The relation between northern employer and employee was purely economic, like that between Frost and his hired man. Employers were animated by acquisitiveness, and in such a society "virtue loses all her loveliness, because of her selfish aims."[18] By contrast, southern slaveholders were true paternalists, who cared for their slaves and who offered them a better economic bargain.

Like South Carolina Senator John Calhoun before him,[19] Fitzhugh offered an analysis of capitalism that was strikingly similar to that of Marx: a labor theory of value, where capitalists appropriated the surplus created by labor, a concentration of wealth in the hands of a few plutocrats, the fall of working class wages in industrial societies, class struggle, and the idea that factory workers were slaves. But while Marx welcomed the revolution that he thought would result, Fitzhugh saw slavery as an antidote to revolution. Southern slavery, with its paternalistic concern for the slave, was the only solution for class conflict, he thought.

At the bottom of every society, said Fitzhugh, was a "mud sill," like the raw earth at the bottom of a mansion, composed of people, white and black, who are incapable of anything other than the most menial responsibilities. This underclass (for Fitzhugh, fully 95% of the population) supports the small group on top to which a society looks for its culture, refinement, and progress. Where the underclass does not seek to rise above the mud sill, a civilization such as that of Greece or Rome may flourish. However, said Fitzhugh, this can happen only if the underclass's political rights are suppressed and a paternalistic safety net substituted in their place. The members of the underclass "have 'a natural and inalienable right' to be taken care of and protected, to have guardians, trustees, husbands, or masters; in other words, they have the natural and inalienable right to be slaves."[20] Thus, said Fitzhugh, the best thing a philanthropist can do is buy slaves.[21]

One might too easily regard the slaveholder's paternalism as a cynical device to suppress slave dissent and rebellion. Certainly the slaveholder's smug self-satisfaction is repellant. But there are things worse than paternalism, and one of them is Simon Legree's frank racial hatred and his whip. Paternalism imposes a moral discipline, for the paternalist must at a minimum believe that he is acting in the subject's best interests. For the slave, this is a moral victory, argued Eugene Genovese: "Paternalism's insistence upon mutual obligations—duties, responsibilities, and ultimately even rights— implicitly recognized the slaves' humanity."[22]

Many members of the patrician class in the south, before and after the Civil War, seem sincerely to have believed this, and "aristocrats" such as ex-Confederate General Wade Hampton could mount a serious campaign in 1876 for black votes and receive them. The Jim Crow laws that followed, with their segregated schools, trains, and restaurants, were the product not of aristocratic paternalists but of the populist bigots who succeeded them, such as the thuggish race-baiter, "Pitchfork Ben" Tillman.[23] While Hampton seems to have regarded the ex-slaves with a degree of respect and even affection, Tillman led the 1876 Hamburg Riot in which white farmers massacred blacks at will to strike terror and bring an end to Reconstruction.

This is not to defend the paternalism of the former slave owners. If there are things worse than paternalism, there are things a great deal better, notably the autonomy rights that the ex-slaves sought and that the aristocratic paternalists resisted. What the latter offered the ex-slave was a tepid concern and an implicit insurance contract in which black workers ceded political and economic rights in exchange for a very minimal safety net. They would be fed and offered very basic shelter, and when old might rely on an implicit promise that they would not be let go. The problem is that the former slaves had no choice in the matter. They were treated as second-class citizens in a racist state where the threat of violence was never entirely absent and where basic economic freedoms were denied them.[24]

𝄞 Women

Women also labored under paternalistic fetters until relatively recently. They were barred from working at dangerous jobs or from working as long hours as men. Before they could sell or buy property, they required the consent of their fathers or husbands. At marriage, a woman lost her capacity to contract. She had no separate legal personality, and marriage transferred everything she possessed to the control of her husband.

More subtly, tax laws continue to give women an incentive "to stay at home and bake cookies," in Hilary Clinton's memorable put-down of housewives. Housework has a significant economic value, but families are not taxed on the imputed income. However, an income tax is levied if a spouse takes a job outside the house, and no deductions are allowed for the maids and nannies that perform the services the housewife formerly provided. To add insult to injury, families are taxed as a unit on their income, so that two-income families find themselves in higher tax brackets than they would be if they divorced.

Nineteenth-century utilitarians, notably John Stuart Mill, championed the effort to remove the disabilities under which blacks and women suffered. As an economist, Mill recognized the costs that paternalistic restrictions impose, and his *On Liberty* remains the classic statement of antipaternalism. Mill condemned all state interference with individual choice where the sole intended beneficiary is the individual himself. Only harm-to-others could justify fetters on personal choice.

Mill's antipaternalism led him to embrace controversial political causes. He was a passionate abolitionist and one of the earliest feminists. His opponents, such as Thomas Carlyle, ridiculed Mill's concern for blacks and women. Carlyle was a leading Victorian intellectual, but even at the time his 1853 "Occasional Discourse on the N_____ Question" was remarkable for its frank expression of racial contempt. It is often thought that Carlyle's put-down of economics as the "dismal science" referred to the Malthusian belief (to which Mill did not subscribe) that the poor are condemned to starvation wages. In fact, what Carlyle condemned in his "N_____ Question" essay was the antislavery movement, which he said would produce "dark, extensive moon-calves, unnamable abortions, wide-coiled monstrosities, such as the world has not seen hitherto!"[25] What was dismal was not economics but Carlyle's racial hatred and opposition to emancipation.

Within the women's movement, early feminists shared Mill's goals of economic liberty and equality.[26] In the nineteenth century, antipaternalists such as Elizabeth Cady Stanton and Susan B. Anthony sought to remove legal obstacles to women's rights. Christina Hoff Sommers has labeled them as "equity" feminists, along with more recent feminists such as Justice Ruth Bader Ginsburg, who take aim at economic inequalities that prevent women from participating fully in a liberal society.[27] However, late-twentieth-century "gender" feminists abandoned economic liberalism and Mill's ideal of gender-neutral laws. "Radical and socialist feminists," writes Alison Jagger, "have shown that the old ideals of freedom, equality and democracy are insufficient."[28] Similarly, Frances Olsen argues that free contracting rights and antipaternalism might harm women "by encouraging an unrealistic faith in freedom of contract."[29] Olsen supports paternalism when she thinks it helps women (an eight-hour workday law) but not when it hurts them (barriers to women lawyers). Finally, in her introduction to an edition of Mill's *Subjection of Women* and Harriet Taylor Mill's *Enfranchisement of Women*, Kate Soper writes:

> What is likely to jar on today's [1983] readers, however, is the central argument of the essays, that sees the issue of female rights primarily in terms of the opportunity equality will allow for individually talented women to emerge to prominence and realize fulfillment. This is a theme in conflict with that strand of the contemporary women's movement, which stresses not the individual's right to compete, but the iniquity of the competition itself, and which appeals to a collective identity for women in their common struggle against the patriarchy.[30]

Fine sentiments. But the iniquity of competition, so far as women are concerned, was just what prompted the nineteenth-century paternalist to impose his patriarchy in the first place.

We seem to have come full circle, from paternalism to liberalism and back to paternalism. Though separated by an ideological chasm, the paternalism of twentieth-century gender feminists who question the value of freedom of choice is not entirely different from that of nineteenth-century antifeminists. We can draw similar parallels between nineteenth-century apologists for slavery who attacked free markets and free bargaining and the critical race scholars of our day who are no less suspicious of liberal ideals. The affinities between nineteenth- and twentieth-century paternalists were noted by Arthur Leff, who observed that "the benevolent have a tendency to colonize, whether geographically or legally."[31]

Hierarchic paternalism makes sense when it treats children as children and the mentally incapable as mentally incapable. Where it treats adults as children and distinguishes between a superior class of paternalists and an inferior class incapable of self-governance, paternalism has been employed to justify repressive institutions such as slavery and the subjugation of women. This explains the bad odor that surrounds paternalism today.

There is nevertheless a revival of interest in paternalism. However, unlike the hierarchic paternalism discussed in this chapter, the new paternalism would impeach everyone's judgment. It might draw the net more widely, but at least it does not discriminate. And to this egalitarian paternalism we now turn.

THREE

Cognitive Paternalism

I stumbled when I saw.

Shakespeare, King Lear

THE CURRENT REVIVAL OF PATERNALISM builds on an extensive literature in experimental psychology that challenges the idea that people always act rationally. "Rational choice" scholars assume that people have a fully specified set of stable preferences, consistent over time, and always prefer the greater to the lesser payoff. Such people would not seem to need many fetters on their choices. They can look after themselves. In experiments, however, people often appear to act irrationally. We make what seem to be computational errors.

- We might buy a lottery ticket because we overweigh small probabilities.
- We might violate the rules of probability theory and misjudge the likelihood of getting AIDS.
- If a coin came up heads five times in a row, we might expect it to come up tails next time.
- We're willing to spend a lot of money to save a dog that we don't know which is stranded on a ship adrift on the ocean but seem callous when it comes to spending money on human victims who aren't identified.

A new school of law-and-economics, called behavioral law-and-economics, takes these anomalies as a starting point and asks whether they might justify restrictions on individual choice. If we make computational errors about the risk of illness, perhaps regulatory rules should steer us straight and encourage frequent handwashing. If we are too optimistic about our retirement nest egg, perhaps tax laws should give us incentives to save our earnings. When we are biased in any of these ways, the unbiased paternalist might "de-bias" us by nudging us away from mental errors.

Just how rational are we, then? That depends on how we define rationality. If we mean the reasoning ability of an infinitely powerful computer, no one would be rational, so that can't be right. We need a standard of rationality in which nearly all of us are rational, nearly all of the time. Besides, we'd never want to emulate a computer in our daily lives. Even simple tasks, like looking across the room, would become impossible if we could not abstract from all the information we process. As it is, we can distinguish a large far away object from a small one close by, even if both project the same image on our retinas. We do this through unconscious geometrical calculations that incorporate an understanding of the structure of the world. We can frame a picture of a stable world that persists through our eye and bodily movements. We can also process out "floaters" and impedimenta that are found in our eye and that project on our retina.[1] We select what we need to make sense of the world and focus only on a small part of all we experience; beyond that, our instincts and patterns of perception and thought take over. Otherwise, we couldn't walk and chew gum at the same time.

We can drive down the highway with our minds occupied with plans and ideas and our instincts guiding the steering wheel. We arrive home on autopilot, without fully remembering how we got there. We never notice how our hunches guide us, not because we don't use them but because they work so well. We only notice how the hunch takes over when it leads us astray, where we drive to our familiar Safeway store without turning for the unfamiliar Whole Foods we had really meant to visit.

✺ Heuristics, Instincts, Emotions

Hunches are intellectual short cuts, and might be seen as *heuristics*. A heuristic device is a tool for learning, such as a teacher's prop; and judgment heuristics are the props or mental shortcuts we employ in all our decision making. They are the unreflective or even unconscious hunches, the pervasive and indispensable rules of thumb we employ when we see everything at a glance, when we infer from scattered bits of evidence. Without them, we could not move at all. The mental costs of concentration, information acquisition, information marshalling and evaluation, calculation and decision would paralyze us. To economize on all this, we rely upon judgment heuristics, preferring a rational irrationality to an irrational rationality, a wise ignorance to foolish learning.

Heuristic devices economize on information costs as well as calculation. It is costly to produce the information we need to get through life. Sometimes we need precise answers, but for the run-of-the-mill case precision is a luxury we can easily do without, and there our hunches serve us well. We can gauge how high a ceiling is without breaking out a measuring tape, and estimate Ted Williams's batting average without looking it up. Even if our hunches are sometimes in error, we would prefer to go with them if the cost of searching for better information exceeds the benefits.

The French mathematician Pierre Laplace assumed away information costs by positing an omniscient super-intelligence that, knowing everything there was to know and possessing limitless intelligence, could predict the future with certainty.[2] When Napoleon asked Laplace where God fit into his scheme, the mathematician answered "Sire, I have no need for that hypothesis." The only problem is that's not the world we live in.

Over time, our calculations may turn into *instincts*. We begin by working out the details of a complex decision, evaluating and weighing all possible outcomes, finally arriving at an overall best solution. When a similar problem arises in the future, the best outcome suggests itself naturally and immediately. Similarly, we feel an instinctive aversion to what resembles a bad choice from the past. Been there, done that. G.E. Hinton concludes that "people seem capable of taking frequently repeated sequences and eliminating the sequential steps so that an inference that was once rational becomes intuitive."[3]

Intuitions are instinctive judgments that seem immediately obvious and that seem to beckon us. Mario Bunge describes how scientific discoveries are often made through a quick inference that seems to integrate all prior knowledge into a grand vision.[4] We see it all at once and say "aha!" Or "eureka!" We accumulate a host of facts, but the last leap that gives us the answer seems to come from elsewhere, another part of our brain. As indeed it does. The left hemisphere of the brain accumulates knowledge and engages in analytical thinking; the right integrates it, places it in its proper context, takes account of nuance, nonverbal cues, and arrives at an overall decision.

Alexander Dumas portrayed the need for instincts in *The Man in the Iron Mask*, the sequel to *The Three Musketeers*. Truth be told, Porthos was never the sharpest knife in the drawer, and in the sequel, he flubs a very simple task. With his fellow musketeer, Aramis, Porthos is in a prison and surrounded by enemies. Aramis tells him to light a powder keg of gunpowder, throw it amongst their enemies, and then run for safety. That's three things, one more than Porthos can comprehend at any one time. He lights the fuse, throws the powder keg, and then is paralyzed into inaction. When the explosion comes, the prison walls collapse over Porthos and kill him. What he lacked, along with intelligence, was the simple instinct to run from danger.

Apart from heuristics and instincts, our *emotions* also economize on calculation costs. Paul Slovic's "affect heuristic" permits us to arrive at decisions swiftly when an argument "doesn't pass the smell test" or when our emotional state shuts down our calculations and brings us to a decision.[5] Our distaste for liars is both an aversion and a sense of the harm they impose upon us, with the emotion economizing on cost-benefit analysis. We don't have to calculate the harm—we simply know we don't like them. The distinction between feelings and calculation is often blurred, and many of our judgments are as much one as the other.

At times, a simple preference or aversion takes charge and tells us to stop calculating and get on with it. Our sense of boredom prompts us not to spend too much time at what seem like pointless tasks. We can estimate without calculating to the fifth decimal, and we don't need to know exactly how many stories a tall building is. We might spend an endless amount of time in search of the perfect mate, but falling in love tells us to stop. As does our mate. A friend of a friend decided to marry, but feared that the regular dating process offered too small a sample. So he set out to date a different woman each week for a year, after which he would make his choice. And as he was a rational choice economist, he explained what he was doing to every woman he dated. Curiously, the dates were less than satisfactory, until the fifth date, when the woman took pity on him and married him.

One of neurologist Anthony Damasio's brain-damaged patients illustrates the need for a stopping impulse. The patient lacked any sense of emotional commitment and spent inordinate amounts of time on trivial tasks. One day, Damasio asked him when their next session should take place.

> I suggested two alternatives dates, both in the coming month and just a few days apart from each other. The patient pulled out his appointment book and began consulting the calendar. . . . For the better part of a half-hour, the patient enumerated reasons for and against each of the two dates: Previous engagements, proximity to other engagements, possible meteorological conditions, virtually anything that one could reasonably think about concerning a simple date. . . . [H]e was now walking us through a tiresome cost-benefit analysis and endless outlining and fruitless comparison of options and possible consequences. [W]e finally did tell him,

quietly, that he should come on the second of the alternative dates. His response was equally calm and prompt. He simply said: "That's fine."

Damasio concluded that "deciding well also means deciding expeditiously, especially when time is of the essence."[6]

We also free ride on mental calculations made by others. We observe the decisions others make, and if they seem successful, follow them. If they're unsuccessful, we don't. We abandon fruitless searches when others have stopped looking.[7] It's good to learn from our painful experiences but better still to learn from someone else's bad choices. At times, this might seem like a herd instinct that sets past mistakes in stone and leads us to repeat failed strategies. We might fail to recognize that a novel situation calls for rethinking past strategies. Generals always fight the last war, it is said. But when they do, they tend to lose the war.

🕮 Judgment Biases

That's not to say that our heuristics, instincts, and emotions always get it right. The cognitive psychology literature of the 1970s and 1980s identified several areas where our hunches seem biased and might lead us astray.[8] Daniel Kahneman and Amos Tversky—the leaders of the cognitive movement—devised experiments in which people's hunches violated the rules of probability theory and the axioms of rational choice.

The following is a nonexhaustive selection of cognitive heuristics where our biases are said to mislead us.

- *Availability Heuristic.* When predicting the future, we'll base our judgment on how quickly past instances come to mind.[9] For example, we were much more likely to expect a terrorist attack on the United States in October 2001 than in October 2008.
- *Anchoring Heuristic.* Like a ship's anchor, mental anchors or reference points tie us down. In one test, a roulette wheel was spun to generate a number between 0 and 100. Subjects were then asked whether this number was higher or lower than the number of African members of the U.N. When the roulette number was 10, the median estimate of African U.N. members was 25; when the roulette number was 65, the median estimate was 45.[10] The number turned up by the roulette wheel shouldn't have mattered, but it did.

- *The Gambler's Fallacy.* The roulette wheel has come up black for the last five spins. What is the probability that it will come up red on the next spin? Assuming that the wheel is unbiased, the correct answer is 50 percent. The wheel has no memory of previous spins and the probability of red on the sixth spin is the same as it was on the first one. Nevertheless, most people seem to think it must be higher than 50 percent, as though a red were "due."
- *The Hot Hands Fallacy.* Many basketball fans believe that players go on winning streaks, where they develop "hot hands" that make all their shots, even though there is no evidence of this.[11]
- *The Endowment Effect.* In experiments, people seem to value goods more once they own them. In one experiment, two groups of students were shown mugs worth about $5. One group was given the mugs and then asked what price they would want if they were to sell them. The other group was not given the mugs and was asked how much they would pay to buy them. The selling price exceeded the buying price, which suggests that we value goods more once we possess them.[12]

At first glance, experiments like these make people look stupid. However, this conclusion would be misleading, and it isn't the view of most behavioral scientists who work in the area. Kahneman and Tversky themselves regarded judgment hunches as highly efficient rules of thumb that work quite well in the average case. Nevertheless, many scholars, especially in law, have ignored these reservations and have seen a justification for paternalism in our cognitive biases. We rely on our hunches at our peril and, instead, should defer to the expert with his perfect information and manuals of probability theory. We'll call this *cognitive paternalism.*

※ The Counterrevolution in Cognitive Psychology

Over the last twenty years, hundreds of law review articles have embraced cognitive paternalism. First, they identify a judgment bias from the cognitive literature. Second, they propose fetters on free choice to de-bias us. The race is always to find a new area where our judgment is defective and where the law professor will steer us right. For the paternalist with a vested interest in impeaching our judgment, the always-successful search for a judgment bias might be thought an example of its own kind of bias, the self-serving bias where we find what we happen to be looking for.

However, the cognitive paternalist overstates his case. In the real world to which he so often refers, our heuristics are far more sophisticated and accurate than he concedes. What he has ignored is a more recent counterrevolution in cognitive psychology that emphasizes the overall efficiency of our judgment hunches and that suggests four arguments against cognitive paternalism. I label these the argument from *design flaws*, the argument from *indeterminacy*, the *ecological rationality* argument, and the argument from the *paternalist's biases*.

Design Flaws

Some experiments seem designed to show that we have judgment biases. They cook the books and ignore benign explanations of the findings.

- The manner in which the questions are posed might elicit the answers the cognitive paternalist wants to hear, so that we're made to seem more helpless than we really are. The judgment bias might disappear when the questions are posed in *neutral settings*.
- People might take more time to eliminate errors in *real-world settings*, where the stakes are higher than they are in an experiment.
- A one-shot experiment might also fail to capture the way we *learn* from our mistakes in the real world.
- We might *discount the facts* as they are recounted to us by the experimenter.
- How we *assess risks* may reflect how we feel about the event itself.
- We might take the experimenter's questions as prompts that *signal* useful information, so that we follow his lead.
- Judgment biases might be corrected in *market transactions*.[13]

Neutral Settings

Laboratory tests have been found to depend on the manner in which the questions are posed, with the bias disappearing in neutral settings. One example of this might be the endowment effect, which we saw above. If people want to hold onto things they have been given, this might be because they thought they were gifts and that it would be churlish to sell them. Or they might think that the decision to sell reveals that they are hard up and in need of cash. When these and other flaws are addressed, and the test is administered in a more neutral fashion, the endowment effect has been found to disappear.[14]

Real-World Settings

People spend more time avoiding calculation errors in real-world settings than in experiments. Paying subjects even a moderate amount for the correct answer gives them an incentive to work out the calculation and increases the accuracy of predictions.[15] Where the stakes are higher, as they are in real-world decisions, people can be expected to do better still.

Learning

People learn from their mistakes and adjust their hunches. If a newly married young couple underestimates the probability of divorce, those on their third and fourth marriages probably get it right. And if someone keeps feeding me a misleading anchor, I'll simply stop relying on him.[16] Fool me once, shame on you; fool me twice, shame on me. By taking choices away from us, the cognitive paternalist ignores these feedback loops and reduces the information about preferences that comes when we deliberate about what we want.

Discounting the Facts

People might discount the facts in the problem set before them. The experimental psychologist presents his subject with a set of facts and assumes that he accepts them as true. In some cases, however, the subject might reasonably question the facts, and this might account for the bird-in-the-hand fallacy in which we seem to have an irrational preference for goods received sooner rather than latter.

In an experiment, subjects were presented with two options with the same expected value (probability times magnitude, adjusted for inflation) but with payoffs at different times. Even though they were worth the same, subjects preferred the bird-in-the-hand, in the form of the front-end-loaded option where they were paid off earlier. Though this at first glance seems irrational, the front-end-loaded choice might in fact be more valuable where there is a positive probability of default at the back end. The experimental psychologist might assure us that this will not happen, but we seem hard wired to mistrust people who tell us the check is in the mail. We live in a world where the future is uncertain and where we rationally discount later events and prefer the immediate payoff.[17]

The conjunction effect might similarly be self-correcting in the real world. The conjunction effect refers to the way in which we seem to miscalculate when figuring out the probability that two unconnected events will both occur. The right way to do this is to multiply the two probabilities together. For example, if we're told that there is a 50 percent chance that a Democrat will be the next president and a 2 percent chance that the Washington Nationals will win the pennant, there is a 1 percent chance that both will happen. In tests, however, most people seem to guess higher,[18] and this mental error is labeled the conjunction effect.

Outside the experimental lab, however, people might correct for anticipated judgment biases by adjusting probability estimates of the separate events. If they overestimate the probability that two conjunctive events will occur together, they might reduce the probability assigned to one of the events. For example, they might underestimate the likelihood of a Nationals pennant victory and come up with the correct 1 percent estimate that both will occur. An earlier literature on "conservatism" (the tendency to discount events) suggests just this possibility.[19] In real life, the conjunction effect might thus be self-correcting in ways that escape the attention of the experimental psychologist.

Assessing Risks

Dan Kahan has noted that risk perceptions often are a proxy for how we feel about the event in question.[20] People opposed to abortion might have an exaggerated view of its dangers to women, while pro-choice advocates might minimize these. The same is true of many other contentious issues, such as gun control, global warming, and the danger of contacting HIV. In short, individual differences in the perception of risk might not reveal irrationality but only differences in how the outcome is perceived.

Signaling

The subject may take an anchor as a signal that is coded with useful information. This might explain why tort reform statutes that cap damages for pain and suffering don't seem to have affected what courts award.[21] If the legislator sets a maximum damages award of $1,000,000, a judge who formerly awarded $500,000 might now double his award, and this is evidence of the anchoring bias. But something more than a simple anchoring effect might be going on. What this ignores is the informational content of the legislation. Even as the judge who formerly awarded $2,000,000 will realize that his awards were too generous, the parsimonious judge who formerly awarded $500,000 will read in the legislation a signal that his awards were too low. Further, both judges may see in the $1,000,000 figure a focal point to which both should reach if they think that an even-handed justice system means that plaintiffs should receive the same award for the same injury, without regard to the identity of the judge before whom they appear.

Market Transactions

A business that consistently made bad decisions because of faulty heuristics would tend to be squeezed out by competitors.[22] Business rivals have an incentive to correct consumer misperceptions so that a sustained substantial error about consumer products is unlikely to persist. This might not eliminate judgment errors because there is reason to believe that they are found in the most efficient markets, such as the stock market. There is a lengthy literature on stock market bubbles, irrational exuberance, and other stock price anomalies.[23] That said, there is a good deal of evidence that violations of rationality norms are abated in market transactions.[24]

Indeterminacy

Before he has standing to fetter our choices, the cognitive paternalist must do two things: he must identify a judgment bias that deflects us from our true preferences, and he must tell us what these preferences are. If he can't satisfy the second of these requirements, he won't be able to tell us what we really want, and his policy prescriptions will be indeterminate.

The indeterminacy problem arises when the paternalist identifies heuristics that might lead us astray but cannot tell us what we really want to do. Russell Korobkin ironically offers an example of this error. Korobkin suggests that customers usually ignore nonsalient (i.e., boring) terms in contracts and therefore "a cautious brand of paternalism" that imposes mandatory contract terms is justified.[25] However, that doesn't get us very far unless we know which terms consumers want, deep down. One of the more boring terms concerns choice of law: Is the contract to be governed according to the law of a particular state, such as New York. Just about all consumers gloss over choice of law clauses so as to kick-start Korobkin's cautious paternalism. But then what state law would they want? The example might seem trivial, but when it comes to more important terms, such as product safety, the same indeterminacy roils the paternalist. Just what kind of warranty rights would consumers want? The paternalist thinks he can tell us—but can he?

Thomas Jackson's argument for fresh start rights in bankruptcy is another example of this kind of indeterminacy. Jackson suggested that the debtor's right to discharge his debts in bankruptcy and start afresh responds to the conjunction effect, where we overestimate the probability of conjunctive events (a *and* b).[26] In Jackson's view, upsides are generally conjunctive (my gold mine will succeed if interest rates are low *and* the price of gold is high). If there is a 50 percent chance of each, the probability that both will happen is $(.5 \cdot .5 =)$ 25 percent. Because of the conjunction effect bias, however, we tend to assume that there is a greater likelihood that both will obtain and that my mine will succeed. At the same time, said Jackson, we tend to underestimate the probability of disjunctive events (a *or* b), as where my gold mine will fail if exploration costs are high *or* the chance of finding gold is low.

If Jackson is right, people will systematically overestimate upside gains and underestimate downside losses. They will too readily court financial ruin and too often tumble into default. Mandatory bankruptcy protections protect debtors from this bias by limiting what they can borrow to finance a project. If bankruptcy law protections weren't mandatory, debtors would waive them and pledge all their future earnings to secure a project. Because they can't do this, under current bankruptcy law, they'll borrow less and take smaller risks.

However, we needn't suppose that the world will systematically line up the way Jackson says. Jackson assumes that upsides are characterized by conjunctive probabilities and downsides by disjunctive ones, but there is no reason to assume this is so. In choosing between two upsides, a worldly and an ecclesiastical career, *Le rouge et le noir*'s Julien Sorel had different alternatives in mind so that his upsides were disjunctive (le rouge *ou* le noir). Similarly, a person's downside risks will often be conjunctive and depend on the combination of separate events. Antonio, Shakespeare's Merchant of Venice, could withstand a single shipwreck but not several independent ones. In short, Jackson fails to show that debtors are more likely to underestimate rather than overestimate the chances of default, with the result the policy prescription is indeterminate.

The endowment effect provides another example of the indeterminacy problem. Just how should the cognitive paternalist respond if people value goods more after they possess them? Should the desire to retain what one has be seen as a deep preference, to be respected and vindicated by the paternalist? In that case, the doctrine of adverse possession, which awards property rights to the person in long-time possession,[27] would make sense. We shouldn't take property away from people in possession. But suppose instead that we see the endowment effect as a judgment bias. In that case, the endowment effect would look like "an unwanted impediment to trade,"[28] to be debiased by the cognitive paternalist. That would mean that there's nothing special about possession and that people can be adequately compensated with money damages if their property is harmed by a nuisance. They wouldn't need special property rights, such as an injunction against the harm. So is the bias the problem or the solution? The paternalist can't have it both ways. And if he can't tell us which is right, the policy implications are indeterminate.

Sometimes two separate hunches, taken together, resemble Stephen Leacock's *Nonsense Novels*, where Lord Ronald "flung himself from the room, flung himself upon his horse and rode madly off in all directions." One example of how two hunches might point in opposite directions is optimism and risk aversion.

- *Optimism Bias.* We seem to discount the risks we face, for example by underestimating the probability of divorce. Because of this, people might be too ready to marry.
- *Risk Aversion.* When it comes to gambles about favorable outcomes, people are risk averse: they prefer a sure thing over a risky bet with a higher expected monetary value. For example, people might prefer $1,000 with certainty to a coin toss with a payoff of $0 for heads and $2,100 for tails.*

The overly optimistic are too quick to gamble and the risk averse are too slow to gamble. This doesn't offer much guidance for policy prescriptions. Like the Oliver Wendell Holmes' *One-Hoss Shay*, the biases might even be in equipoise so that the entire apparatus hums along nicely. When my impulses balance each other off, my aim is true.

That's speculative, of course, but it illustrates the paternalist's problem. While he can identify heuristics that might lead us astray, he cannot tell us which heuristic we will employ in any particular case. Will we use the

---

* With an expected monetary value of $1,050.

availability or anchoring heuristic or simply rely on our emotions? If the paternalist doesn't know, how can he say what we want? Without an understanding of the ways in which we deploy our heuristics in particular cases, the cognitive paternalist cannot hope to persuade us to fetter our choices.

Ecological Rationality

Our hunches can only be evaluated in the ensemble. What matters is how they work together, not the solitary nudge in a particular direction. A heuristic that misleads in one case, especially in a laboratory experiment, might perform very well in the mass of real world cases for which it is employed. Moreover, what matters is the fit between our hunches and our environment. Hunches should be evaluated according to their *ecological rationality*, on how well they serve us in the world as we find it.[29] The cognitive paternalist derides the *homo economicus*, whom he compares unfavorably with his "real people." But these don't turn out to be very real either, when their hunches are seen in isolation and independently of their natural and social environment.

Gerd Gigerenzer offers a richer understanding of mental hunches, as a collection of decision rules and heuristics, fitted for our environment, which he calls an *adaptive toolbox*. In making choices, we pick and chose from a toolbox of decision tools that are adapted to our environment. One of these is Gigerenzer's Take the Best heuristic. When faced with a puzzling question, we search through cues according to their probability of giving the correct answer. We look at the most promising cue, and if it answers the question, we stop there and decide accordingly. For example, if asked whether more people live in Seattle than Louisville, one might consider two cues: which city has a major league baseball franchise and which has a major horse race. Taking the Best means selecting the first cue and picking Seattle.

In Gigerenzer's Recogntion heuristic, one picks the familiar over the unfamiliar answer. When asked whether San Diego or San Antonio had the greater population, German students got the right answer (San Diego) all the time. They recognized San Diego as an American city but had never heard of San Antonio. By contrast, only 62 percent of Americans got the right answer. They knew more about both cities, and the additional information just got in the way.[30]

One of the most striking examples of ecological rationality is the way in which we employ heuristics to judge how to catch a fly ball in baseball.

Where the ball will land will depend on a number of factors, which the physicist could solve through a set of differential equations. He would want to know the angle at which the ball was hit, its velocity and spin, the air resistance and wind direction, and he'd have only a few seconds to compute all this. Ball players don't do this, of course. Instead, they instinctively follow what Gigerenzer calls the gaze heuristic: once the ball is high up in the air, look at it and run toward it in such a way that your angle of gaze remains constant. Do that, and the ball will land in your glove.[31]

We unconsciously do the same thing when we drive. Highway fatalities have declined dramatically in the last twenty years, in large measure because cars and highways are safer than formerly. Nowadays, most highways have speed bumps along each lane to tell us when we stray into the wrong lane. Where there aren't speed bumps, and even where there are, we gauge how to keep to our lane by watching the yellow or white line on the side of the lane. Where we see the line bob and weave as it disappears on the hood of the car, we're driving erratically. Where it doesn't, when it always disappears at the same point on the car's hood, we know we are keeping a constant distance from the line, even when rounding a curve. And we do this without thinking about it, when we're thinking about last night's baseball game or the latest styles in *Vogue*.

The adaptive toolbox has three special features. First, its guidelines are ecologically rational, in the sense that they fit the world as we find it. This in turn means that we must take the long view. Mental hunches may be likened to programs we adopt at birth and can alter only with difficulty thereafter. To evaluate them, we must examine their overall effect on our welfare because a hunch that seems to err in a particular case today might nevertheless be a valuable heuristic. A test of the anchoring bias in an experiment doesn't tell us very much if the bias suits us well over our lifetime.

Ecological rationality provides an explanation for seemingly irrational biases. Consider the phenomenon of regret, which is said to be an example of judgment bias.

- *Regret*. You arrive at a theatre and sit in the third row. This seems a little close so you move to the fourth row. Before the play begins, the manager announces that everyone in the third row has won a ticket for next year's entire series. You say, "If only I hadn't moved!"

Regret might seem a highly inefficient emotion.[32] The decision to change seats made sense at the time, and in any event, the past can't be changed. Ignore sunk costs, says the economist, and we're also told to pay no attention to water under the bridge. But we don't do that. When things turn out badly, we imagine a counterfactual world, where we acted differently and where things turn out better for us. This might seem silly, but it's often a valuable exercise. The anxiety we experience through regret is a useful reality check that pierces through our self-esteem and forces us to scrutinize our behavior for signs of error. Without regret, there would be no learning from past errors and an increased likelihood of future errors.

Second, we adjust our decision rules to new environments. People learn how to deploy different heuristics when first hunches mislead with feedback mechanisms that adjust old heuristics for new tasks. The submariner learns how to keep his head down, after a few bumps. The batter learns how to recognize the curveball. More generally, we can learn from the mistakes of others, in adapting our heuristics. We don't even have to see their mistakes. It suffices to see how others have adapted to a new environment and follow their example.

Third, the adaptive toolbox is "fast" and "frugal." *Fast* heuristics do not require much mental computation, and *frugal* heuristics do not need much information. While fast and frugal rules might seem to sacrifice computational ability, they can accurately mimic complex mathematical calculations— as my dog does when she catches a Frisbee on the fly. Fast and frugal heuristics also permit us to store and integrate a large amount of information that we can use thereafter. We can disregard extraneous data and bring to mind only the relevant information. We can also make inferences from past experiences without literal recall through simple cognitive tools. The cook who knows just how much spice to add does not remember past successes and failures but only what feels right between his fingers. The experienced lawyer with his situation sense can recognize patterns and analogies that elude the book-smart researcher.

Fast and frugal decision rules can outperform more complicated decision structures that require more information. To gauge the seriousness of the risk, a hospital in San Diego measured nineteen symptoms when a heart attack patient was admitted. However, a rival test that asked only three of the nineteen questions provided better answers.

- Is the patient's blood pressure below a critical level? If so, we don't need to ask any other questions and the patient is high risk.
- If it's not, is the patient less than 62.5 years old? If so, the patient is low risk.
- If the person is more than 62.5, and displays an elevated heart rate, then the patient is high risk.

Taking more information into account would give us a less accurate measure of risk. Sometimes "ignoring information can save lives."[33]

Many of the cognitive paternalist's judgment biases can thus be seen as fast and frugal rules that efficiently exploit information for the task at hand. The availability heuristic has us base our judgments on how quickly we think of past instances and is useful in the general case precisely because it brings general information to mind. We need it most for the situations with which we are most familiar, and there it is most helpful. The taxi driver knows his shortcuts, and the computer programmer his stratagems. For the idiosyncratic problems, the heuristic might mislead the lay person but advantages the expert, and this strengthens economies of specialization. In such cases, we rely upon the expert and discount lay opinions.

No one prizes rationality more than the cognitive paternalist. For him, hunches are always a second-best tool, where calculation and information costs get in the way of the perfectly rational solution. But this short changes the value of hunches, which might outperform the "rational" decision-making processes of logic, mathematics, and decision theory when it comes to real world decisions. "Despite widespread claims to the contrary, the human mind is not worse than rational . . . but may even be better than rational."[34] Our mental shortcuts permit us to solve complex mathematical problems quickly and accurately. This is even true of bumblebees, which engage in probabilistic induction that the human brain is too limited in capacity to perform.[35]

Finally, many real world problems can't be solved by rational deliberation. A super-computer can't tell me how to live my life or whom to marry. And when I want to know whether a person will be loyal to me, I'll take him aside and tell him an off-color joke. If he's my friend, he'll laugh. Not a fake laugh either, but a heart-easing laugh that can't be mimicked by car salesmen and politicians. Evelyn Waugh understood this. "Men who have loved the same woman are blood brothers even in enmity," he said. But "if they laugh together . . . orgiastically, they seal their friendship on a plane rarer and loftier than normal human intercourse."[36]

The Paternalist's Biases

Behavioral theories might even support antipaternalism because judgment biases seem at least as likely to affect the paternalist as his subject. The paternalist asks legislators, judges and juries to evaluate individual choices, without pausing to reflect that the same judgment biases might color their decisions. One example of this is the hindsight bias:

- *Hindsight Bias.* Hindsight is not 20-20, and looking backward, we are apt to ascribe a false wisdom to our decisions. We knew precisely when we would have pulled the pitcher in yesterday's ball game—just before he gave up the home run.

If we were asked in August 2008 who will win the November presidential election, we would give one answer. But if we were asked in August 2009 what we thought a year before about who would win, we would credit ourselves with far more foresight than we in fact had. That's the hindsight bias at work. We all voted for it before we voted against it.

The bias is most likely to mislead when we sit in judgment over others. For juries, a lawsuit is a one-shot judgment, without learning or feedback loops. As we have seen, however, people learn from their mistakes over time. In addition, there is little parallel in the courtroom to the self-correcting tendencies of market processes, particularly where the stakes are high. Not surprisingly, therefore, much of most sophisticated work in behavioral law-and-economics deals with jury error[37] and is thus more antipaternalist than paternalist in its direction. For example, if courts took account of the hindsight bias, they'd be less ready to impose liability on manufacturers for negligence.[38] Because of the bias, a 1 percent probability of an accident might look like a 100 percent probability after the accident has occurred. The result is that too many defendants will be held liable.

The hindsight bias also explains the business judgment standard in corporate law that absolves managers from liability for good faith breaches of the standard of due care. When corporate managers are in bad faith, it's easy to impeach their decisions. When they're in good faith, however, we'd like to encourage them to gamble on valuable but risky opportunities. They won't do this if they can be sued for every gamble that comes up blank. And that's just what might happen because of the hindsight bias. Even if some ex ante decisions to take up an opportunity might be imprudent, it would be dangerous to permit a court to second-guess them. Because of the hindsight bias, the court would be too likely to impeach business decisions that were in fact prudent at the time, with the result that firm managers will be excessively cautious.[39]

The hindsight bias is a form of a more general egocentric bias, in which people overestimate their abilities. We live in a Lake Wobegon world, where we're all above average. This might lead us to be too optimistic when it comes to estimating our chances of success in our jobs and our marriages. However, the egocentric bias might also affect the paternalist's judgment. The egocentric judge, who is the hero in his own private movie, will have little self-doubt about his ability to determine the facts and gauge the veracity of witnesses. He sees and understands all at a glance. He need not pay overmuch attention to the law or to the evidence. He simply knows, from the start, who is right and who is wrong. He also knows, if an accident has occurred, that someone did something wrong and is going to pay for it.

An egocentric judge with the robust self-confidence of a Lord Denning might then be too ready to impeach a consumer's judgment. At the moment of contracting, when the future lies ahead and an infinite number of outcomes are possible, the consumer might wisely discount the possibility of a one-in-a-million defect and waive legal remedies against the seller. But looking backward, after the future has revealed itself, the judge is apt to think that things had to happen just as they did. Doing so, he might disregard the waiver and find the seller negligent for a design flaw. This plausibly explains the judicial fascination with contractual exemption clauses where consumers waive the right to sue a seller for product defects. Beforehand, the likelihood of the event that would trigger the clause might have been exceedingly small; but after the accident, it always seemed inevitable to Lord Denning, who was quick to find the seller liable. Ironically, it was the paternalist whose judgment was off.

Because adjudication is retrospective and legislation prospective, one would expect legislators to be forward looking and less swayed by judgment biases than judges. However, the gripping stories which attract newspaper coverage ("if it bleeds, it leads") appear to result in excessive statutory and administrative regulation, as the availability heuristic would predict. One example is Superfund liability for environmental clean-ups where the clean-up costs exceed the benefits of a cleaner environment.[40] From an economic perspective, it makes little sense to get the last particle of a pollutant out of the ground. Nevertheless, the salience of the story attracts public interest groups who find it easy to bring their story to the media and pressure the Environmental Protection Agency for action.

🎞 Conclusion

During the 1990s, cognitive paternalists identified judgment hunches that in laboratory settings seem to lead us astray and suggested fetters on choice to "de-bias" us. The hunch was always the problem and paternalism the solution. However, this literature now seems dated, after a counterrevolution in cognitive psychology that saw heuristics, instincts, and emotions in a more positive light and highlighted cognitive paternalism's shortcomings.

Cognitive paternalists can point to experiments where our hunches seem to misfire. However, they lack a grand theory that tells us what hunch will be employed and when. Outside of the psychologist's laboratory, we simply don't know which hunch a person will pull out of his toolbox to employ for any particular choice. In addition, different hunches seem to tug in opposite directions, so that the paternalist's policy prescriptions are indeterminate.

The cognitive paternalist misses the richness of our hunches. We are prompted to act by our instincts and emotions, which tell us when to stop thinking and get on with it or when something doesn't pass the smell test. They guide us through the most important decisions in life, what job to take, whom to trust, whom to marry, by instincts that a computer could not hope to mimic.

Our hunches are also much more sophisticated than the cognitive paternalist supposed. They not only economize on costly calculation but can even outperform the most powerful computers, as Gary Kasparov showed when he beat the "Deep Blue" chess program on the first round. At a more prosaic level, a set of fast and frugal decision rules can identify high-risk heart attack patients more accurately than a test weighing a much broader range of factors. We're not always better off with more information or more calculation. Sometimes less is more.

Finally, the same judgment biases of which the paternalist complains also infect the paternalist's judgment, and the beam in his eye is often greater than the mote in the consumer's eye. In particular, judges are more apt than consumers to be misled by the hindsight bias, where they assume that things just had to turn out the way they did and that consumers foolishly failed to assess risks properly. Taking choices away from consumers by refusing to enforce the agreements they have entered into would plausibly make them worse off.

Before second-guessing our hunches, therefore, we should ask Jack Nicholson's question: Do you suppose that it doesn't get any better than this?

FOUR

Akrasia

Make me chaste and continent, but not yet.

St. Augustine

COGNITIVE PATERNALISM ASSUMES THAT PEOPLE know where they want to go but are misled by mental biases about how to get there. Their error is a mental or computational one. Telling them about the error would get them get back on track. An older form of paternalism addresses a more intractable problem and focuses instead on the need for strength of purpose or will to choose rightly. Telling the weak-willed person that he is making a bad decision wouldn't cure the problem.

Imagine a person whose mind is unclouded by judgment biases. She knows precisely what she must do to achieve his highest ends. She can measure every possible end-state and knows her best ends along with the best means to get there. Would she always choose rightly? Not if she lacks the strength of will to put her best life plan into effect. Telling the swinish Grille what is good for him would not accomplish much. With no external impediment blocking his way and with a clear vision of the good, his lack of inner resolve would still prevent him from reaching his goal, and his *akrasia* or weakness of will supplies a second possible justification for paternalistic restraints on free choice.[1]

We encounter akrasia every day. The weak-willed person is the problem drinker, the binge-eater, and the drug user. He is the credit card junkie and the gambler. He is the child whose preferences are all in the present, the expectant heir through whose pockets money burns a hole, and the prodigal son for whom the spendthrift trust was invented. He is the short-sighted criminal, for whom the prospect of tomorrow's punishment weighs lightly against the benefits of today's crime. He is St. Peter hearing the cock crow. He is you and me.

🎕 Varieties of Akrasia

Akrasia might take one of six different forms.

- The akrates might be in the grip of an irresistible and *overpowering passion*.
- He might be unable to resist reaching for an experience to which he is *addicted*.
- He might be *self-deceived* about his strength of will, and court temptations which he cannot resist.
- He might be a *divided self*, where a strong- and weak-willed person battle for control.
- He might undergo a *reversal of preferences* in which a later self regrets choices made by a prior self.
- He might be a *hyperbolic discounter* who overconsumes in the present and doesn't save enough for the future.

In all of these cases, the soft paternalist might seek to overrule choices to vindicate the person's deepest preferences.

Overpowering Passions

The akrates might firstly be overpowered by his passions. While I see this as weakness of the will, Aristotle distinguished between akrasia and what he called impetuosity.[2] For Aristotle, the weak-willed person deliberates about what he should do but cannot follow through because of his weakness. He might perhaps be an addict who regrets his addiction but is powerless to overcome it. By contrast, the impetuous person does not deliberate and simply acts on his emotions. No thinking, just do it. Weakness of the will doesn't come into it because the impetuous person's impulses kick in too quickly for his will to have a chance to intercede.

For my purposes, impetuosity is simply an extreme form of an overpowering passion. However, Jean Racine's *Phèdre* is a more difficult problem because it suggests a second kind of impetuosity, one that seems strong willed. Here the strong-willed person deliberates and knows what is best but does not do it. He is not weak but still cannot resist an overwhelming emotion.[3] Because her lust for her stepson, Hippolyte, is so fierce, Phèdre must confess her love to him. Her passion is more than anyone could bear and, for this reason, seems less than weak-willed or sinful. "Her crime is more a punish-ment of the gods than an act of will," explained Racine.[4]

Because she cannot be blamed for her passion, Phèdre is a "righteous sinner" whose moral fate is beyond her control. She is damned but not for anything which she had the power to change. As such, she testifies to the teachings on the indeterminacy of God's grace that Racine learned at the Jansenist school in Port-Royal. For Jansenists, "those people, celebrated for their piety and doctrine," God's grace is a free gift that He can bestow upon or deny to anyone, whatever their moral worth, and the righteous sinner will be condemned, however blameless he might be.[5]

That kind of thinking might lead to immoralism. If it's all in God's hands, why bother? But it might also lead to the strictest moralism, as it was with the austere Jansenists. As they saw the theatre as an occasion of sin, Racine broke with them when he wrote for the stage. His life became worldly, his morals lax. He took a cynical mistress, La Champmeslé, whom he was forced to share with others. His success on the stage inspired rivals, his personal life invited ridicule. Now, with his greatest play, he would make amends. The play portrayed an adulterous passion, with his mistress in the role of Phèdre, but now, wrote Racine:

[T]he slightest faults are severely punished, and the mere thought of crime is regarded with as much horror as the crime itself. The weaknesses of love are shown to be true weaknesses. The passions are presented only to show us all the disorder to which they give rise. And vice is portrayed everywhere with those colors which cause its deformity to be known and detested.[6]

From his friend, Nicholas Boileau, Racine learned that Antoine Arnauld, the Jansensist leader, admired the play. Racine arrived unannounced at Arnauld's door and submitted his will to the Great Arnauld before a crowd. Racine said nothing, but in tears knelt before Annual, who, kneeling in turn, embraced him.[7]

Even the most overwhelming passion might thus be blameworthy. We might pardon involuntary acts performed under the compulsion of an exter-nal threat but not acts that are prompted by our passions. "Concupiscence does not cause involuntariness," said Aquinas, "but rather makes something to be voluntary."[8] And the most deep-rooted character trait may still be con-demned, as La Bruyère noted. "To say of a man who is bad-tempered, moody, quarrelsome, sullen, touchy and capricious: 'that's his temperament,' is not to excuse him, as it is intended to do, but to admit unwittingly that such great faults are irremediable."[9] Our passions do not excuse moral faults but seem more like moral faults in themselves, if we cannot resist them.

The same is true of weakness of the will, however powerful the passions might be. Before we call weakness of the will a fault, however, must we assume the existence of a faculty called the will? In describing promissory institutions, "will" theorists have argued that undertaking an obligation to perform a promise requires a special mental act—the "act of will." What they have in mind, however, seems nothing more than a private resolution, possibly accompanied by teeth-clenching. A person who forms such a resolution might intend to be bound, and might even perform out of what he perceives as a sense of duty. But there is no special *act* of willing, apart from deciding to perform.

If promissory institutions don't require acts of will, neither does akrasia. We can call people weak-willed without positing a special faculty called the will. The strong-willed needn't grit their teeth to resist temptation. Just the opposite. They show greater self-control when they dismiss temptation without an agony of self-doubt and hesitation. We judge whether people are weak-willed by the ease with which they tumble into sin, not by observing some interior mental act.

At the same time, we do need to know something about people's feelings before we can call them strong-willed. Dispassionate people who are never tempted are not strong-willed. The innately moderate person who lacks the disposition to misbehave might live a virtuous life, but as she has not been tested, he does not display strength of will. Perhaps no such people exist because we all have an inclination to sin. But some of us lack the desire to indulge in a particular vice, and there is nothing strong-willed about abstaining from sins that do not tempt one. Not being tempted to smoke, I don't display will power when I turn down a cigarette. Nor does it take much willpower for the aged courtesan to abandon vices that in reality have abandoned her. "When vices leave us, we flatter ourselves with the belief that it is we who leave them."[10]

Addiction

The overpowering passion might be an addiction, where a person seems unable to stop repeating destructive behavior. Addictive goods might mean different things, including hard drugs, sex, the Internet, and my BlackBerry, but what is common to all definitions is the idea that the desire for the good increases with use and that after a time withdrawal becomes very difficult.

One of the most common addictions seems to be to work. When asked whether they were workaholics, about 30 percent of all Canadian adults say yes;[11] and one can only imagine what the figure would be for the Japanese. This comes at a cost, for longer work hours are correlated with stress that results in high blood pressure and an increased likelihood of heart disease. The workaholic's family also suffers, and he is far more likely to become divorced.

From a psychological or physiological perspective, the experience of withdrawal imposes enormous emotional costs that have physical correlates in the brain. For example, alcohol stimulates the release of the neurotransmitter dopomane that is associated with pleasureful feelings and produces a temporary sense of euphoria. However, the brain adjusts for this by weakening serotonin receptors, with the result that the drinker will suffer from depression unless he drinks again. The need for a drink and the anxiety associated with withdrawal increase with use, and the chemical dependency constitutes a form of addiction.[12]

By contrast, the economist's definition of addiction focuses on the price elasticity of addictive goods. Prices are elastic when small changes in price are associated with big changes in how much of the good we consume, and inelastic when big price changes don't produce big consumption changes. If an addict has an irresistible psychological craving, we'd expect that her demand for the addictive good would be highly inelastic. She has to have the good and will pay almost anything for it. Economists, however, have shown that in most cases it doesn't turn out that way. Though most psychologists consider cigarettes addictive, smokers cut back on consumption when the price of a pack goes up.[13] The same thing happens when higher taxes slightly increase the cost of alcohol and people cut back a lot on their drinking.[14] The message seems to be that kicking the habit is a lot easier than the psychologist thinks.

Those of us of a certain age will perhaps side with the economist. Many of us knew someone who took hard drugs in the 1970s. They held regular jobs, partied with us, and on occasion snorted or shot up. We looked askance at this—and yet they were our friends. Thirty years later, they're still around. They've kept their jobs (often in the high tech or advertising fields) and traded a harmful addiction for beneficial ones—jogging or yoga.

Self-deception

The akrates might also be self-deceived about his strength of will.[15] Newspapers report that 98 percent of Americans think they are going to

Heaven and that only 70 percent think that Mother Teresa made it. We seem to inflate our own worth relative to everyone else, and the self-deception might lead to akratic behavior if the self-deceiver tumbles into vice because he overestimates his self-control. We can have that extra piece of pie because just one piece won't make a difference—and we'll have it again and again.

Self-deception might take the form of an emotional cascade. An informational cascade refers to the way in which we tend to play follow the leader. One person stands up to applaud a performance, then another, and then we all do. A few people head down a path, and then there goes everyone—a cascade where one person influences another. But cascades may be wholly internal as well. A person might come to a party with the firm resolve not to have more than one drink. After the first drink, however, he will permit himself to take two more, and after that three more. Were he more self-aware, he would know that his resolution would fail after the first drink and that in reality he has a choice between no drinks and six.

Self-deception might be a useful adaptive strategy for those who want to present an attractive image of themselves. To signal high worth, we'll want to accentuate the positive and eliminate the negative; and these less than truthful signals become more credible when we believe them ourselves. It is, after all, a little painful to know what others think of one or (what may be worse) how little they think of one, and psychologists report that the people with the most accurate understanding of how they are viewed are the clinically depressed.[16] The self-aware will then have a disadvantage in the competition for a mate as compared with the self-deceived who are full of themselves, thus suggesting an evolutionary explanation for self-deception.[17]

Not every weak-willed person is a self-deceiver. The self-aware akrates might know he is weak-willed and still give in to temptation. The person who overconsumes in the present and does not save for the future might know that he'd be better off if, like La Fontaine's ant, he put something away for retirement. If he doesn't, he knows that he'll regret it later. And yet he is weak-willed and fails to do so. If he is aware of his weakness, his self-knowledge might even make his destructive behavior seem tragic. We are attracted to people like Phèdre because we think they are powerless to resist their fate. By contrast, true self-deceivers are often figures of fun, like M. Jourdain in Molière's *Bourgeois gentilhomme*. After getting a bluffer's guide to literature, Molière's comical bourgeois thinks himself educated and is delighted to learn that he's been speaking prose all his life.

Nor is every self-deceiver akratic. Self-deception might be morally blameless and even admirable when the self-deceiver thinks too little of himself.

Heroes often deny that they have been brave, and generous people often think they have given too little. Ordinarily, this kind of self-deception enhances the virtuous behavior and makes it more laudable still. Nevertheless, self-deception can become so extreme as to consume a person's life and shut out any possibility of happiness. The strong-willed self-deceiver might be a moral martinet who maintains an overrigid code because he underestimates his power of self-control. He might refuse to look at the dessert cart even though he possesses the power to resist ordering, or he might abstain from desserts completely even though he could indulge on occasion without making a practice of it. Because he is self-deceived about his self-control, he adopts rules of unbending and joyless austerity.

We can easily bring to mind cases where we seemed self-deceived. As an explanation for akrasia, however, self-deception is problematical. The akratic prefer p and not-p, and that's hard enough to fathom. They want something, and yet they don't want it. But the self-deceivers believe in p and not-p, and that seems harder to understand. I am deceived if, on a clear day, I think it is raining. I am *self*-deceived if I both believe that it's raining and yet believe that it's not. Before akrasia can be attributed to self-deception, then, we need to explain how people might simultaneously believe in inconsistent things.[18] How can I believe I have the strength of will to resist temptation, when part of me believes otherwise?

There are at least three answers. First, we need not define self-deception to mean a belief in inconsistent things. Instead, the self-deceived might simply be mistaken about their worth or strength.[19] They might think that the first drink at the party won't lead to five more and overestimate their strength of will. They are not merely deceived but are self-deceived because the deception concerns themselves.

We like to think we know ourselves, but the most self-aware of us are often surprised to learn things about ourselves. With a better understanding of our character, we might see our faults more clearly. Instead, we are often pulled up short when reminded of some act of heartless betrayal or callous indifference. Of all things, we might expect to know when we're in love, but even then we might be mistaken. We can't be in love if we can easily move on and forget the lover, and yet, like *The Red and the Black*'s Julien Sorel, we might think we're in love and do just that. We might also be in love and not know it, like Mme de Rênal, who remains unaware of her love until she discovers that she is jealous of her maid's crush on Julien.

Second, we might recognize an inconsistency between believing in p and not-p, but work to change our beliefs. Where we think it in our interest to do so, we might consciously set out to weaken one set of beliefs and promote another in its place. This was what Pascal recommended to the skeptic who did not believe in God but wanted to do so. Pascal's *Pensées* is a work of apologetics that seeks to persuade the reader of the utility of belief. Pascal asked the nonbelieving skeptic to assign a positive probability that God exists. If the skeptic does so, and thinks that believers have a chance at infinite happiness, then she'll think that it's better to believe. If she could, she'd place a bet on God's existence. And she must bet, said Pascal.

The argument (Pascal's wager) fails, but let's suppose that it persuades the skeptic. The problem is that that this doesn't make her a believer. Thinking that religious belief is good for one does not produce belief. So what can the skeptic do? Pascal's answer was that one who wants to believe should go through the motions and act as though she believed. She should say the rosary beads aloud and bless herself with holy water. She should turn off his mind and let her passions and animal instincts take over (*s'abêtira*). In this way she can silence the doubts prompted by her reason.[20] "Nothing so conforms to reason as this disavowal of reason."[21]

If she did this, the skeptic would not hold simultaneous inconsistent beliefs. Over time, however, one set of beliefs would replace another. Surrounded by pious believers and clutching her beads, the later self will forget the doubts that seemed insurmountable to the former self. Or the later self might remember them and thank God for the gift of grace that permitted her to overcome them. She might even remember that the grace was accompanied by a strong dose of self-help, that she manipulated her beliefs, and yet adhere to her new beliefs. She can know that she formerly believed in not-p, and now believes in p, and that she tricked herself to produce the new belief, and still believe in p. She can do this if her new belief in p is accompanied by a belief in the wrongness of believing not-p. Of course, if she thought *that* belief a product of self-deception, the new belief structure might unwind. However, she might cut off this possibility by consigning that question to oblivion through simple forgetfulness, throwing away the ladder once she had ascended to his new belief.

Third, a belief in inconsistent things is not hard to understand when facing the truth about oneself imposes emotional costs. Denial is not a river in Egypt, and Pascal's observation that "ordinary people have the ability not to think about things they do not want to think about" is generally accepted by psychologists.[22] We might be stronger than we know, or weaker too, happier or sadder.*

---

* Psychologists report that patients may exhibit the physical symptoms of depression before they realize they are depressed. Michael Lewis, Shame 15–16 (New York: Free Press, 1992).

Our self-love might blind us to our weaknesses and lead us to the false belief that we are strong-willed or that our sins are not grave. We might tuck away the knowledge of our lapses into some dark corner of our consciousness, and parade our pretended virtues in the sunlight. The self-deceiver is then a divided self, where one self deceives and the other is deceived.[23]

The Divided Self

A unified self has a consistent set of preferences, but a divided self might have simultaneous conflicting ones. Like Spenser's Guyon, we are torn between good and evil counselors, between palmers and tempters. The strong-willed part of our psyche might hate gambling in general while the weak-willed part loves blackjack in particular, especially in Las Vegas and after a few martinis. The strong will sets the rules, and the weak will breaks them.

The idea that we might be inhabited by different people is not a novel one, and Freudian psychologists will identify the different parts of our personalities as the strong-willed super-ego and the weak-willed ego. St. Paul made a similar distinction, between spirit and flesh. "For the flesh lusteth against the spirit: and the spirit against the flesh; for these are contrary one to another: so that you do not the things that you would."[24] When we are conflicted, we feel two people warring within a single breast.

The divided self figures prominently in accounts of conversion experiences, including the most famous *Confession* of all. St. Augustine describes how two wills fought within him, and how he wanted the will to goodness to triumph—but not too quickly.

> The new will which I began to have was not yet strong enough to overcome that other will, strengthened by long indulgence. So these two wills, one old, one new, one carnal, the other spiritual, contended with each other and disturbed my soul. . . . It was myself indeed in both the wills. . . . Still bound to earth, I refused, O God, to fight on thy side, as much afraid to be freed from all bonds, as I ought to have feared being trammeled by them. . . . For I was afraid thou wouldst hear me too soon, and heal me at once of my disease of lust, which I wished to satiate rather than to see extinguished.[25]

One of the best-known modern conversions happened in 1935 when an alcoholic overcame his weakness of will. Bill Wilson's drinking had cost him a promising job on Wall Street and landed him in a hospital. For years he tried to quit but always found himself drinking again. In desperation, he begged God for help. "If there be a God, let him show himself," he cried. And then he saw the room fill up with white light and experienced a sense of ecstasy and freedom. He never drank again and went on to found Alcoholics Anonymous (AA).[26]

With over two million members, AA is far and away the best-known support group for alcoholics who wish to stop drinking. There is no formal organization but only local chapters, all of which subscribe to Wilson's Twelve Step program. The first step asks members to admit that they are powerless over alcohol. Subsequent steps are explicitly religious. The alcoholic must make a decision to turn his will and life over to the care of God. He must admit to God the exact nature of his wrongs and be wholly ready to have God remove his defects of character. He must through prayer and meditation seek to strengthen his contact with God. The religious character of AA has drawn criticism from some, but the movement remains the most effective self-help strategy for alcoholics who seek to stop drinking.

The divided self might seek integration by eliminating one set of preferences. If it could, the calmer self would replace the preference for gambling with, say, the desire to read morally uplifting law review articles. These preferences about preferences (or "metapreferences") are common to all of us and an essential prelude to the task of reforming our character. When we seek to change our preferences in this way, it might not be clear who the "true" self is and whether the desire to quit gambling is more than a pose. Yet the familiar sense of deliberating about which set of preferences should be satisfied reminds us of the conflict in our desires.

When the will to goodness wins the battle for self-control, when the other self disappears and one no longer feels divided, a feeling of relief and peace often descends. The stress of conflicting emotions is gone, and one feels as though one has come home. As with St. Augustine and Bill Wilson, the sense of integration is often associated with a religious experience.

The change might not be toward holiness. The integrated self might have cast off religious belief and embraced a life of earthly joys, as Joyce's Stephen Dedalus did in *A Portrait of the Artist as a Young Man*. We might also be corrupted, with one sin weakening our moral sense and increasing the likelihood that we will commit other sins. Our emotions are bound together, not separated into watertight compartments. One emotion might rub up against another, either to dull or sharpen it. We might become prey to every kind of misbehavior.

The gateway sins which lead to other sins are the theologian's cardinal sins. For economists, they're called "internalities."[27] Unlike externalities, whose effects are felt by third parties, internalities affect the subject himself, by changing his tastes and preferences. When the internalities are positive, he is changed for the better, as where his character is strengthened through good habits. And when the internalities are negative, he has been morally corrupted.

The divided self is prominently on display in the choice between spending money today versus saving it and spending it at a future time. If prudent, a person will seek to smooth out consumption between different periods, avoiding periods of feast and famine. In Milton Friedman's life-cycle model, the goal is a flat or constant level of consumption throughout one's life, with nothing left over at death.[28] For Friedman, the 1990s bumper sticker had it wrong: the person who dies with the most toys is not a winner because he has oversaved and underspent during his life.

We might not be so prudent, however. Because she myopically prefers present to future rewards, a person might be more closely allied to today's self. She might sing in the summer and starve in the winter, like La Fontaine's grasshopper. Though free of judgment biases, today's weak-willed self might be unable to implement the frugal ant's utility-maximizing life plan. She might transfer excessive wealth from future to present periods, overconsuming in the present and underconsuming in the future. When the future becomes the present, she will regret her choice, but by then it is too late.

Reversal of Preferences

The divided self has two simultaneously conflicting desires. A self might also undergo a reversal of preferences over time. The kinds of plans we make before a religious conversion, before we fall in love, before a child is born are very different from the plans we make afterward, and a later self might regret choices made by a former self and ascribe them to weakness of will.

The *Baby M* litigation is a prominent example of a reversal of preferences. Mary Beth Whitehead agreed to be artificially inseminated for a fee of $10,000 in a surrogacy contract that specified that she would give up the child at birth to a childless, professional couple. She wanted the money, and she also wanted to give the other couple "the gift of life." She did not think she would regret her decision. But when the child was born, Mrs. Whitehead was a very different person (even though this was not her first child). She realized she could not part with her child. She surrendered it but soon became suicidal. She received permission to see the child, and fled with it a thousand miles away, where she lived in hiding in a series of motels until the police found her three months later.[29]

Mary Beth Whitehead did not succumb to an overpowering temptation when she signed the surrogacy contract. Instead, she made her decision after calm deliberation, unlike her frantic decision to run off with her child. In that sense, her initial decision might not seem weak-willed or a suitable case for the soft paternalist. This is not to say that the perfectionist would approve it, for he might think it an objectively bad choice. For the perfectionist, the problem is not that her initial decision failed to reflect her preferences but rather that she had had bad preferences.

Nevertheless, there is a sense in which we might see her decision as weak-willed. The surrogacy decision conflicted with her subsequent preferences. Today's self had not undergone the transforming experiences of the child's birth and loss and came into conflict with tomorrow's self. If we accept the second set of preferences as better reflecting the true Mrs. Whitehead, then a restriction on surrogacy contracts is a form of soft paternalism.

When people's preferences have radically changed, on whose side should the paternalist be? The second Mrs. Whitehead had strong preferences about the surrogacy contract, but so did the first Mrs. Whitehead. How should the soft paternalist choose between them, in the name of vindicating her preferences? The paternalist might nevertheless take sides, either to free or fetter a choice, if he knew which choice would make the person best off overall, treating her as a unitary and not a divided self. In the case of Mrs. Whitehead, the question answers itself. There is no question but that the pain she experienced when she gave up her child dwarfed the pleasure she took a when she entered into the contract.

Were all surrogates like Mrs. Whitehead, the argument for banning surrogacy contracts would be difficult to resist. But it is by no means clear that most women would react as she did. The Baby M case received enormous publicity, and this might have been expected to reduce the supply of surrogate mothers. That doesn't seem to have happened, however, and a casual surf of the Internet suggests that the practice is thriving. Women who choose to become surrogates report that they know that giving up the baby will be not be easy. Nevertheless, they appear to think that the experience on the whole is worthwhile, and they are likely better judges of this than the paternalist. Again, it is sometimes said that surrogacy contracts should be banned because the confusion about who his parents are will harm the child.

That might be so, but if the alternative is not to be born at all, the child must be presumed to be emphatically in favor of surrogacy.

Reversals of preferences can be distinguished from the divided self phenomenon. The alcoholic who loses the taste for alcohol experiences a reversal of preferences. The alcoholic who gives up drinking, but never loses the desire to do so, is a divided self. Apparently, the desire for drink never disappears, which is why the ex-drinker describes himself as an alcoholic. He is a divided self.

Hyperbolic Discounting

The *hyperbolic discounter* prefers present to future selves by overconsuming in the present and undersaving for the future.[30] As between a smaller payoff today and a larger one tomorrow, the hyperbolic discounter wants it now. In preferring present to future selves, he discounts the latter's pleasures and this might seem weak-willed and a special case of divided selves.

The strong-willed saver might want to enjoy an equal amount of pleasure (the economist's utility) during each period of her life. She does not discount future pleasures and thus might be called a *zero discounter*. Most people do discount future pleasures, however, and those who do so at a constant rate are called *constant discounters*. Ten percent next year, ten more percent the year after, and so on. But that's not how we seem to behave either. In experiments, we apply a sharply declining discount rate to pleasures in the near term and a much lower discount rate in the long term. For example, we might apply a 50 percent discount when the choice is between consumption today versus tomorrow, 20 percent when the choice is between tomorrow and six months from now, and 10 percent when the choice is between six months from now and a year from now. That is, we'll be indifferent between $100 today versus $50 tomorrow, between $100 tomorrow and $80 six months from now, and $100 six months from now versus $90 a year from now (with inflation-adjusted dollars in all cases). The resulting curve resembles a hyperbolic function in mathematics, and such people are hyperbolic discounters.

Whether hyperbolic discounting really exists has been disputed. In experimental tests, subjects are more likely to discount hyperbolically when small sums of money are at stake,[31] and this is consistent with the informational problems we saw in the last chapter. When we're talking about large amounts of money, people have an incentive to calculate present values; but for small amounts of money, the difference might not be worth the mental effort.

If this was all that was happening, hyperbolic discounting would be classified as a judgment bias and not as a form of akrasia.

Tests of hyperbolic discounting might also suffer from a design flaw. The hyperbolic discounter might reasonably prefer to take the money and run when he thinks that the promisor might default on his promise to pay up in the future. As we saw, a bird-in-the-hand bias is rational if there is a positive probability that the bird in the bush will fail to materialize. When the promisor might default, when the check in the mail might never arrive, $100 in cash today might be worth more than a promise of $150 tomorrow. Even if the experimenter tells us that the future payment is a sure thing, this might not overcome a healthy, ingrained suspicion about cheap talk.

Status concerns might give rise to another design flaw. Preferring $150 tomorrow over $100 today might reveal an ignoble concern for chump change. People with an aristocratic disdain for trivial difference in payouts will take the money today. Status signals are weakened when both payouts are in the future, and the decision looks more purely financial.[32] The choice between payoffs one year and two years from now doesn't signal that I'm a moneygrubber.

Nevertheless, the real world decisions of individuals do seem consistent with some form of discounting the future. For example, we would expect zero discounters who value future rewards as much as present ones to take full advantage of tax shelters which permit people to lower their tax burden by saving for the future. Because many taxpayers fail to do this, the message from the Tax Code seems to be that some of us are weak-willed and some of us are not.*

Procrastination might amount to hyperbolic discounting. The procrastinator delays performing an unpleasant task that he believes should be done now. This might be prudent when the problem might take care of itself in the future even if the person does nothing now. At times, however, the procrastinator postpones a task which he knows he will have to perform, when the choice is between a small effort today versus an even larger future effort, and

---

* Other tax decisions might seem strong-willed. A large number of people receive tax refunds each year from the I.R.S. As they have overpaid their taxes by withholding too much from their paychecks, they might have increased their current income by reducing their withholding payments. Presumably, they do not seek to make a gift of the float to the fisc. This is consistent with a zero-discounter's strong-willed self-binding strategy because it reduces the temptation to overspend in present periods and ensures there will not be a cash crunch when the tax bill is due.

this suggests hyperbolic discounting. Small leaks in the basement, fixed early, can avoid major floods in the future, but still we procrastinate.

Once, at dinner, I heard some newly installed bookshelves tumble down in our library. They had not been properly fastened to the wall. "Why don't we simply close the door to the library?" I suggested to my wife. It's not as though we were looking at the books very much. We might close the door and finish our dinner, without even inspecting the damage. Alas, my wife rejected this eminently sensible suggestion.

There is an overlap between the different kinds of akrasia I have identified. A person with an overpowering passion might be an addict, who in turn might be self-deceived about how serious his addiction is. The hyperbolic discounter might also be self-deceived, and might be an example of a divided self. Certainly, he'll have a reversal of preferences when he has overconsumed in the present and left too little for his old age. Nevertheless, it is helpful to distinguish between the different forms that akrasia might take.

𝍌 Does Akrasia Exist?

Aristotle doubted whether weakness of the will exists because he found it difficult to imagine how someone with knowledge of the good would lack the strength of purpose to reach for it.[33] For most of us, that might not seem like much of a puzzle. We know that the marshmallow sundae should be resisted, but give me that spoon! More troubling is the idea that the akrates does things he really does not want to do. Is the person who reaches for the sundae weak-willed? Or does the desire for the extra scoop of ice cream constitute his deepest desire? He might afterward tell us that he regrets overeating, but the sense of having succumbed to temptation is not akrasia because we often regret acts that were truly desired at the time.

It is, after all, possible to be rationally fat. The lawyer at her desk might think that she doesn't have the time to exercise. She might take comfort in advances in medical technology that will keep her alive a few extra years (though not so long as her svelte know-it-all nephew).[34] Is it really so unreasonable to trade off a few extra years at the fag end of life at the nursing home for lunches of pâté de campagne on a hot baguette fresh from a Parisian baker, over a Moulin-à-Vent? When Lampedusa's *The Leopard* lovingly described a glistening bowl of macaroni, topped off with tartuffo, and baked in a shell of sweet pastry, were we meant to be shocked by the quivers of admiration it evoked from the dinner guests?

Akrasia does not require that the act be actively regretted in the present, as we are doing it. Otherwise it would be difficult to see how anyone could be weak-willed. The regret comes later as it did for the second Mrs. Whitehead when she had to surrender her child. However, the sense of retrospective regret does not mean that the first Mrs. Whitehead chose poorly. There are a good many things we regret, but that is not to say that we would have been better off overall had we chosen otherwise. We regret the risk we took, when we come up blank; but without the benefit of hindsight, taking the risk might have been the prudent thing to do. If the second Mrs. Whitehead regretted the contract, the first Mrs. Whitehead would have regretted fetters on bargaining that prevented her from entering into the contract.

Jon Elster argues that a bias in favor of present consumption must be irrational because it will be regretted in the future.[35] But the experience of regret proves nothing because the prudent saver may regret postponed joys. Regret is a byproduct of the conflict between today's and tomorrow's person and does not tell us who should win the contest. Deferred consumption will be regretted by today's person, and present consumption will be regretted by tomorrow's person. However we choose, we will experience regret. The question is not whether the choice is regretted, but whether the decision adds to or subtracts from overall lifetime happiness.

Nor should we assume that rational consumers will seek a stable consumption across all periods, one hundred dollars today, one hundred tomorrow, and so on. This assumes that when adjusted for the time value of money today's dollar provides the same utility as tomorrow's dollar. However, there is no reason to think that this is so. The young might live on the *air du temps* in Charles Aznavour's *La Bohème* and need relatively little money to do so, grouped around their stove and reciting their poetry. When we are old, we shall need more expensive toys to compensate for the decay of life. We might thus prefer to save for a rich old age and underconsume when young. Or we might prefer to take our pleasures up front, rather than wait.

Pleasures have a time dimension. Before we go off on a trip, we experience the pleasure that comes from anticipating the things we'll see.[36] And after we return, we recall the trip with pleasure. If the pleasures of anticipation and remembrance are a wash, they might be ignored in our felicific calculus. In some circumstances, however, one temporal pleasure might outweigh the other and bias us in favor of present or future selves. The pleasures of anticipation often seem more intense than the calmer pleasures of remembrance, and this would argue for postponing our enjoyment so that we may savor the promise of future pleasure. On the other hand, the longer the waiting period, the weaker the sense of anticipation. We might take pleasure in thinking about a trip to Europe that we'll take in six months, but not in six years. Rather than postpone the trip to a time when other joys have faded, we might reasonably prefer to experience it in one's youth when it might be savored more intensely and remembered for a longer period.

Early pleasures that are long remembered, or that shape future preferences or behavior, are like the human capital investments we make in education or skills training. We might use a pleasureful experience as a hook upon which to hang the further pleasures we will derive from it. An eighteen-year-old's European holiday may stimulate a passion for history or literature. A Bach concert heard when one is young might be the gateway to a life-long love of baroque music. And this might point to a preference for present over future consumption.

The difference between anticipated and remembered pleasures has a parallel in anticipated and remembered pains. Amnesic drugs such as Midazolam (better known under its trade name of Versed) reduce but do not eliminate pain during an operation. What they do, however, is erase the memory of the pain afterward, so that it is remembered as a not unpleasant experience. Patients report dreamlike memories of emerging from a procedure and often cannot remember dressing themselves afterward. Consequently, the drug is highly popular among patients, who often ask for it when a procedure such as a colonoscopy is to be repeated. Even the first colonoscopy seems less alarming with the prospect of a pleasant remembrance dominating anticipation of an unpleasant procedure.

Derek Parfit offers another justification for discounting the preferences of future selves.[37] We might care less for future selves because we know that what they will want is not what we now want. The young socialist might imagine that as he grows older he'll become more conservative, and because he feels so strongly committed to his left-wing ideals, might rationally discount future preferences. He might embrace radical causes today rather than prepare himself for a lucrative career. Again, a person in love might prefer to give his lover jewelry today rather than save for himself as a future person, if the future person might not be in love with her.

Akrasia can be distinguished from the judgment biases we saw in the previous section, even if the akratic appear to have an inconsistent set of preferences. Mary Beth Whitehead had inconsistent preferences about surrogacy, and the hyperbolic consumer has inconsistent preferences about saving. If the rational consumer has consistent preferences, inconsistency implies irrational preferences. Rationality, however, does not mean that one must have the same set of preferences all through one's life. Mary Beth Whitehead did not have consistent preferences over time, but she was no less rational for her change of heart. Nor is the hyperbolic consumer necessarily irrational. Instead, he might be weak-willed and unwilling to bear the emotional costs of sacrificing present gratification to make his actions conform to a consistent set of preferences. Or else he might simply favor consumption today to consumption tomorrow, today's person over tomorrow's person. Such time preferences are neither rational nor irrational—they are simply preferences. Some people like vanilla and some people are hyperbolic discounters.

That leaves nasty habits such as smoking. But even this might conceivably be consistent with a person's best life plan. As Gary Becker has noted, addiction may be rational in the sense that one might choose to become addicted with eyes wide open, when the addict's life is happier overall than the abstainer's. Becker defines an addictive good as one whose utility is a function of previous consumption: the more one has consumed in the past, the better one likes it in the present, and the harder it is to give up.[38] So defined, addictive goods include not only cigarettes and liquor but also classical music and romantic love. With its euphoria, heightened awareness, and reduced need for sleep, romantic love affects us in much the same way as amphetamines.[39] The rational, self-aware lover recognizes her addiction and the pain of a possible break-up but nevertheless believes the benefits exceed the costs. To coin a phrase, better to have loved and lost than never to have loved at all.

Figure 4.1 represents three forms of addiction, for classical music, coffee, and heroin, with time measured on the horizontal axis and utility (or pleasure) on the vertical axis. Line OA represents the neutral utility level of the person who abstains from all three goods.

The utility level of the classical music addict is shown in line OB. Since listening to classical music is pleasureful and downloads are cheap, he's always better off with his addiction than he would have been as an abstainer. At no point does the OB line dip below the nonaddict's OA axis. The addiction is also time consistent, in the sense that there never is a time when the addict regrets his addiction.

The coffee addict, represented by line OC, is also better off overall than the abstainer in the sense that her lifetime happiness is maximized by her addiction. The coffee addiction is time-inconsistent, however, because there comes a time when she would rather give up coffee. Where her utility curves drops below the horizontal line, which represents the abstainers' utility level, the addict would prefer not to drink coffee; but being an addict she cannot

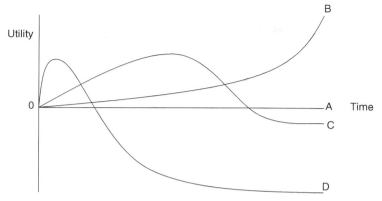

FIGURE 4.1 Rational Addiction

give it up. Withdrawal has simply become too painful. Still, on net, the decision to take the first cup of coffee maximized lifetime happiness.

Line OD represents heroin addiction, which is both time-inconsistent and the source of great unhappiness on net. The heroin addict experiences a preference reversal in which he regrets his addiction decision; and he is worse off overall than the abstainer.*

The Beckerian addict is not irrational because in each of the three cases he is doing precisely what he wants to do at the moment when he becomes addicted. Moreover, the classical music and coffee addicts are not weak-willed; even the strong-willed would become addicted if the diagram represented their payoffs. The heroin addict is not irrational either, although his decision to experiment with heroin requires an explanation because the addiction will leave him worse off.

Four possibilities present themselves. First, the drug user's addiction might result from a calculated gamble, where the good is pleasant and the probability of addiction for most people is very low.[40] The recreational user of soft drugs might reasonably believe that it is unlikely that he'll become addicted. Second, the drug addict might be misinformed about how addictive the drug is and think that people can easily kick a heroin dependency. Third, he might be self-deceived about his strength of will. He might naïvely think that he'll be able to "just say no" when he wants to stop, without realizing that his

---

*   The Becker definition of addition adds a further condition of tolerance: the more the addict has consumed the addictive good in the past, the less pleasure he gets from a given present consumption level. In my examples, this would be true of heroin but not classical music or coffee.

preferences will radically change when he becomes addicted. The fourth explanation, and the one to which Becker subscribed, is that the consumer is a hyperbolic discounter who places a high weight on present gratification and a low weight on later misery.

The first explanation might persuade us to leave well enough alone because the danger of addiction is low. The second explanation might suggest the need for an educational campaign on the dangers of hard drugs. However, the third and fourth explanations might justify a dose of paternalism. The heroin addict might not be irrational, but as a self-deceiver or hyperbolic discounter, nevertheless appears weak-willed. Becker's analysis of addiction suggests prudential limits on paternalism but does not rule all such fetters out of order.

✌ Does Akrasia Argue for Paternalism?

The different kinds of akrasia implicate different forms of paternalism. If the hyperbolic discounter has an objectionable set of preferences when it come to saving money, overruling his choices would constitute hard paternalism. Whenever the paternalist disregards the subject's preferences, deep or shallow, he is a hard paternalist—and a perfectionist. When, however, a person is subject to an overpowering passion, when she is addicted to something harmful, when she is self-deceived about her strength of will, when she has inconsistent desires or conflicting desires over time, the paternalist might be thought to take sides with her deeper preferences, and this would amount to soft paternalism.

The akrates might welcome the soft paternalist's fetters on choice to remedy his weakness of will. Fearing he will succumb to an overpowering passion, he might seek to put it out of bounds through legal barriers. The potential addict might want to criminalize dangerous drugs to increase the cost of taking the fatal first step. Profligate nonsavers might support tax incentives to salt money away in a pension plan. The hard paternalist cannot enlist the subject's support in this way. Even here, however, the interference with individual choice might nevertheless seem justified when the paternalist can plausibly assert that his fetters will benefit the subject.

Whether hard or soft, the paternalist must respond to four objections from the akrates.

- The restrictions are unjustified if the paternalist is in *bad faith* and doesn't care about the subject's well-being.

- The paternalist might not be able to overcome the *informational hurdle* of showing that he, more than the subject, knows what is in the subject's best interest.
- The paternalist might be an officious intermeddler if he ignores the possibility that the akrates might cure the problem on his own through *self-binding strategies.*
- Even if private self-control strategies sometimes fail, we might still prefer to let the individual wrestle with the problem of resisting temptation because of the positive value ascribed to *free choice.*

Bad Faith

Paternalistic fetters are in bad faith when they are motivated by concerns other than the subject's best interests. An obvious example was the slaveholder's argument that slaves were better off in bondage, but other examples abound. Nineteenth-century temperance laws that restricted the sale of alcohol were denounced by immigrant groups as bigoted attacks by Know-Nothing nativists. The Maine Law, passed in 1851 to prohibit the sale of all alcoholic beverages, might just possibly have had something to do with the desire to repel Irish immigrants. Today, the disproportionate burden that drug laws impose on the African-American community prompts the same complaints. Where such concerns are justified, the paternalist's bad faith is a fatal flaw.

There are lesser forms of bad faith, where the paternalist's ostensible concern for his subjects masks a partisan or self-interested political agenda. The leading American teacher's union, the National Education Association (N.E.A.), opposes publicly financed vouchers for private and religious schools, ostensibly for public-spirited reasons. However, it doesn't take a great deal of cynicism to see self-interested motives behind the union's opposition to competition from other educational providers. The N.E.A. is not a paternalist, of course. It does not enact laws. However, it is a major political force, and it is not unreasonable to suppose that its views influence many legislators whose concern for children is suspect. The same point might be made about businesses that wrap themselves in the American flag when they propose import tariffs.

The Informational Hurdle

The paternalist who claims he knows what is best for the subject faces a daunting informational hurdle. It is often difficult to identify akrasia because the choice of one's best life plan is a vastly complicated matter. Those who seem weak-willed might simply be making their best personal choices. They might be addicts, but addicts for whom the addiction on net leaves them better off. They might have divided preferences, or experience regret, but still choose better for themselves than any paternalist could do for them.

The choice of how best to live one's life is immensely nuanced. Everyone has his own way of flourishing, and the one-size-fits-all rules of the paternalist who can legislate only for the average man, the homme moyen sensuel, cannot possibly satisfy everyone's needs. This is especially true when one remembers that what a person might need to flourish can change over time. My own goals are very different today from what they were when I was young, and neither I nor the paternalist could have predicted how things would turn out. The difference is that I had the flexibility to adapt to changed circumstances. By contrast, the legislator is not apt to change direction. His laws stay on the books for an interminable time. He does not react quickly to new information.

Self-Binding

The third objection to paternalism is that the subject might employ his own self-help strategies to avoid akratic behavior. Through self-binding or pre-commitment devices, people can narrow the range of their future options by making it more difficult or expensive to succumb to temptation.[41] The canonical example is Ulysses, who wished to hear the song the Sirens sang on their rock-reefed island. The problem was that sailors who heard the song felt compelled to sail to the reefs, where their ship crashed and they drowned. Ulysses solved this by binding himself to the mast and stopping the ears of his crew with wax. As they rowed past, he heard the music and cried out to his crew to release him and sail to the reefs. But because they could not hear either him or the Sirens, they rowed safely on, oblivious to the pleas of their enchanted captain and the Siren song.

Like Ulysses, we might adopt ex ante strategies that limit future options and protect us from ex post self-destructive behavior. We might simply avoid occasions of sin or make an addictive substance difficult to obtain. We might avoid bars or casinos and stay away from places where we are likely to run into a former lover. We might break up a harmful relationship brutally and violently to remove any possibility of reconciliation.

We might shelter money in a pension plan that imposes a penalty for early withdrawal. We might pay excessive withholding taxes so that we receive a pleasant check from the fisc when we file our tax returns. We might even think this a present and forget that it's our money that is returned to us and that we made a present to the state of the float.

We might enlist friends and mentors in our self-control strategies. The alcoholic will attend her AA meeting regularly and rely on a support group of sponsors she can call when tempted to act out on her compulsion. The person addicted to Internet porn can configure his computer so that a list of all the websites he visits is sent to a friend. For modern epistolatory romances, we might give a friend our BlackBerry and ask him to change our email passwords. For practicing Catholics, the need to confess one's sins as a precondition to taking Communion binds them to walk the straight and narrow.

We might form a New Year's resolution that we cannot relax without a sense of private shame. Or, because private shame might easily be forgotten, we might form a side bet by telling a friend that we've gone on a diet so that we suffer an additional humiliation when we gain weight.[42] Joining a diet club with weekly weigh-ins also shames us into losing weight. Indeed, there isn't much point to paying the membership dues apart from the humiliation of the weight-in if we don't lose weight. The loss of public face pierces through our self-love and reveals the weakness to ourselves as well as others.

Kay Jamison offers a dramatic example of a self-binding strategy.[43] Jamison is a psychiatrist who suffers from bipolar disorder, and who can become suicidal when off her meds. The problem is that, when off her meds, she loses her desire to go back on them, in order to experience the intense exhilaration of the manic stage. And so she entered into a bargain with her family. If they see her off her meds they have the power to commit her to a psychiatric facility against her will. The additional incentive is enough to keep her taking her pills.

Forming the stable preferences that constitute one's character is also a self-control device. By refraining from temptation today, I make it less likely that I will succumb tomorrow. My character is toughened, my resolve made firm, by the repeated practice of self-denial. The qualities so hardened form our idea of virtue, and many of our moral rules might be explained as precommitment devices where a present and future self deliberate about how to govern their behavior. The future self proposes strict rules because a more flexible standard would permit cheating by the weak-willed present self, which in turn adopts the rules precisely because it knows itself to be weak willed.

Calls for paternalistic intervention tend to ignore the possibility that precommitment strategies suffice. One example of this is Thomas Jackson's explanation for mandatory bankruptcy laws that prevent borrowers from waiving the right to bankruptcy relief.[44] I cannot make an unqualified promise to repay money I borrow, because my promise that I will never discharge my debts in bankruptcy cannot be enforced. Jackson's justification for this restriction on the borrower's bargaining freedom is that absent mandatory fetters on choice the hyperbolic consumer would mortgage his future to fund present gratification. To prevent this, the bankruptcy discharge would make it impossible for a person to transfer all his assets to a lender upon default. Because the creditor knows he will not get everything on default, he will lend less to the borrower.

This assumes that that the debtor cannot solve the problem of akrasia by adopting his own self-help strategies. Mandatory legal barriers are unnecessary where present selves can bind future selves on their own. And, so far from constituting weakness of will, borrowing might be just such a strategy.

Borrowing to fund a long-term investment is a self-binding device because we tie up our earnings to repay the debt. Otherwise, our paycheck would burn a hole through our pockets. Home purchases are one example of this. Though borrowing is usually thought to transfer money from future to present periods, the direction of the wealth transfer is reversed in home mortgages. While the debtor lives in the house, he consumes a portion of its value. But he is also saving for future consumption because houses are durable goods that appreciate in value and therefore represent an investment.

Self-control strategies can at times seem excessive as George Ainslie has noted.[45] The moderate drinker might limit himself to one glass of wine at dinner, but the alcoholic may find it necessary to abstain completely. He'd be better off if he could limit himself to one glass of wine but perhaps that is not an option. "One glass is too much, and ten bottles is not enough." In this way, the natural spendthrift might become a miser and the natural sluggard a health fanatic. I am by nature unobservant and apt to miss appointments. To correct for this, I diarize everything on several different calendars and rely on associates to remind me of meetings. I tend to be tardy, if left to my own devices, and compensate for this by arriving at the airport an hour early.

These examples show how self-control may shade into overcontrol, how a person might sacrifice present real pleasures because he fears they might lead to future overindulgence. George Stigler is said to have observed that a person who has never missed a plane has spent too much time in airports.

Perhaps. But for me the choice is between missing no planes and missing a lot of them.

The possibility of overcontrol indicates how difficult it might be to identify akrasia. Is my compulsive attention to my schedule a bubblehead's reasonable coping mechanism or a comically excessive overreaction? When the abstainer takes a glass of wine at dinner, is he displaying weakness of the will or is he wisely relaxing an excessive self-control program? It may be hard to say, and it might be equally difficult to stigmatize the first cigarette as weak-willed.

Compulsive overcontrol is not a prescription for a particularly joyful existence. For those who might safely imbibe without descending into alcoholism, an adherence to overstrict rules turns them into Henri Bergson's machine-man. They take a few principles and absurdly extend them beyond their reasonable scope. What they have forgotten is that "willpower is an awkward expedient, not the ultimate rationality."[46] A mixed strategy that avoids extremes of overcontrol and uncontrolled behavior might then offer greater happiness. A person might follow a self-control strategy but allow for occasional backsliding, and provided the exceptions do not eat up the self-control rules this might permit him to achieve a higher level of well-being than fanatical abstinence or dissolute intemperance.

The Value of Free Choice

There is a final reason why the argument for paternalism from akrasia might fail. Personal autonomy has an intrinsic value, quite apart from the choices we might make. It strengthens our self-control and permits us to flourish in our own unique way.

When the paternalist takes choices away from us, he also deprives us of the ability to adopt our own self-help precommitment strategies. Mill analogized the will to a muscle, which atrophies when not used.[47] By deliberating over one choice, even or especially when this is painful, a person might subsequently find it easier to make the correct choice over an entirely different matter, and this strengthens and forms our characters.

Self-control is a source of pleasure in itself. It permits us to feel a justifiable sense of self-worth and self-esteem. By taking control of our lives, we make them *our* lives and no one else's. We achieve the moral freedom of an adult, free from the tutelage of parents and the state, and feel just what a child does when he assumes control of his destiny.

Free choice also offers new horizons of possibilities, never glimpsed by the rule-bound life. We flourish only when we make our own path not when we follow one set for us by the paternalist. The paternalist cannot possibly know what I need to flourish and achieve a worthy goal in life, a goal that is my goal and no one else's. I myself will not know where I should go until I embark on my journey. I might seek to enlist the aid of a mentor or confessor to guide me, but that choice is mine.

This kind of freedom is especially valuable for the eccentric people Mill had in mind, the people who live their lives against the grain, the moral heroes of *On Liberty*. Socrates, Christ. For moral progress, said Mill, we look to them for guidance. To be sure, the eccentric might simply be the kind of wacko Edith Sitwell described in *English Eccentrics*, such as Mad Jack Mytton, who drove his carriage into the ditch when he learned that his traveling companion had never enjoyed that exhilarating pleasure. Or Richard Porson, who chased his students with a poker when they came ill prepared for his tutorials. But they might also be William Wilberforce, who endured the ridicule of his parliamentary colleagues to push for abolition of the slave trade. And in most cases, we can tell the two kinds of eccentrics apart.

🖋 Conclusion

The argument for paternalism from akrasia asserts that we are sometimes too weak-willed to pursue the good even when we recognize it. Akrasia might come in several different forms, such as an overpowering passion or addiction. We might be self-deceived about our ability to resist temptation, or we might see our selves as divided, with two persons with conflicting passions inhabiting the same body. We might undergo a reversal of preferences and bitterly regret an earlier choice. Or we might simply be unable to defer present gratification to reap a greater future reward.

Before the restriction on choice can be justified, however, the soft paternalist must show that his good faith efforts to benefit the subject will indeed make him better off. First, the paternalist sometimes acts in bad faith, to advance a purpose other than the subject's well-being. Restrictions on ex-slaves and women are obvious examples. Second, the case for fetters on choice is weak when there is some doubt whether the paternalist knows the subject's deep preferences. In such cases, people can decide best for themselves. For example, a person might rationally decide to engage in addictive behavior because not every addiction is harmful. Third, paternalism is unwarranted when the subject may remove temptation on his own through self-help devices, such as precommitment or self-binding strategies. Some of these devices, such as leveraged home purchases, have been mislabeled as weak-willed, which should give us pause before we fetter choices. Finally, when the issue is close, the presumption in favor of liberty argues for letting people make their own decisions.

FIVE

Information Costs

He who deliberates lengthily will not always choose the best.

Goethe

ANTIPATERNALISTS ASSUME THAT PEOPLE best satisfy their preferences when they choose for themselves rather than when the paternalist chooses for them. This in turn assumes that the individual's choice is freely made and not vitiated by defects of consent such as fraud. Fraud corrupts all, says the common lawyer, and a contract tainted by a fraudulent misrepresentation will be set aside. The badge of consent that permits an inference that the contract would make the innocent party better off is absent.

Defects of consent such as fraud bear a family resemblance to the defects of mental and moral capacity we saw under the headings of judgment bias and akrasia. In all cases, there is a disconnect between a person's true preferences and the choices he makes. We enforce contracts because we assume they'll make people better off. When we can't assume this, we don't enforce them. There is only one reason to honor a choice, and one reason not to.

Fraud vitiates a contract because one party entered the agreement with flawed information. Does this mean that a contract should be set aside if there isn't a completely level playing field, with all the relevant information equally shared by both parties? If so, we could never enforce a bargain, because there are always asymmetries of information. Moreover, information itself is a product, with a cost of production, and if it always had to be shared, there would be no incentive to produce it.[1] The prospector would not search for the Treasure of the Sierra Madre, and there'd be a lot less research and development.

Information costs might nevertheless suggest three different kinds of paternalistic restrictions, even in the absence of fraud. First, contracts that appear to impose extreme burdens upon a party, such as contracts of slavery, might be banned because of the information production or *screening costs* that a court would incur in determining whether the party really consented to be bound. Perhaps one person in a billion might really want to become a slave; but for everyone who truly consents, one hundred people might foolishly agree to be bound without really understanding what this entails. They might have been misled by their owner, or subjected to force or undue pressure, or mistaken about what they were getting into. The court would then have to distinguish between the two kinds of contracts, and screening cost considerations then would argue against enforcing all such contracts. The burden of distinguishing the first from the second group might easily exceed any plausible benefit the one-in-a-billion slave would receive. And that's not even counting the error costs if the court gets it wrong and improperly enforces the contract against a person who did not really consent to it.

Second, the plethora of choices offered a consumer might be thought to impose the excessive *search costs* of finding exactly the right goods to buy. We are presented with a dizzying number of products at the supermarket and must pick the one brand of soap we want from a vast array of choices. How difficult this must be, says the paternalist, who would take choices away from people to economize on the consumer's information production costs. Fewer choices would mean less time spent shopping and more time spent on the more worthwhile pursuits preferred by the paternalist: bowling with others, going to the candidates debate, or doing any one of the countless socially useful things the American paternalist might want us to do.

Third, a person might have an incentive to bear excessive *signaling costs* in revealing information about himself unless paternalistic rules prevent him from doing so. To signal that we are brave we might consent to take part in a duel or play hockey without a helmet. We'd all be better off if we agreed to ban dueling and mandate hockey helmets. Could we write a contract to that effect with everyone else, we would all do so. As we can't, as they are too many of us to do so, the only alternative is to enact laws that take such choices away from us by criminalizing duels or mandating helmets. Such laws are paternalistic but seem benign if they permit us to realize our deepest wishes.

𝍂 Screening and Unfair Bargains

Screening refers to the information produced by one person about another or about a bargain where the other party is less than wholly trustworthy.

When a slightly suspect seller offers us a used car, we might screen by enquiring into the seller's reputation. Without even thinking about it, we'll go to a respected car dealer even if other dealers seem to offer lower prices. Alternatively, we might take the car to be vetted at a garage before we buy it. This will impose costs but is nevertheless prudent if the alternative is the higher costs of a bad bargain.

The buyer who bears screening costs will seek cost effective ways to reduce them. He will shop for the cheapest competent garage to vet the car. He might also hire a lawyer to read the contract to make sure that it does not contain oppressive terms. And rather than hire a lawyer, he might prefer a rule of paternalism in which a court strikes down extremely one-sided terms. The court system and the machinery of litigation also impose costs, even if these are borne in part by the state's judicial system. However, asking a court to conduct an ex post review of the relatively few contracts that rise up to bite one might be less costly than hiring a lawyer to conduct an ex ante review of all contracts, fair and unfair. It's a lot cheaper to look at one oppressive contract than the thousands of fair bargains.

The more extreme the unfairness, the more plausible the rule of paternalism. As an example, Richard Hare suggested a screening cost justification for why courts should set aside contracts of slavery.[2] What Hare had in mind was a consensual surrender of one's freedom and not a nonconsensual binding of a slave against his will. When the relationship is based on force, we don't presume that the slave is made better off because he had no choice in the matter. That's an easy one. But what if a person voluntarily consents to be a slave? Contracts to which the parties have freely consented are presumed to make both parties better off. Should a voluntary slavery contract then be enforced?

The answer is no, of course, but it is useful to distinguish three reasons why we would strike it down. First, we might think the contract *substantively unfair* because it is excessively one sided and harmful. Even if the slave freely gave his consent, this should be ignored because slavery is inimical to personal flourishing and moral responsibility. This is a rule of hard paternalism or perfectionism which second guesses the slave's preferences.*

---

*   Mill would not have enforced such an agreement on libertarian grounds, on the theory that the assertion of freedom to become a slave is self-defeating when one's freedom is forever lost. On Liberty at 101. This sounds like a logical point, but it nevertheless seems to come down to perfectionism, with personal autonomy held up as an essential element

Second, we might question whether the slave's signature on the contract really reflected his preferences. If it did not, there is no reason to think that it would leave the slave better off. We would then strike down the contract, not for its substantive unfairness, but rather for its *procedural unfairness*. This is not a matter of paternalism, hard or soft, but of the traditional vices of consent, such as fraud. A contract of slavery might be procedurally unfair because the signature on the dotted line was fraudulently induced.

Screening theories provide the third reason why we might refuse to enforce the contract. Let us suppose that only one man in a billion would ever consent to become a slave. Before we enforce the contract, we would want to make sure that he really was that one-in-a-billion case. We would examine him closely to see if there were any evidence of fraud or some other defect of consent such as force that would impeach the contract.

What makes this a screening problem is that it focuses on the informational costs born by the courts and the parties in proving the validity of the consent. Because the stakes are so great, the costs of satisfying the evidentiary burden would be enormous. Ordinary standards of proof would not apply, and we would have to prove the slave's consent to the hilt. Otherwise, we might mistakenly enforce a contract of slavery against a person who did not really consent or whose consent was tainted by a judgment bias. What if the agreement we signed hurriedly at the car rental booth provided that we'd become the slaves of Hertz if we came back with less than a full tank of gas? Even with the strongest of standards of proof, the courts would inevitably get it wrong on occasion and condemn to slavery someone who really didn't want to be a slave.

As compared with the costs of enforcing the contract of slavery, the benefits from enforcing the one-in-a-billion contract could only be trivial. Given the enormous burden that the contract imposes on the slave, the benefit he would derive must be presumed vanishingly small. On screening grounds, this argues for a complete ban on contracts of slavery because this would eliminate the wasteful information production costs that enforcement would entail.

Screening theories explain why other very harsh contracts are banned as a matter of public policy. A contract to subject oneself to physical abuse will not be enforced because it is very unlikely than anyone would freely agree to this. Even if someone did, we'd still want to ban such contracts, as a matter of perfectionism, because it is degrading. I have in mind here something like dwarf tossing (which seems to be a pressing social problem in several Canadian provinces, where it is banned).

One-sided terms are most to be feared in noncompetitive markets and in one-shot transactions where the seller needn't worry overmuch about her reputation. For example, in *Thornborow* v. *Whitacre*,[3] the defendant borrowed £5 and in return promised to give the plaintiff two grains of rye-corn in the first week, four grains in the second, eight grains in the third, and so on for a year. At trial, the defendant argued that if the promise were enforced, there would not be enough grain in the world to satisfy it. The contract was set aside. Special terms for the method of payment sometimes serve useful purposes but clearly did not do so here, and refusing to enforce such contracts usefully reduces screening costs.

🖎 Search Costs and Constrained Choice

Political philosopher Isaiah Berlin famously distinguished between negative and positive liberty. Negative liberty means that choices are not curtailed by legal constraints as they are when particular options are banned. Positive liberty means that the range of possible choices has expanded so that I can do things formerly closed to me.[4] When freed from jail, my negative liberty is enhanced; when I sprout wings and fly, my positive liberty has expanded. Positive liberty is antipaternalism in spades. If the paternalist wishes to narrow our range of options, positive liberty gives us more options.

Compared with fifty years ago, we might be thought to have less of Berlin's negative liberty today. A number of things that were permissible then are now illegal. That might not be a bad thing—we can well do without racism and sexism. What has expanded, however, is our positive liberty. Today, we have many more choices. We can move about more freely. Travel is cheaper, and countries once closed to visitors have opened their doors. We can more easily settle in another part of the country, and our choice of careers depends far less on what our fathers.

More than others, Americans have prized this kind of freedom. Historian Frederick Jackson Turner thought this came from the country's origins as a frontier society. Western states hungry for settlers competed for people by offering them free and democratic institutions. In time, eastern states lost people and began to compete by becoming more liberal. The result was a fresh start country, where everyone could always begin anew.

Few things are more appealing that the idea of starting over afresh, the slate wiped clean. In John Ford's *Stagecoach*, we cheer when the lovers are permitted to escape their past (jail for John Wayne's Ringo Kid, a bordello for

Claire Trevor's Dallas), and ride off together into the sunset. The dead hand of the past is cast off, and possibilities we thought foreclosed are opened.

Expanded choice or greater positive liberty would seem an unambiguously good thing. Imagine a range of options, like a row of levers, a thousand in all, offered to a group of people. Assume further that adding one more choice would make one person better off. He'd prefer the new lever to the thousand old ones. No one else would be affected, as they all would prefer the existing choices. The result is that the new choice would make one person better off and leave no one else worse off. This is the very definition of efficiency (or Pareto-efficiency) for the economist, and leaving aside the spiteful (who are better off when another is worse off) and the envious (who are worse off when another is better off), expanded choices seem an unmixed blessing.

Up to a point. The kinds of choices that commercial societies offer us, the unending array of gadgets, the cornucopia of food and drink, the parade of image and sound, Vanity Fair in all its glorious vulgarity, offend puritans at both ends of the political spectrum, the anticapitalist radical and the conservative declinist. Restricting choices on cultural grounds amounts to a hard paternalism or perfectionism that mistrusts our preferences. This is the perfectionism of John Ruskin, who lamented the banal choices of modernity. We'll take up perfectionism later and for now ask only whether consumer choices should be restricted to economize on *search costs*.

Search costs are the costs of acquiring and processing information about choices. Suppose that a new product is brought to market. Consumers will be asked to evaluate it and compare it with the next best choice, and this task might involve information production and computation costs. These costs, moreover, will be borne not only by the person who selects the new option but also by those who reject it. A person can't tell that the choice isn't for her until she examines it; and if she turns it down, these costs are, with the benefit of hindsight, a pure loss.

To return to my example, suppose that a thousand options are offered to a group of people, and one more choice is added to the mix. One person in the group might prefer the new choice, but everyone else would pass it by. For them, the new choice offers no benefit but instead imposes the cost of evaluating it. These search costs, borne by everyone in the group, might exceed the gains of the solitary person who takes up the new choice so that on net it makes people worse off.

Experimental tests of the costs of expanded choice suggest that more options don't always help. As the number of choices increases, people search less and consider fewer choices. They feel themselves conflicted and often simply decide not to choose. In one study, people were presented with a tasting booth that featured upscale brands of jam.[5] One group was shown six kinds of jam and the other group was shown twenty-four kinds, all in the same price range. A greater percentage of passers-by (60% to 40%) stopped at the larger display, but fewer people bought. Nearly 30 percent (31 people) at the smaller display bought jam, while only three percent (4 people) did so at the more extensive display. Too much choice seems to chill the desire to buy.

However, this is a long way from making the case for paternalistic fetters on choice. In a market setting, sellers have both the incentive and means to cure the problem by offering consumers an optimal number of choices, one that will maximize the number of sales. We wouldn't expect to see 1,000 items on a menu, but a much more limited number. A larger number of dishes confuses the patrons and sends a signal that no particular dish is especially good. Sellers don't need the state to tell them how to make money.

The argument from search costs sees the consumer as a helpless victim, swooning over a dizzying array of supermarket choices. So many choices, so little time. Yet somehow we manage to buy our cereal and laundry detergent without an intellectual crisis. Our heuristics, especially the availability heuristic, help us. We look for the cues that are most available to us: the same brand as the one we bought last week, the same color on the shelf. The availability heuristic constrains our choices, and for this reason, the paternalist is troubled by it, as we saw in Chapter 3. But by limiting our choices, the availability heuristic usefully economizes on informational costs.

The consumer can also economize on informational costs by his choice of stores. Looking for a book, he might visit a mega-store, where many thousands of books are indifferently arranged. Or he might visit a boutique bookstore which caters more closely to his tastes. Because so many purchases may be made over the Internet, he can use search engines that locate the particular goods he wants. The dominance of search engines such as Google is a consequence of their ability to find what we want quickly, and the next generation of search engines will be even better at intuiting our poorly expressed desires.

I'm a great fan of amazon.com, but because my choices are eclectic, it can't figure me out and its recommendations often leave me cold. It does know that, while I like Raymond Chandler and Georges Simenon, I consider most detective novels infra dig. With a more sophisticated search engine, however, Amazon might recognize that Michael Connelly's Harry Bosch novels would suit snobs like me just fine.

A plethora of goods for sale is a response to consumer demand. Man does not live by bread alone, noted Lionel Trilling. He also needs strawberry jam. And not just Smuckers either. We seek out the store that stocks several kinds of strawberry jam, to say nothing of quince and boysenberry. We sort ourselves out by our tastes and pick the jam we want. And then there is the simple joy of seeing the row of jams spread out before us on the shelf. We might not want boysenberry, but somewhere deep inside we like to be reminded that we're not living in the U.S.S.R. We shop to consume what we buy. But we also shop because shopping is a pleasurable consumption activity.

Were it otherwise, there'd simply be less for sale. Space is at a premium, and the size of a store is a function of the taste for variety. If we wanted only one kind of cereal, a 40,000 square feet Safeway in Alexandria, Virginia (with its 24,000 different items), would shrink to the size of a 10,000 square feet Monoprix (with its 6,000 items) in Paris, where high ground rents constrain store size and shelf space. Given the choice, we'll take more of everything, please. We'll pay for this by paying prices that reflect the store owner's higher rental costs for more space; and if the desire for variety might offend the puritan, it's precisely our tastes which disturb him.

The concern about search costs also overstates the information needed for inexpensive consumer purchases. We don't spend an inordinate amount of time worrying about which kind of jam to buy because the stakes are so low. In such cases, consumer purchases are more like a form of entertainment and less like a search cost. Where we do invest in information is when we are faced with big-ticket purchases, such as cars, houses, and university education. There we do take time. We read consumer guides, we search on-line, we ask around. It is highly misleading to suggest that there is any comparison between this and the search for a better brand of toothpaste.

Nor is it the case that producers manipulate consumers and dictate their tastes to manufacture a frivolous and wasteful taste for diversity. If that was true, notes James Twitchell, we'd be stuck with their duds. We'd be driving Edsels, listening to an eight-track tape, and drinking New Coke.[6] Instead, manufacturers are exquisitely sensitive to consumer tastes and package goods in the hope that among the thousands of products offered to the shopper, theirs will catch her eye. Consumers drive the economy, and it is misleading to portray them as passive recipients of goods foisted upon them.

Competition on markets also reduces search costs. Because they bear these costs, consumers seek products with the lowest information costs, all other things being equal. When offered similar goods, consumers prefer the one easiest to evaluate. We'll take the car with a proven track record over the one we know nothing about. Producers have thus an incentive to make their products easy to find and compare. We complain about the mass of fine print on labels that we're asked to digest and wish there were laws to make things simple, without realizing that laws are often the reason for the fine print.

Markets also permit consumers to free ride on the searches other consumers have performed. We don't have to read *Consumers' Reports* every time we buy something. Instead, we can ordinarily assume that other consumers will have identified defective products, which will have disappeared from the shelves. When vitamin A was recently found to be harmful when taken in large quantities, manufacturers were quick to lower the amount of it to acceptable limits. Retailers also have an incentive to cure the informational problem by stocking only high-quality products. If shoppers think there's a problem in the produce department, they won't buy the baked goods either.

The search cost argument for paternalism therefore overstates consumer search costs. At the same time, it understates the paternalist's own informational problem. If consumer sovereignty is said to be problematical, the proper response is "compared to what?" So long as the paternalist seeks to mimic the tastes of consumers and not his own, he faces the same informational problem that consumers do. He also must wander down the aisles of the supermarket, picking some items and rejecting others. The problem is that he can't possibly know the tastes of all consumers.

It used to be thought that economic planners could learn what consumers want and save them the cost of choosing for themselves. Since the collapse of communism, such arguments find few supporters. Instead, we've all come to accept Frederick Hayek's point that a single person can't possibly aggregate the knowledge of consumer tastes that is impacted in market processes.[7] Even Mikhail Gorbachev understood this before the collapse of the Soviet Union. Communism would prevail everywhere, he said. But they would need to leave New Zealand with a free market to see what goods to produce.

※ Oversignaling

By signaling, I tell you something about myself. That's different from screening. Screening refers to the information produced by the promisee to whom the promise is made, when the promisor is less than wholly credible. By contrast, signaling refers to the promisor's efforts to persuade others to rely on him and believe his promises. Both promisor and promisee have an incentive to take cost-effective steps to cure the informational problem because both stand to gain from the bargain, and both will lose if information costs get in its way.

We might too easily imagine that promisors give nothing away. On a naïve view of human relations, we hold our cards tightly to our vest, like W.C. Fields in *My Little Chickadee*. Before us the mark nervously holds his hand open, for all to see. "Is this a game of chance?" he asks. "Not the way I play it," answers Fields. We are Fast Eddie in *The Hustler*. "Looks like a church!" enthuses the sidekick, as they enter a pool hall. "Yeah," says Eddie. "The Church of the Good Hustle."

The films (and Georges de la Tour's paintings of the card sharp) remind us of a time when we were young ourselves and foolishly taken in by someone older and more unscrupulous. We have learned our lesson and will not be tricked again. Or if we are tricked, we'll know that we are in large measure to blame. In a world comprised of Fast Eddies, we approach strangers with a degree of rational mistrust.

That's a simple enough message, and George Akerlof used it to write a brilliant article and win a Nobel Prize.[8] Akerlof described how the used car market might unwind in a "market for lemons" because of rational mistrust. To simplify, he supposed that there are only two kinds of goods: good and defective used cars ("lemons"). There are an equal number of both, and the buyer can't tell them apart. The seller has driven his car and knows its quality, but that doesn't help the buyer. And bringing the car to a mechanic won't help either because we assume that the only way to determine its quality is to own one and use it for a while.

The buyer would be would be willing to pay $10,000 for a good car if he was sure that that's what it was. Lemons are worthless, however, and the buyer would pay nothing for them. What he does know is that there is an equal number of the two kinds of cars and might think that he should pay $5,000 for the car (since he'd have a 50% chance of getting a car worth $10,000). He might think that—but he'd be wrong.

What he'll have missed is the game-theoretic nature of the problem. If the car was randomly selected from the pool of all cars, its expected monetary value would indeed be $5,000. But the car isn't randomly selected. Instead, it is being sold by a seller who knows its true value and who, moreover, has a choice whether to sell or not. If the car isn't a lemon, the seller won't want to sell it on the cheap. He'll want more than $5,000 for it because it's really worth $10,000. But if the seller knows that it's a lemon, $5,000 will seem a great price to him. The seller's willingness to sell the car at $5,000 therefore signals that it's likely a worthless lemon. Because of this, the buyer will offer a lower price for the car, which in turn will squeeze out any remaining sellers of good cars. In the end, buyers will assume that only the lemons will be offered for sale and will not bid for them. In this way, the market for all used cars will unwind.

There. That's a Nobel Prize explained in a few paragraphs. Things always seem simpler afterward, don't they?

Who is hurt by the disappearance of the market for used cars? We instinctively sympathize with the buyer, but as nobody buys a car no buyer is hurt. There is still a loss, however, because both parties will have lost the benefit of the bargain. Buyers can't buy the good cars they want, and owners can't sell them. The seller has thus an incentive to cure the problem by signaling the car's true quality. This explains why the seller might be willing to assume the risk of legal liability by granting the buyer warranty rights for a defective product. Ex post, when product quality is revealed and defects are revealed, the seller will regret that he must pay up; but ex ante, before the car is sold, he will realize that the car cannot be sold unless the buyer receives warranty protection.

The seller's willingness to assume the risk of defects credibly signals product quality. Sellers of high quality cars are more likely to offer the warranty because they know they won't have to pay up (or at least are much less likely to do so). By contrast, sellers of lemons would resist the warranty because they know they'll be sued. Even before the buyer sues on the warranty, the mere willingness to offer it provides valuable information.

One of my friends (an economist) applies this lesson when he buys a used car. He shops around and, when he finds a car he likes, asks about extended warranty plans. If the seller is willing to offer a two or three year plan, he'll buy the car—without buying the warranty. He knows that what signals product quality is the offer of the warranty and not the warranty itself. Besides, warranties are usually overpriced. That's the punch line of a joke in *The Simpsons*. Homer submits to a procedure to reduce his already subnormal IQ. We know the procedure has worked when he says "Extended warranty! How can I lose?"

As a signaling strategy, unenforceable promises are far less credible than binding legal warranties. Not everything said in the context of a negotiation involves legal liability. Instead, the statement might be a "mere puff" or simple commendation ("The car's a real beaut!"), which is no more binding that the car salesman's lupine grin. Or the statement might be promises made in Thomas Hobbes' state of nature where the courts are corrupt or powerless and the rule of law does not obtain. In that case, said Hobbes, the promise is void:

> For he that performeth first hath no assurance the other will perform after, because the bonds of words are too weak to bridle men's ambition, avarice, anger, and other passions, without the fear of some coercive power; which in the condition of mere nature, where all men are equal, and judges of the justness of their own fears, cannot possibly be supposed. And therefore he which performeth first doth but betray himself to his enemy.[9]

The difference between the two signals—the offer of a warranty and a mere puff—is that the former, but not the latter, separates out the true and false signaler. When backed with legal force, the promise becomes credible; but when it's simply cheap talk, the buyer relies on it at his peril. The signal only works if it's going to hurt.

The signaling strategy that I have described employs costly or Spence signals, named after Michael Spence, who first wrote about them.[10] Spence signals have two characteristics. First, they are messages intentionally sent, as opposed to mere indicies. An index is an observable characteristic, such as a dent in a used car. That might provide useful information, but it's not a signal. The last rose of summer may signal autumn but does not count as a Spence signal. Instead, a signal is a device intentionally employed to make a promise credible. Second, the signal must permit the promisee reasonably to rely on the promise. That is, it must be believable or credible so that promisees can separate the sheep from the goats. For this to happen, promisors must sort themselves out, with true signalers in one camp and false ones in the other and a *non-mimicry constraint* that prevents false signalers from aping true ones.

In Spence signals, the sorting device is the cost of signaling, which is unequally borne by low and high quality signalers. For example, a low quality borrower (with a high probability of default) might not agree to bear a penalty on default, while a high quality borrower might be willing to do so because his probability of default is so low. The willingness to bear the penalty will then constitutes the non-mimicry constraint that separates the two kinds of borrowers. For low quality signalers, the cost of the almost certain penalty will exceed the gains from the contract. By contrast, high quality signalers will expect to derive greater benefits from the contract than the cost of the penalty, which they are unlikely to bear. The result is that only high quality signalers will have an incentive to assume the risk of the penalty, and their willingness to do so credibly signals their quality to promisees.

Costly signals have to hurt, if they are to separate the two kinds of promisors. Costless signals, such as mere puffs, won't do the trick. In that case, the signaling costs would be the same for low and high quality signalers, and the willingness to bear them would not permit recipients to tell them apart. The result would be a *pooling equilibrium* in which everyone looks the same. The promisee won't be able to distinguish them and will not rely on the promise. But when signaling costs are lower for faithful than faithless signalers, the result may be a *separating equilibrium*. Here only the trustworthy signaler has an incentive to signal, and when he does so, his promise is credible.

The signaling strategy Spence had in mind was education. Why is it, he wondered, that a person might study hard to receive top grades in a course that doesn't train one for a career? Reading Greek classics might be enjoyable, after a very difficult language is mastered, but that doesn't wholly explain why a person might strive to be at the top of his class. Or why an A in classics might matter to an employer (other than a classics department). The answer is that top marks might correlate with other qualities that an employer prizes, notably intelligence, industry, and possibly a gift for languages. If such attributes come easier to the student who receives an A+ than one who coasts along with a C, then the grade provides the non-mimicry constraint that permits the employer to rely on it as a signal.

There. That was another Nobel Prize, explained in a few paragraphs.

Spence signals might explain what otherwise might seem anomalous behavior. We've come a long way from blue-collar sweat shops, and Fair Labor Standards legislation prescribes a forty-hour maximum work week for covered employees. But that doesn't help young lawyers or doctors who are often asked to work extremely long hours, for years at a time. An associate lawyer might regularly put in eighty hours a week, and hospital residents might work even longer hours. A few years back, hospitals voluntarily agreed to ask residents to work no more than twenty-four hours at a stretch, rather than the forty-eight hours that had formerly been the norm.

Back when, we used to complain that factory workers toiled impossible hours to support the idle rich. That's certainly not the case today. Right now, it's the associate securities lawyer who is overworked and in need of paternalism—provided anyone feels sympathy for him.

All of which raises the question why the best and the brightest would agree to spend their salad days working slave hours. This would seem to be enormously costly, in terms of foregone happiness. And why would a hospital ask a resident to work such impossible hours that the quality of his medical judgment must suffer? The answer is that the associates and residents are in an arms race with each other for a scarce number of slots as law firm partners or as doctors at prestigious clinics. Those who stay the course and do not burn out signal that they have the qualities of determination and drive that correlate with what the law firm or clinic seeks in its partners and senior doctors—none of whom would themselves work those kind of hours.

Because they are costly, Spence signals are employed only where there is a shortage of information. Faced with two bright-eyed borrowers, the lender may not know who the better risk might be. And the law firm that wants to invest in training an associate lawyer won't always know which candidate has the grit to make partner. Spence signals are therefore most likely to be used where the informational problem is impacted.

Informational problems are especially severe in honor cultures. In the kind of primitive honor society portrayed in *The Iliad* or in Mallory's *Morte D'Arthur*, we know relatively little about other people. There are no credit checks or Google searches—what takes their place is personal reputation. People signal their character through unbending rectitude, which must always be on public display. In Homeric Greece, for example, the sense of shame (*aidôs*) was an all-powerful incentive to bravery, superseding even love of family. When Andromache implores her husband, Hector, to quit the battle lest she and their child be left unprotected, he replies that he would feel nothing but shame if he did so. And so he goes to his doom—and theirs too.

Anthropologist Ruth Benedict called such societies shame cultures in contrast to guilt cultures.[11] In a guilt culture, the sense of shame is internalized and people feel pain whether or not their transgression is observed. Their conscience bothers them. By contrast, in a shame culture, such as Benedict's Japan, the sanction for breach is the reputational loss when others notice the fault and revise their opinion of one. In that case, we might agree with Iago that a person has lost his most precious possession.

> *Good name in man and woman, dear my lord,*
> *Is the immediate jewel of their souls.*
> *Who steals my purse steals trash:' tis something, nothing;*
> *'Twas mine, 'tis his, and has been slave to thousands;*

But he that filches from me my good name
Robs me of that which not enriches him,
And makes me poor indeed. (Othello III.iii.155-61)

Post-Revolutionary America was an honor culture, according to historian Joanne Freeman.[12] The American Revolution destroyed or weakened many of the institutions around which colonial society had been built, and in the self-created and fluid society which emerged, people sought to signal their place in the pecking order. An extreme example of this was the duel. Alexander Hamilton was killed in a duel with Aaron Burr in Weehawken, New Jersey, but this was not the first duel Hamilton had fought. He had participated in ten duels before this, and his son had been killed in a duel. When Burr challenged him (in a manner which did not permit a graceful apology), Hamilton wrote that he disapproved of the institution but felt compelled to defend his honor.[13] He intentionally missed Burr by discharging his pistol into the air, but Burr took aim at Hamilton and did not miss. In an anarchic and duel-happy Ireland, things were taken a step further. In the Irish *Code Duello,* no apologies could be received after the parties had taken their ground, and firing into the air was strictly condemned. In the not unlikely event that the seconds quarreled, they were to exchange shots at the same time as their principals, and at right angles to them.

In honor societies, dueling was a Spence signal employed to guarantee the accuracy of the information about a person's integrity. A gentleman didn't fight a duel with a servant because the latter's inferiority was apparent to all. But among gentlemen, the willingness to defend one's honor on the dueling ground credibly revealed a person's character.

With perfect information about others, the institution of dueling would never have been introduced. A false slight upon an honorable person's character would be recognized as a misrepresentation and would not tarnish his reputation. Only the libeler would see his reputation suffer because his lie would be apparent to all. Where perfect information does not obtain, however, the parties will seek to signal their qualities, and might adopt costly Spence signals such as dueling to do so.

The dueling example illustrates how Spence signals might seem rational and irrational at the same time. In dueling societies, it might be rational to challenge a libeler to a duel, if the alternative of a damaged reputation is more costly still; and for the same reason it might be rational to accept a challenge. But what is individually rational for both parties might not be collectively rational for the society as a whole. Given the choice, everyone might prefer to ban the institution of dueling. It might be criminalized, as it was in Hamilton's New York (but not New Jersey), so that no dishonor would attach to people who refuse to invoke it. This would amount to paternalism because it takes choices away from people with the goal of satisfying their deeper preferences. More precisely, it would be a form of the collective choice paternalism we saw in Chapter 1. We'd all be better off if we could frame a general bargain in which dueling is banned. As that is impossible, a legal prohibition is the best we can do.

Dueling seems an easy case for the paternalist. Other examples of oversignaling also suggest a need for paternalistic fetters. In 1959, Jacques Plante became an object of ridicule in the hockey world when he donned the first face mask. Plante, the goalie for the Montreal Canadiens, had tired of catching Bobby Hull's slap shots with his teeth. In time, the practice of face masks for goalies caught on; but it would have happened faster had the National Hockey League mandated face masks. And the goalies themselves would plausibly have wanted the choice taken from them. They might have saved their teeth without losing face.

Athletes would likely agree to ban steroids, if the ban could be made effective. An individual player can tower over his competitors through steroids, but when everyone uses them the comparative advantage is lost and everyone would look like Canadian sprinter Ben Johnson. That wouldn't be so bad, except for the very harmful side effects of steroids. They can stunt an adolescent's growth, alter sex characteristics, lead to premature heart attacks, kidney failure, and serious psychiatric problems. This is why a flat prohibition on their use is something all athletes might want, if frequent drug testing could ensure that the ban would be effective.

For similar reasons, bikers might also want to mandate motorcycle helmets. Motorcycle accidents are a leading cause of death among young men, and helmets save lives. If bikers would refrain from wearing helmets when given the choice, out of a macho desire to signal bravery, then laws that require them to do so might accord with their deepest wishes. Plus they get to wear German WWII helmets.

There are limits to the oversignaling case for paternalism, however, once one moves beyond the threat of serious bodily harm. Most associate lawyers who work eighty hours a week do so to signal their worthiness for a partnership, but it doesn't follow that all law firm associates would want to mandate shorter hours. While a forty-hour week is the norm for most union jobs, and France mandates a thirty-five hour week, some associates would doubtless prefer to work longer hours, and not simply for signaling purposes. They might simply enjoy their work or see the long hours as a reasonable human capital investment. That's what one has to do to master a difficult subject and be on top of one's profession at age thirty-five.

For such people, fetters on working hours would represent a striking restriction on personal freedom, one directed at the most industrious and entrepreneurial people among us. To see this, imagine how such laws would be enforced if they are not empty shams. Would work police conduct midnight raids of law offices? Or would they monitor work done at home, for those with home offices? To be wholly effective, such laws would require a surrender of personal liberties associated with a police state. And this would be true of many of the signaling strategies people adopt. There are so many different ways in which a person might seek to rise above the crowd that the paternalist would have his hands full. Would he penalize the snappy dresser, the more cultured person, the more eloquent lawyer?

The examples illustrate the absurdity of trying to police every signaling strategy. On the other hand, there are less intrusive ways of nudging people to work shorter hours, without invoking the specter of work police. Progressive tax rates could remove much of the incentive to strive to acquire wealth and to work eighty hours weeks to signal one's desire for wealth. More intrusive laws would impose luxury taxes to curb conspicuous consumption, mandating generous parental leave periods or restricting consumer advertising. Such laws might not criminalize oversignaling but would nevertheless amount to paternalism as they are motivated by a desire to make people better off. Whether they would accomplish this goal is a subject, we take up in the next chapter.

SIX

Happiness

What's so good about happiness? It doesn't buy you money.

George E. Jessell

THE PATERNALIST CLAIMS that he knows best what will make us happy. If he's wrong, we'll have a better idea than him about our future happiness. But to the extent he's right, wouldn't it be sensible to let him choose for us?

Just how good are we are predicting our future happiness, then? All our important decisions have long-term consequences and involve a prediction about future states of mind. Whether the choice is wise will depend upon the accuracy of the prediction. And we are far from infallible. St. Teresa observed that "there are more tears shed over answered prayers than over unanswered prayers." More recently, Tibor Scitovsky suggested that people get addicted to unsatisfying base comforts and sacrifice the higher pleasures of novel experiences. They simply don't understand that the rat race is less than entirely satisfying.[1]

If there's any prediction about future happiness in which we'd feel confident, it's that more money would make us better off. That's also the basis of rational choice economics. More is better, says the economist. That's not to say that the relationship between wealth and happiness is one-to-one, and the economist's idea of diminishing marginal utility suggests that the "bang from the buck" gets smaller as we get wealthier. A marginal salary increase from $100,000 to $150,000 matters less than one from $50,000 to $100,000, in the same way that the second scoop of ice cream is enjoyed less than the first. Diminishing marginal utility means we get smaller increases in happiness as income levels rise. But it doesn't mean we get no increases. Even with diminishing marginal utility, we'd expect people to report greater happiness as they became richer.

It doesn't always happen that way, and that was the theme of a long-ago television show called *The Millionaire*. The show's conceit was that an eccentric

millionaire gave away checks for $1,000,000 to total strangers, and each epi-
sode began with the camera trained on his secretary, Mr. Anthony. "My name
is Michael Anthony," he would say:

> And until his death just a few years ago, I was the executive secretary to
> the late John Beresford Tipton. John Beresford Tipton, a fabulously wealthy
> and fascinating man, whose many hobbies included his habit of giving
> away one million dollars, tax free, each week . . . to a person who had never
> met him; indeed, had never even heard of him.

All we saw of Tipton was his hand. He'd offer Anthony the check, telling
him that he wanted to play a new kind of chess game "with human beings."
And then we'd follow Anthony as he gave the check away and disappeared
himself. The chess game was to see whether the money made the recipients
happy, and as often as not it didn't. For every person who got an expensive
life-saving operation, there was someone who squandered the money and
lost all his friends. This probably accounted for the show's popularity.

That's a television show, but here's a real story. Mack Metcalf was a forty-
two-year-old forklift operator in Kentucky, who in 2000 won a $65 million
Powerball jackpot.[2] He quit his job and never worked again. He bought a
forty-three acre estate for more than $1 million, where he collected expen-
sive cars and exotic pets. Trouble started right away. He was sued for child
support by a former wife, and cheated out of another half million by a girl-
friend. He became an alcoholic and died only three years after he won the
lottery. It was the worst thing that ever happened to him.

〽 Empirical Studies

That's one anecdote. But an anecdote is not the singular form of the plural
data. To do a proper study of how wealth correlates with happiness, the
economist needs data and will look at hundreds or thousands of cases. And
in recent years, a fascinating empirical literature has assembled the data and
questioned the notion that more money equals more happiness. In 1974,
economist Richard Easterlin reported that average reported happiness levels
for Americans had not risen for decades, notwithstanding a doubling of average incomes.[3] Since then, the "Easterlin paradox" has spawned an enormous
literature on the relation between income and happiness and represents
a serious challenge to antipaternalists. If free bargaining rights and free

markets that make people richer don't make them better off, then what's the point? The economist's norm of efficiency, where bargaining gains are exploited, would be an empty symbol, the way someone described the Eucharist at a posh dinner party attended by Flannery O'Connor. "Well, if it's a symbol," said O'Connor, "to Hell with it."[4]

Empirical studies of happiness are generally conducted through surveys of subjective well-being (SWB). For example, the U.S. General Social Survey asks people "Taken all together, how would you say things are these days—would you say you are happy, pretty happy, or not too happy?" Economists regard survey data as distinctly second-best. They prefer reported preferences, what people do and not what they say, objective to subjective findings. For good reason. Self-reported data is subject to fudging. A person might be embarrassed to report that he is unhappy. And what he reports about his happiness today might not be the same thing that he remembers at a future time. Across different languages and cultures, happiness doesn't translate well and questions about well-being don't elicit the same responses.[5]

But while self-reported happiness levels are necessarily subjective and prone to uncertainty, most people answer the surveys, and not everybody answers "very happy." In other surveys, one might worry that people are self-deceived, but it's hard to see how one can be mistaken about whether one is happy. In addition, a person's answers tend not to change much from one survey to the next, and people who describe themselves as happy tend to be so described by their friends. They are also more likely to behave as happy people do, by making friends and helping others, and less likely to suffer from emotional stress. People who report that they are very happy will smile more, while people who say they are unhappy have higher physiological signs of stress.[6] As far as empirical evidence of happiness goes, it doesn't get much better than SWB surveys.[7]

So what does the SWB survey data show? The Easterlin paradox suggests that more money doesn't translate into more happiness. However, the paradox disappears when we compare individuals or countries at a single point in time. On average, rich people are happier than poor people, and people in rich countries are happier than people in poor countries. In the 1994 United States General Social Survey of individuals, 44 percent of people in the highest income class reported themselves very happy, compared to only 16 percent in the lowest.[8] When we turn from individuals to cross-country comparisons, there is also a significant correlation between measures of happiness and gross domestic product per capita.[9] People in first world countries report that they are a good deal happier than those in developing or third world countries. Even within the first world, there does not seem to be a leveling off at the top end of the scale.[10]

These results are unsurprising because higher income correlates with basic material goods such as better schooling, food and health care. Quite apart from these findings, self-reported measures of happiness generally ignore one of life's basic goods: longevity. The survey questions simply ask people whether they are happy at the time and don't adjust for the length of time during which the happy person will enjoy life. They don't survey dead people. And because life expectancies range from eighty in first world countries such as Australia, to thirty-nine in underdeveloped Zimbabwe, the omission understates happiness levels amongst long-lived people in the richest, entrepreneurial countries. To some extent, the benefits of longer lives in the future are reflected in present reports of happiness because a thirty-eight-year old with a life expectancy of thirty-nine won't be terribly happy. But if future happiness is good in itself, this is left out of snapshots of well-being. A longer happy life is preferable to a shorter happy life.

Even if wealthier people tend to be happier, this doesn't show in which way causation works. More money might make people happier, but happy people might also be wealthier because they enjoy their work more. Causation probably works in both directions, and there is independent evidence that more money makes people happier from studies of what happens when people win lotteries.[11]

ℳ The Hedonic Treadmill

These are point-in-time snapshots, which compare different groups of people or countries at the same time. However, this doesn't tell us what happens to people over time as they become wealthier, and here there is stronger evidence for the Easterlin paradox. Studies of what happens to individuals over time suggest that we are on a "hedonic treadmill," and that the pleasure of new possessions or accomplishments fades as we become accustomed to them. As our income increases we become happier, but after a time we revert to the mean. We keep walking, but stay in the same place on the treadmill.[12]

Turning from the individual to the national level, several recent studies suggest that people in market economies have grown richer but not happier.[13] The percent of Americans who described themselves as "very happy" declined from 34 to 29 from 1972 to 1994, a period during which real income increased by nearly 50 percent. Overall, happiness levels have remained fairly constant during the period.[14]

Two explanations for the hedonic treadmill have been offered. First, we might each have an innate *adaptation set-point* of happiness, determined by character or genes, to which we revert after every gain or loss. Major events, such as a marriage or job loss, will move us from our equilibrium, but we quickly return to our natural state, neither particularly happy or unhappy, joyful or joyless.

If happiness levels are coded in our genes, trying to make ourselves happier is as futile as trying to make ourselves taller, as University of Minnesota geneticist David Lykken noted.[15] To determine the role genetics plays, Lykken and his colleagues surveyed pairs of twins in a study called, inevitably, the Minnesota Twins experiment. They questioned pairs of identical (monozygotic) twins with the same DNA, some of whom were separated at birth and raised apart. Remarkably, there was little difference between twins raised together and twins raised apart for most of the measured psychological traits, suggesting that these traits are a product of heredity and not environment.

In particular, Lykken found that genetic factors played an important role in happiness levels.[16] He reported that in predicting a person's future happiness levels, one can use the happiness levels of identical twins interchangeably. In other words, the happiness of twin *A* in year one predicts twin *B*'s happiness in year nine as accurately as it does twin *A*'s happiness in year nine, even for identical twins separated at birth and raised apart. Remarkably, Lykken could predict twin *B*'s happiness level much more accurately by looking at twin *A*'s happiness level nine years earlier than by looking at twin *B*'s current income or marital status. He concluded that our genes fix a set-point of happiness to which we tend to revert.

That set point is never one of perfect happiness. If our genes condemn us to a hedonic treadmill, they are a kind of original sin that dooms us to strive in an always unsuccessful search for satisfaction. We cast about restlessly in search of what Blaise Pascal labeled "diversion." "All man's misfortunes derive from one single thing," said Pascal, "his inability to remain at repose in a room."

This might be useful from an evolutionary perspective, as an adaptation set-point prevents us from lapsing into the life of self-contented indolence, like the Tahitians Paul Gauguin portrayed. We must get out, make discoveries and do things. Our restlessness produces wealth, empire, and civilization. Nevertheless, the unending search for pleasure seems self-defeating in the end. We flip through magazines, channel surf television, or Google the Web, and in between sneak in a game of spider solitaire. And when that fails we go shopping.

The second explanation for the hedonic treadmill is that, as our material goods increase, so do our aspirations. When we grow wealthy, we have more, but want more still, and get no closer to our goals. Our reach never exceeds our grasp, and we are never satisfied. This *aspiration adjustment* hypothesis was Richard Easterlin's preferred explanation for why happiness levels are sticky, and he gave a striking example of this in an experiment which asked participants to go down a list of consumer goods and pick the ones that formed their idea of the good life. They then were asked to identify the ones they had already. When the survey was repeated with the same people sixteen years later, they possessed more goods, but the gap between what they had and what they wanted remained about the same.[17] The Promised Land always recedes as we approach it. With more money, we simply want more things, and while the twenty-year-old might have been happy with a week in the Caribbean, the sixty-year-old wants a month in Tuscany. More money is never entirely what it's cracked up to be.

In *The Joyless Economy*,[18] economist Tibor Scitovsky explained why more money doesn't seem to bring more happiness: we get bored. When our desires are met we experience momentary bliss. But our joy turns into satiety, and satiety into mere comfort, and comfort soon begins to bore, and after a while boredom is disquieting. Every new pleasure palls when it becomes routine, as they almost always do.

However explained, the hedonic treadmill might be thought to justify paternalistic interference with personal preferences. If we want things that don't make us happy, then taking away the chance to get them won't make us worse off, and might make us better off. At least we wouldn't waste our efforts pursuing them. Suppose that Robert Lane is correct in arguing that "people are not very good judges of how, even within the private spheres of their own lives, to increase, let alone maximize, their happiness."[19] We chase after wealth, says Lane, but never really find the contentment we seek through material goods. If so, the case for individual autonomy is weakened, and fatally so if SWB happiness is the summa bonum.

∰ Relative Preferences

The hedonic treadmill assumes that increased wealth doesn't result in increased happiness, either for individuals or countries. There's another possibility, which is that increased wealth makes individuals happier but not their countries. This might be attributed to *relative preferences*, where people care about how they are doing relative to other people. They have absolute preferences, in the sense that they want more wealth—but they also have relative preferences and worry about keeping up with the Joneses.

Suppose you were given a choice between two states of the world. In state *A* you'd earn $50,000, and everyone else would earn $25,000; in world *B* you'd earn $100,000, and everyone else would earn $250,000. (We're assuming that prices are the same in both worlds.) In absolute terms, you'd be better off in world *B*, where you could buy more goodies. Relative to everyone else, however, you'd be ahead in state *A*. Which would you pick? In an experiment with Harvard graduate students, more than half the people chose world *A*. Their relative preferences—how they'd compare with others—dominated their absolute preferences for more wealth. And to satisfy their relative preferences, they were willing to take a deep pay cut provided everyone else took a deeper cut. They preferred to be poorer so long as others were poorer still.[20] La Rochefoucauld understood the sentiment when he observed: "In the misfortunes of our best friends we always find something not altogether displeasing to us."[21]

In my university, salaries have recently been posted on the Web and made accessible to everyone on faculty. Imagine how you'd feel when you discover that your $6,000 pay increase was dwarfed by a colleague's $20,000 increase. While knowing what your colleague got might give you a few bargaining chips when the next salary increases are made, you might prefer blissful ignorance. Mightn't you have been happier before the salaries became a matter of public knowledge?

Economists describe relative preferences as externalities because the change in one person's wealth has an external spillover effect on others. For the altruist who feels better when others do well, the externalities are positive. For the envious who feel worse when others do well, the sign is reversed and the externality is negative.

Envy externalities magnify happiness effects. The well-off are happy because they are rich; and they are happier still because they are richer than the poor. And this works in reverse for the poor. They are less happy because they are poor and less happy still because others are rich. Tertullian has left us with a striking vision of relative preferences. One of the particular joys of Heaven, it seems, will be the ability to peer down from on high and observe the sufferings of the sinners in Hell.[22]

The paternalist might see in relative preferences an argument for a ban on certain kinds of conspicuous consumption that fan other people's envy.

One example of this is the Elizabethan sumptuary laws which banned "outrageous" double ruffles, gilded spurs, and other fripperies that constituted the status goods of the time. More recently, Robert Frank has suggested that luxury goods such as yachts are wasteful, with the wealthy purchaser's increased happiness exceeded by the unhappiness of the envious rowboat owner.[23] For Richard Laylard, status goods are a form of pollution that impose costs on those who cannot afford them, and deserve to be taxed.

> If a person works harder and earns more, he may himself gain by increasing his income compared with other people. But the other people lose because their income now falls relative to his. He does not care that he is polluting other people in this way, so we must provide him with an automatic incentive to do so. Taxation provides exactly this incentive.[24]

ℳ Does This Argue for Paternalism?

Hedonic treadmill theories don't make a very strong case for paternalism. First, aspiration adjustment theories overstate the evidence about how we adapt to changed personal circumstances. The hedonic treadmill assumes complete adaptation, with people always returning to the same set point. However, the adaptation never seems to be complete. While quadriplegics rebound from their accident and are happier than one might have expected, they are significantly less happy than healthy people.[25] And notwithstanding Easterlin's findings, acquiring more toys does seem to make us happier. A study of ownership and desire for big-ticket material goods (cars, travel, vacation home, etc.) for people at eighteen, thirty, and forty-five found that people wanted relatively fewer goods as they acquired more of them.[26]

Second, the hedonic treadmill assumes that life choices don't affect happiness levels, and that seems to be wrong. Married people are happier than unmarried people, religious people are happier than nonreligious, and charitable people are happier than noncharitable.[27] Moreover, we get happier as we get older.[28] Self-reported happiness increases with age, which is consistent with an income effect because we almost always get wealthier as we get older.

Finally, neither set-point nor aspiration explanations of sticky happiness levels make much of a case for paternalism or for any change in social or economic policies. If happiness levels are a constant, if as Yeats thought we're completely self-appeasing and self-arighting, neither paternalism nor antipaternalism is going to make much of a difference in our lives. To the extent that the paternalist, with his laws designed to make us happier, inspires hopes that are bound to be frustrated, the effort would leave us worse off.

As compared with hedonic treadmill theories, relative preference explanations seem to have more going for them. In particular, they offer an intriguing explanation for flat happiness levels at the national level. If, as a nation, we don't seem to get happier as we get richer, this might be attributed to the negative externalities that the rich impose on the poor. The rich become happier, the poor unhappier, and on average it's a wash. Relative preference arguments for paternalism, however, are problematic.

First, people can drop out of the rat race on their own. If a particular status competition turns out to be a mug's game, people can always switch to another. Status is measured in many different ways: income, education, physical strength, relationships with others, art, music, dance, sport, and for each dimension, a sustaining community of friends seek status and applaud accomplishments. Everyone concerned with status has an incentive to find his own niche, whether it be a knowledge of baseball trivia, a skill at fishing, a knowledge of poetry, or a collection of art. Those who cannot afford the expensive baubles by which the rich signal status might nevertheless find other equally satisfying ways to compete for attention.

Second, relative preference theories assume that the competition is a zero-sum game, that the loser's loss always equals the winner's gain. There is little reason to think this is so, especially where the competition is for status or fame. Those who compete for Nobel Prizes, for honorary titles, and for academic honors usually benefit others through their efforts—which is why the prizes and honors were created in the first place. Where the competition hurts other people, we don't award prizes. There are no awards for best crime or worst movie (although MTV reality shows might give one pause).

When the competition is for material gain, the spillover effects are also generally benign. The inventor of a new miracle drug that saves or prolongs life might gain enormous rewards, but we all also benefit. To succeed, his invention must be patentable, and patents are not awarded unless the invention is both new and useful. Whether patentable or not, new technologies will not be brought to market unless they respond to human demands. Apart from material gains, successful entrepreneurs gain higher status, and this also provides them with an incentive to succeed. Without the status gain, write Nobel laureate Gary Becker and Kevin Murphy, there would be an underinvestment in entrepreneurial activity.[29] In all such cases, there are externalities, but these are more plausibly positive than negative.

Third, efforts to promote happiness by eliminating status competitions might be self-defeating. By calling attention to wealth differences, they might excite more class envy than they curb. For example, a scheme of progressive taxation might reduce envy by flattening out wealth differences. But at the same time, a populist campaign to erase wealth differences might result in resentments that remain unsatisfied by the tax increase.

This assumes that preferences are shaped in part by the legal regime in which we find ourselves. In the jargon of economists, these are *endogenous preferences* because they are "born from within" the legal regime. What we want depends in part upon the laws that govern us. The opposite of endogenous preferences are *exogenous preferences*, which are born from without, in the sense that the legal regime does not affect them.

The argument that legal rules shape our preferences turns out to be an argument for paternalism, as we will see in the next chapter. If our desires can be manipulated, we might perhaps be legislated into wanting what is good for us. When it comes to relative preferences, however, endogenous preferences are an argument against paternalism. Differences in wealth and status can never be eliminated, and calling attention to them might make the more fortunate worse off without making the less fortunate better off, if the envious remain envious.

Because envy is destructive of individual efforts to get ahead, it is universally condemned. In the Catholic tradition, it is one of the seven capital sins; and in the Jewish tradition, covetousness is the only sin of intention, where the mere desire is wrongful even if it is not acted on. As the desire to deny goods to one's neighbor, envy is the opposite of the principles of sympathy and benevolence which Adam Smith and Bishop Butler thought the foundational moral sentiments. It is also the sin against capitalism, which infected the backward Italian town—"Montegrano"—studied by Edward Banfield in *The Moral Basis of a Backward Society*. Banfield's Montegrano was so riddled with envy that any form of economic progress was unthinkable. The Montegranese thought that every politician was on the take, that every priest was corrupt, and that every employer cheated his employees. Only the most basic forms of economic cooperation were possible.

All those who stand outside the small circle of the family are at least potential competitors and therefore also potential enemies. Toward those who are not family the reasonable attitude is suspicion. The parent knows that other families will envy and fear the success of his family and that they are likely to do it injury. He must therefore fear them and be ready to do them injury in order that they may have less power to injure him and his.[30]

In an envious society, where your gain is my loss, my only sensible course is to refuse to bargain with the enemy. All gains from joint cooperation would thus be lost, and what would remain would be Max Weber's "universal reign of absolute unscrupulousness" that is wholly destructive of economic growth.[31]

Policies that seek to satisfy class envy might thus be self-defeating, exciting as much envy as they dampen. As we noted, the class hatreds unleashed by populist attacks on the wealthy and privileged might not be dissipated by schemes of progressive taxation meant to bring about equality of outcomes. There is never a promised land, where envy is satisfied. Differences in outcomes persist after every attempt to equalize them, and the populist never lacks for targets or the envious for their rancor.

Not surprisingly, there is a strong correlation between happiness levels and cultural norms of individualism which constrain envy. If there are Montegranos, there are also anti-Montegranos which prize personal accomplishment, which give priority to the individual and his desires, which discount envy, and which place a smaller weight on a person's relation to the collectivity. And they tend to be happier than envious societies.[32]

All this will come as a surprise to Marxists, who describe people in bourgeois, market societies as unhappy and alienated; and to communitarians such as Charles Taylor, who think that the emphasis on individual rights results in an atomistic society where people are cut off from one another. That's not what the evidence shows. People in individualistic societies report they are happier than those in collectivist societies that subordinate individual to group feelings.[33] Caring about other people doesn't make people happier if their care takes the form of envy.

These findings might evidence a wealth effect, where people in individualist societies are happier because they're wealthier. But that doesn't seem to be the only thing going on. Within first world countries, relative preference theories predict that people are happier where there aren't great disparities in wealth. However, there doesn't seem to be any evidence of this. Rich people are happier than poor people, but the difference doesn't seem to have anything to do with the size of welfare payments. The generous payouts of welfare states don't seem to affect happiness levels.[34]

More to the point, the happiest societies are also the freest, economically and politically. Across the board, a 1 percent increase in the Wall Street

Journal/Heritage Foundation measure of freedom is associated with a 2 percent rise in the percent of people in the country who say they are happy.[35] And individuals who favor democracy and free markets are also happier than those who don't.[36] If any message can be taken from the empirical evidence, it is that repressive regimes are miserable ones.

At the individual level, there is a lot of evidence that free people are happy people. In a study of a Connecticut nursing home,[37] psychologists gave one group of residents a few seemingly innocuous choices. They could decide which night of the week would be movie night. They were also asked if they wanted a plant and given a choice about which one they wanted. On another floor, with a similar set of residents, people weren't given these choices. The movie night was chosen for them, and they were simply handed a plant. The first group of residents immediately perked up and seemed happier than the first group a year and a half later. The paternalist made people unhappy.

A fourth difficulty is that the evidence from charitable contributions is inconsistent with relative preference theories. Were we obsessed with status differences, we'd feel better when others were worse off. We'd then be the last people to donate to charity for the less well-off. But that is just what Americans do, more than anyone else. The most individualistic and richest nation—America—is also considerably more generous than more collectivist European societies. After accounting for differences in standard of living, Arthur Brooks reports that Americans give almost three times as much of their income to charity as the French and more than ten times as much as the Italians. Nor does American generosity stop at the checkbook. The monetary value of volunteer efforts by individual Americans also exceeds that of Europeans.[38]

In sum, there is little evidence that relative preferences weight heavily for Americans. And this is why Seymour Martin Lipset thought that socialism did not take hold in the United States.[39] Unlike Europeans, Americans are not burdened by class envy. Instead, they believe they have a shot at moving up the ladder; and because America is a more mobile society, such beliefs are not irrational.

𝑀 What's So Good about Happiness?

A final difficulty with relative preference explanations, or with either of the hedonic treadmill theories, is that self-reported measures of happiness might ignore other of life's goods which those who strive for success are more likely to attain. SWB snapshots might not reflect friendship, love, excellence in one's job, or success in a worthy endeavor. For that, one must turn from subjective to objective measures of happiness, such as those Aristotle provided in the *Nicomachean Ethics*.

Aristotle thought that happiness—*eudaimonia*—was the highest good, to which all men aim. However, he defined happiness objectively and contrasted it with amusement (*paidia*). Happiness refers to a successful life that conforms to man's end or function; amusement is simply a light and ephemeral pleasure, and that's not what a successful life is all about, thought Aristotle.

> It would, indeed, be strange if the end of life were amusement, and one were to take trouble and suffer hardship all one's life in order to amuse oneself. To exert oneself and work for the sake of amusement seems silly and utterly childish. (Nicomachean Ethics 1176^{b}28)

A life filled with amusements very possibly ranks high on SWB measures of happiness. Looking backward, however, we might like Aristotle think our life ignoble and unsatisfying if we have little to show for it. On Aristotelian or eudaimonistic measures of happiness, the oversignaler whom we saw in the last chapter, who works long hours and has greater accomplishments, would likely rank ahead of the do-nothing fainéant.

Aristotle's eudaimonia was not a subjective good but the exercise of a man's soul in accordance with excellence or virtue, and in this sense Aristotle's moral theory was perfectionist. It saw the moral end as the perfection of the total nature of man, with full happiness achieved through the realization of his capacities. This is the work of the man who experiences the thrill of discovery when he tackles a new project, who enjoys the sense of mastery as he develops his skills, or who strives for perfection in his tasks.

Psychologists have recently sought to give content to eudaimonistic well-being (EWB) and distinguish it from hedonic SWB measures of happiness. Carol Ryff has developed self-reported surveys to evaluate EWB on six dimensions of objective well-being: purpose in life, environmental mastery, autonomy, personal growth, positive relations with others, and self-acceptance. To this might be added such related goods as fulfilling one's potential, self-flourishing, and the practice of virtue. These are all important elements of happiness, even if they are not captured by SWB's more immediate snapshot of one's feelings. Not surprisingly, young adults with higher education, who are more likely to be strivers, report low SWB but high EWB happiness.[40]

There are, in short, different dimensions of happiness, and the oversignaler is likely to rank more highly on EWB than on purely subjective measures.

EWB measures of happiness are also coded with a sense of intrinsic worth. They give us not merely a sense of happiness but of a happiness that is deserved, of which we might be proud, and this must be the more satisfying. EWB happiness is the happiness of justified rather than fatuous self-esteem. It's the happiness of wealth that is earned rather than given to one, as to the lottery winner. To a nation in the midst of an economic crisis, Franklin Roosevelt said in his First Inaugural that "happiness is not in the mere possession of money; it lies in the joy of achievement, in the thrill of creative effort." We should therefore hesitate before we deprive the achiever of the rewards of his efforts, through the sharply progressive taxes Robert Frank proposed.[41]

Even this does not exhaust the goods of the world. SWB and EWB measures of happiness are an important measure of the good life, but the search for happiness might include other goods more likely to be found in the competitive societies that paternalists decry. One such good is joy, which is as different from happiness as love is from friendship. Joy shares one attribute with happiness and pleasure, said C. S. Lewis: experience them once and you want them again.[42] Yet next to joy, mere happiness seems pallid, almost weightless. Happiness lacks ecstasy's bittersweet release, and we would never trade it for joy. Happiness is a suitable goal for those who are content with a quotidian life, slouched before the television set. The quest for happiness might even seem a little banal. "I feel sorry for you," wrote Baudelaire to a critic, "that you are so easily made happy."[43]

Happiness is a secular concept, and joy aspires to the condition of the sacred. It seeks something more than everyday pleasures and is unsatisfied with anything less than the awe-inspiring mystery and religious ecstasy Rudolf Otto described:

> The feeling of it may at times come sweeping like a gentle tide. . . . It may burst in sudden eruptions up from the depths of the soul with spasms and convulsions, or lead to the strangest excitements, to intoxicated frenzy, to transport, and to ecstasy.[44]

That's not to say that religious people cannot be happy people, and indeed there's a lot of empirical evidence that they're happier than people who don't practice a religion.[45] However, the gulf between the sacred and the profane is not so easily bridged. The sense of the holy, the feeling of awe before God, is not captured by a feeling of happiness, and indeed might seem more like agony, as it did in Richard Crashaw's *Hymn to St. Teresa*.

O how oft shall thou complain
Of a sweet and subtile pain?
Of intollerable joyes?
Of a death in which who dyes
Loves his death and dyes again,
And would for ever so be slain.

As between an ordinarily pleasant life and the saint's ecstatic life, might we hesitate before choosing mere happiness? Might we ever prefer a life touched with tragedy if the alternative asks us to forget the pathos of the world?

However, what does all this say about paternalism? Not much, in my view. I concede that there are objective goods, things worth pursuing for their own sake. What I don't concede is that the paternalist is particularly helpful in getting us there.

First, there is a very large overlap between the list of EWB objective goods and what people prefer. Go down any list of objective goods—family, friends, joy, laughter, health—and ask who wouldn't want them. Do people want to be friendless and sick? Could we, without difficulty, walk away from a joyous experience? What puts something on the objective list of goods is that, for the most part, people in fact prefer it. This is to say that they don't need paternalist's help in order to choose it.

Second, even if our preferences don't match up exactly with the objective list, just how would the paternalist remedy this? Joy cannot be commanded by the legislator, and giving him the power to try to do so might easily lead him to overreach. Of all the different kinds of paternalism, the most dangerous is perhaps that which purports to give our empty lives meaning, a power claimed only by the most oppressive of regimes, the kind that seeks to create New Soviet Man or the Fascist hero.

Finally, the most obvious message from the EWB objective goods standard is that strivers and oversignalers who rank lower on SWB, but higher on the EWB standards, should not be impeded by the paternalist.

𝄞 Conclusion

A recent empirical literature on self-reported happiness levels for people and countries suggests that we'd be better off if we spent less time striving for wealth, as oversignalers are apt to do. On closer examination, however, happiness studies provide little basis for paternalistic interference with individual choice. The evidence is at best ambiguous because the wealthy really are happier than the poor. In addition, the happiest societies are those with the greatest economic and political freedom and, consequently, with the smallest degree of paternalism. Finally, self-reported happiness studies ignore objective measures of well-being that offer deeper and more permanent personal satisfaction and which the oversignaler is more likely to experience.

SEVEN

Endogenous Preferences

One's own free, unfettered choice, one's own caprice—however wild it may be. . . . What man wants is simply independent choice, whatever that independence may cost and wherever it may lead.

Dostoyevsky, Notes from the Underground

WE SAW ENDOGENOUS PREFERENCES in the last chapter, when we considered whether relative preferences argued for paternalism. There we asked whether populist legislation that seeks to reduce feelings of envy might be self-defeating by perversely arousing more envy than it satisfies. The legislation would tend to equalize incomes, which might make people less envious; but at the same time, by reminding people about differences between rich and poor, it might lead to more envy.

Preferences are endogenous to the legal regime when they are shaped by it, as they would be when populist legislation makes people more envious. When preferences are unaffected by the legal regime, they are exogenous. Antipaternalists generally assume that preferences are exogenous and arise from within ourselves, or perhaps our families, schools, and churches, but never from the state. Otherwise, paternalism might seem difficult to resist. It becomes harder to claim that the state should not constrain choices when it has already done so, determining what we choose by shaping what we prefer. The horse would already have left the gate.

It is difficult to deny that people's preferences depend in part on their legal regime. Of all people, Americans are perhaps least likely to believe that their citizenship has anything to do with their preferences. But think how easy it is for a non-American to spot an American tourist in foreign country. Whatever their race, religion, or politics, Americans stand out, in their fundamental decency, self-assertion and core democratic values. And why are they so alike? It can't be genetic, given America's diversity. So it must have something to do with a common set of norms and institutions of which legal norms and institutions are presumably important factors.

For example, the Civil Rights Act of 1964, which penalized certain forms of discrimination, plausibly changed people's attitudes to race relations in areas beyond the scope of the statute. Racial prejudice is far weaker today than it was then, and the change in the laws likely had something to do with this. Of course, one is never sure about the direction of causation, and a prior change in preferences about race might have produced the statute, rather than the other way around. The bill was enacted when racial prejudice had weakened and would not have been passed fifty years earlier, when racial prejudice was far stronger. Nevertheless, it is not implausible to suggest that causation works both ways in such cases and that the legal change shaped our preferences.

That's not to say that, by themselves, endogenous preferences make the case for paternalism. Laws might change our preferences, but this doesn't necessarily justify state laws designed to interfere with people's preferences. There is a logical leap from the claim that the state does shape our preferences to the assertion that it should do so and that it has free rein to interfere with our choices. Otherwise, everything would be up for grabs. The state could intervene whenever it saw fit, and no one could complain of this. It could promote its own vision of religion, high culture, or diet. It might establish an official church, promote "official artists," and ban the triple-decker McWhopper, just because some of our preferences are shaped by the legal regime. Like a moth to a flame, a facile paternalism is drawn to the idea of endogenous preferences; but something more is needed before the state might legitimately interfere with personal choices. The possibility that preferences are endogenous is not a permission slip for the paternalist.

A strong antipaternalist might therefore want to roll back past interference with preferences and return to a regime of the strictest possible neutrality. As between two proposed laws, he would prefer the one which least shapes our preferences. But is it as easy as that? Some laws, such as the 1964 Civil Rights Act, will inevitably change our preferences. But had the bill not been enacted, that too might have shaped our preferences by sending a signal that racial prejudice was acceptable. Both legislative action and inaction might affect our choices.

However, this argument seems to confuse the different forms that legislative inaction might take. Sometimes the failure to pass legislation resembles action more than inaction. Had the 1964 Act been defeated, after the lengthy filibuster by southern Democrats, this would plausibly have fueled racial prejudice because the filibuster was a very public act. At the time, *Life* magazine published excerpts of the long-winded speeches southern senators made to filibuster the bill, their recipes for Brunswick stew, their memories of the old swimmin' hole, alongside stories about what was really happening in places like Selma and Montgomery. Defeat of the bill would have sent a strong signal about the dismal state of racial relations. It would also have had profound political consequences, for example, by making it difficult for the federal government to enforce existing federal civil rights laws over the objection of southern states that wished to segregate their citizens by race.

When the legislator fails to pass legislation in spite of strong political clamor for passage, this is better seen as action than inaction. By resisting the call for change, the legislator takes a stand and sends a message. Where there is no demand for change, on the other hand, it is hard to see how legislative inaction might affect preferences. There are an infinite number of hypothetical bills not passed in any session of the legislature—bills to subsidize virtue, bills to criminalize vice, bills to subsidize vice, and bills to criminalize virtue—and a failure to enact any of them would not have the slightest effect on people's preferences unless there is a public demand for and awareness of them. And in that case, it is the popular pressure for the law and the resulting sense of frustration over an unaddressed need that produces the passion and the preferences.

Expressive Effects

Let's back up and ask just how legislation might shape our preferences. The most plausible answer is that it does so by expressing the legislator's views about what is just. We are influenced by the views of our friends and associates and by the opinions held by society at large, and they in turn are affected by the opinions expressed by societal institutions, including most prominently the legislature.

The *expressive* function of a law extends beyond the act in question to related behavior, behavior in the penumbra of the statute.[1] For example, we ban trading votes for money because this would corrupt the political process. We'd no longer be a democracy but instead a plutocracy and ruled by the wealthy. In part, however, such legislation might be prompted by a concern for expressive effects. It signals that voting is the cornerstone of the democratic process and that everyone who can vote ought to do so.

For economists, voting is a puzzle. My vote won't affect the outcome of an election unless I cast the tie-breaking vote. That's just not going to happen, however. It didn't happen in Florida in 2000, and it's not going to happen to me in my lifetime. So why should I go through the trouble of trudging to the polls? The answer is that social norms encourage voting, and as I have internalized these norms I'd feel guilty if I didn't vote. That wouldn't have happened without preference-shaping norms and legal institutions, such as the prohibition of vote-selling, that affirm our support for democratic institutions and the moral duty to vote.

The belief that the law should concern itself with expressive effects transcends ordinary political labels. Liberals support laws that seek to shape our preferences about racial and gender issues, and many conservatives have their own expressive agenda. After the Supreme Court set aside a law which criminalized flag burning, some conservatives proposed a constitutional amendment to restrict free speech rights when it comes to desecrating the flag. Quite possibly more flags would be burned by protestors were the law enacted, but that wouldn't be the point. What would matter is that most people might feel greater respect for a national icon. Similarly, conservative opposition to same-sex marriage is premised on the belief that were it legalized heterosexuals would think less of marriage. For that matter, lifestyle liberals who support same-sex marriage do so because they'd like to see more positive attitudes to homosexuality. People who disagree strongly about social issues nevertheless agree that legal rules should seek to mold our preferences.

The antipaternalist cannot ban expressive effects. Whether he likes it or not, laws necessarily express approval or disapproval. At most, the libertarian might ask the legislator to ignore all such effects. Yet even this seems dogmatic. In evaluating a statute we should be entitled to take all consequences into account, including expressive ones. Suppose that an ostensibly benign law seems perverse when expressive effects are taken into account. When a law that seeks to reduce racial tensions would in reality exacerbate them, it would be foolish to enact it.

We cannot ignore expressive effects, then. Yet even this might concede too much to the paternalist. Ostensibly expressive legislation to which penalties are attached can be oppressive, and there is ample evidence that well-intentioned expressive laws have been perverted. This is especially true of Canadian human rights codes, which in recent years have assumed a life of their own.

Canadian human rights codes were initially enacted as a milder version of the American Bill of Rights. The *Canadian Bill of Rights*, passed by a Tory government in 1960, affirmed the existence of certain basic rights but was not enshrined in the Constitution (unlike the 1982 *Charter of Rights and Freedoms*), and was employed only once to strike down federal legislation.[2] It nevertheless served as a model for provincial human rights codes across the country. These enjoyed broad popular support. After all, how could anyone but a benighted bigot object to the goals of the Alberta Human Rights Code, as described in the preamble to the Alberta statute.[3]

Whereas recognition of the inherent dignity and the equal and inalienable rights of all persons is the foundation of freedom, justice and peace in the world;

Whereas it is recognized in Alberta as a fundamental principle and as a matter of public policy that all persons are equal in: dignity, rights and responsibilities without regard to race, religious beliefs, colour, gender, physical disability, mental disability, age, ancestry, place of origin, marital status, source of income or family status;

Whereas multiculturalism describes the diverse racial and cultural composition of Alberta society and its importance is recognized in Alberta as a fundamental principle and a matter of public policy;

Whereas it is recognized in Alberta as a fundamental principle and as a matter of public policy that all Albertans should share in an awareness and appreciation of the diverse racial and cultural composition of society and that the richness of life in Alberta is enhanced by sharing that diversity. . . .

This in Canada's most conservative province. No doubt, part of the appeal of such codes, for conservatives in any event, is that they seem toothless. Yet when the *Western Standard* magazine in Calgary reprinted the Danish cartoons of Mohammed that sparked riots in the Muslim world, an Islamic cleric complained and the publisher found himself dragged before the Alberta Human Rights Commission. The Alberta statute expressly states that the Act shall not be deemed "to interfere with the free expression of opinion on any subject," but still the hearing went on, until the complainant withdrew his complaint of his own accord.[4] The Commission also heard a complaint against a hairstyling school after the teacher failed to reprimand girls in the course for calling a male student a "loser."[5] The complainant

felt like an outsider and felt ostracized by the other students. [He] asked the instructor in the third week of class what the final exam would consist of and if he could have an outline. The instructor told him that he didn't need to know that right now and that she would hand it out in the fourth week, but didn't until the fifth week.

No wonder he brought a complaint! In another case, the Commission heard and upheld a complaint by a dredge operator who failed two drug tests and refused to take a third. The complainant's taste for marijuana was a disability, and by firing him his employer had breached the Human Rights Code.[6]

The Commission is clearly out of control. By holding hearings over frivolous complaints and punishing politically incorrect views that are well within the bounds of permitted free speech, the Commission has disregarded basic civil liberties. It is able to do this because its hearings are not governed by the procedural and evidentiary rules that protect defendants in civil and criminal cases. The penalties it has imposed, and the very cost of the hearings to the defendant, have gone far beyond merely expressive effects, and resemble the sanctions of religious police for the promotion of virtue and suppression of vice.

Because expressive legislation can assume a life of its own and turn into a form of illiberal oppression, one must be wary of the paternalist's efforts to shape preferences through expressive effects. Couching fetters on choice in expressive terms does not make them innocuous, when there is a penalty attached or when people can be dragged through costly human rights hearings. At best, therefore, expressive effects commend themselves when they are truly toothless, when there are no legal fetters of any kind, and when the only sanction is the opprobrium of transgressing a social norm.

This leaves us without a firm standard, either for or against preference manipulation by the legislator. A complete ban on taking expressive effects into account would seem both infeasible and undesirable. The antipaternalist who wishes to limit the role of the state might find it easier to argue for smaller government by relying on expressive consequences. The social stigma that is implicit in the expressive function economizes on legal penalties, and makes it easier to get by with a thinner set of legal prohibitions. For example, a hortatory human rights code that condemns discrimination without penalizing it might effectively deter misbehavior through the stigma, and permit a state to promote its vision of a just society without heavy-handed criminal sanctions.

That's not to say that social sanctions can't be burdensome. Might then even perhaps be oppressive and illiberal? John Stuart Mill was on both sides of the question. On the one hand, he preferred social to legal sanctions because the former were "the *natural* penalties which cannot be prevented from falling on those who incur the distaste or contempt of those who know them."[7] We naturally feel distaste for bigots, said Mill, and this economizes on legal sanctions. What Mill objected to were legal sanctions, and he framed his harm-to-others principle as a response to the threat of legal and not social sanctions. Mill even defended social sanctions because they made legal paternalism unnecessary. Where misbehavior is adequately sanctioned by social conventions, we don't need legal fetters.

That's the Mill who liked social sanctions. There's another Mill who hated them and who decried what he saw as the deadening hand of social norms. This was a commonly expressed view in the nineteenth century, when writers like Stendhal complained of the tyranny of social conventions that led people, especially in the provinces and in America, to live crabbed, joyless lives. In Mill's case, there was perhaps an element of personal resentment. When he was twenty-five, Mill met Harriet Taylor, a married woman with two small children, and for twenty years, they continued a liaison that shocked their friends. The relationship was apparently chaste, to the great amusement of Mill's friend, Thomas Carlyle. (Of Carlyle's marriage, it was said that God, in his infinite mercy, had united Carlyle and his wife so as to make two and not four people miserable.) On the death of Mr. Taylor in 1851, the couple married. Nevertheless, the public scandal about his relationship with Mrs. Taylor left Mill embittered against restrictive social norms. Because of "the despotism of custom" and a "dreaded censorship," eccentricity was treated as a crime and a sterile religion of duty shut out avenues of joy. Real progress, which depends on the individuality of men of genius, cannot thrive where we are governed by social norms which require "ape-like" imitation.[8] So Mill both relied on social sanctions and deprecated them. That's one of the "Mill Problems," of which there are several.

This was in the high Victorian era, to be sure. In Mill's day, divorce required a special Act of Parliament, and Charles Stuart Parnell, the uncrowned king of Ireland, was driven from politics when he was named as the co-respondent in a divorce petition. In our day, one in three children is born to an unmarried mother, and in the inner city the ratio approaches 70 percent. What might have seemed a benign plea for toleration when social norms were strict began to seem a squalid defense of deviance when they were wholly relaxed.

The fear of repressive social norms seems to belong to another era, one of antimacassars and horse-drawn carriages. That's not the world we live in.

If Mill's concerns about oppressive social norms now seem dated, that's because we live in a Millian world today, one where Mill's ideas about the primacy of individuality have triumphed.

⑩ How Default Rules Shape Choices

Sixteen people a day die in the United States waiting for an organ donation. In most European countries, the organ shortage is nowhere near so pressing. What makes the difference is the default rule for organ donations. In the United States, people are presumed to deny their consent to an organ donation after death, unless they explicitly agree to become organ donors when registering for their driver's licence. A reverse presumption is applied in much of Europe: people are presumed to consent to an organ donation unless they explicitly opt out.

In both the American explicit and the European presumed consent regimes, free choice governs since people are free to elect the donation regime they prefer. As such, one might expect that the difference in default rules would not much matter. But the differences are dramatic. Where consent is presumed, as in Europe, 90 percent of the people are deemed to have agreed to become organ donors; where consent isn't presumed, as in the United States, less than 20 percent explicitly agree to become organ donors.

How to account for this? It can't be that Europeans and Americans have different preferences about organ donations because polls report that 85 percent of Americans approve of them.[9] Rather, the difference stems from the default rule, which shapes what we choose. Default rules might even be thought to affect our preferences. We prefer to be organ donors under one default regime, not so under a different regime. Our preferences might thus be endogenous to the legal regime. But even if they aren't, even if they are exogenous and independent of the default rule, our choices themselves are endogenous. How we choose depends on how the options are framed.

There are a good many other examples of how default rules shape our decisions. About three-quarters of 401(k) participants stick with default contribution rates even though they are typically very low and a higher contribution rate would shelter more of people's money from taxes.[10] Another example comes from the choice to receive email marketing. About 30 percent fewer people ask for email follow-ups when the default is no email ("Do NOT notify me") than when they are required to check a box.[11] Then there's tort law waivers. Damages awards in civil cases are higher in the United States than in other countries, and this has led to calls for smaller awards. New Jersey responded to this by giving buyers of automobile insurance a choice between a more expensive policy that gave people the right to sue for pain and suffering and a significantly less expensive policy where such rights were waived. The default was the cheaper policy where pain and suffering damages were waived, and 79 percent of New Jersey drivers were deemed to have elected this. That sounds like a ringing endorsement for tort reform, but for the embarrassing fact that when Pennsylvania adopted a similar measure with the other default, 70 percent of drivers opted for the more expensive plan where they could sue for pain and suffering![12]

These results must be troubling to the economist. "Don't look at what people say," he says. "Look at what they do." Translated, this means that we should infer people's preferences from their choices and not from what they tell us about how they would choose. But when their choices depend on how options are framed, choices no longer provide the bedrock upon which the economist would found a theory of preference satisfaction. Were our preferences wholly malleable in this way, there would be little reason to accord them much respect, or to assume that in making one choice over another people have made themselves better off.

Framing effects, where the manner in which the question is posed dictates the answer, might be thought to shape our preferences in two ways.

- *Expressive Effects*. We might be embarrassed to opt out of the default because we take the legal presumption to signal that opting out would be morally irresponsible. The default regime would exercise a moral suasion and change how we feel about the choice.
- *Signaling*. It might be rational to go along with the default regime because we believe it signals valuable information about what is best for us. Our human resources department has put a great deal of thought into our retirement plans, and following its lead permits us to free ride on their knowledge. We might also free ride on the keeners amongst our fellow employees to read the information and keep the benefits office on its toes.

Alternatively, framing effects might affect our choices without really changing our preferences.

- *Bounded Rationality*. Employee inertia about savings plans might be attributed to rational ignorance. In a world of bounded rationality, where we don't know everything and getting and processing information about savings options is costly, people might simply not bother and simply go along with the default regime. We all accumulate a pile of information from our employers about the furbelows of our pension plan, and normally toss it unread. We have better things to do.

- *Preference Uncertainty.* Framing effects might also respond to uncertainty about our preferences. There is no reason to suppose that we know all our preferences with certainty. We don't always know just what we want until a choice is presented to us. And possibly not even then. Instead, we economize on deliberation by making our decisions only when we have to do so. Until then we needn't give the decision much thought. We are boundedly rational not only about what we know but also about what we want, and a default might short circuit the need to arrive at a decision about our preferences.

We might pretend that we know all our preferences, even as we think we know everything about our character, but we can still surprise ourselves. We don't really know much about ourselves until we're tested, as Joseph Conrad's *Lord Jim* was when he abandoned his ship and left its passengers to their fate. Before then, he would have thought himself the last person to betray the trust reposed in him.

When given a choice, it might not even be clear whether we're faced with a good we desire or a bad we dislike. For example, is a fifteen-minute poetry reading of Walt Whitman's *Leaves of Grass* a good or a bad? I have my own opinion. But even people who enjoy Whitman more than I do might puzzle over the question, and their choices would then be susceptible to framing effects. In one experiment,[13] people were randomly divided into two groups. One was an "accept" group that was asked whether it would accept $2 to listen to the poem. People in the group were being bribed to listen to it, and this assumed that the experience was a bad. The second group was a "pay" group that was asked whether members would pay $2 to attend the reading. This assumed that the poetry reading was a good. How the choice was framed affected how people responded when they were asked a second question: would they attend the recital free of cost? In the accept group, 8 percent said they would do so, while in the pay group, 35 percent said they would.

More deliberation over preferences might even be counterproductive, and lead us to make worse choices. Decisions made intuitively or on the fly can lead to better results than choices made after we introspect about our feelings. In one study, people were asked to rate different brands of strawberry jam. The group that didn't introspect picked the jam that experts rated as higher quality, while the group that was asked to analyze why they liked the jam they chose changed their preference from the higher to a lower quality jam.[14]

🖤 Libertarian Paternalism

Default rules matter. They influence our choices and do so in a far less objectionable manner than mandatory rules that do not permit opt-outs. For that reason, libertarians will much prefer default rules to mandatory ones. Even if the default regime steers our choices, opt out rights preserve individual autonomy. Cass Sunstein and Richard Thaler have therefore argued that default rules that direct us to welfare enhancing choices constitute an unobjectionable form of "libertarian paternalism."[15] Their default regimes are libertarian because they do not eliminate freedom of choice; and they are paternalistic because they direct people to choices that make them better off.

There isn't an easy response to this. It is sometimes suggested that framing problems might be cured through "de-biasing" techniques that seek to identify people's deepest preferences. For example, to find out what a person really wants, we might reframe problems in a way that asks people to deliberate over the choice. For savings plan decisions, employees might be asked to evaluate their entire retirement portfolio and to consider best and worst case scenarios. People might also be counseled about their expected life expectancy and the need to provide for themselves after they stop earning. Or they might be required to produce a retirement budget.[16]

Making people deliberate sometimes produces useful results. In one real world test, making people choose their 401(k) savings rate raised the fraction of people who enrolled by 28 percent as compared with a no-enrollment default.[17] Forcing explicit choices makes most sense where information costs are low and people's tastes vary so that a single default regime won't suit a lot of people. Making people choose also forces them to learn about the options, and this provides better information about what they really want. The paternalist pretends that he doesn't need this information, that he already knows what we want. But does he?

There are limits to this, however. Making people choose can be costly, when the information needed to choose isn't easy to come by. And if most people would want the same thing in any event, a default regime would probably make more sense that a de-biasing strategy. The question, then, is not whether but rather what kind of default rules to adopt. So what kinds of defaults would people want? In a world of bounded rationality, where information and deliberation is not costless, people would prefer default rules that nudge them toward the same choices they'd make if they had to think about it. Default rules that mimic what a person would have chosen come as close to respecting individual autonomy as is possible. Not merely would the parties want the default that mimics their choices, they'd also prefer the default regime to one that forced them to bargain for the terms themselves. I'd much prefer to have my benefits department pick the plan that is best for me than have to worry about it myself. Life's too short.

This is consistent with libertarianism and not paternalism. Where the default rules become paternalistic is when they no longer mimic what the person would have chosen, but instead push people toward what is deemed good for them. These are the defaults that "libertarian paternalism" would supply and that make the libertarian paternalist a paternalist.

When it comes to default terms, we might therefore distinguish between libertarian paternalism and simple libertarianism, libertarianism tout court. Both would oppose mandatory terms that take choices away from people, and instead offer default terms that can be waived. But while the libertarian's default rules would seek to mimic the choices people would make were they required to do so, the default rules of the libertarian paternalist would direct people toward choices the paternalist thinks good for them.

Part of the appeal of libertarian paternalism is that this often comes down to the same thing as pure libertarianism. In other words, what people really want is often what is good for them, and default rules that mimic people's preferences are often those that the paternalist would propose. Nor is it always easy to distinguish between libertarian default rules that mimic preferences and paternalistic default rules that don't. For example, it is not clear what 401(k) savings presumption better accords with our true preferences.

If we are to make sense of libertarian paternalism, then, we need to find a case where default rules clearly don't mimic preferences, where they seek to reform us against our will. But how to tell the difference? Four criteria suggest themselves, as badges of possible paternalism.

- *How hard is it to opt out?* Imposing a strong evidentiary burden before default rules can be waived can turn a default rule into something resembling a mandatory one, and this might be what the paternalist desires all along. For example, the Brady Bill would have required a five-day waiting period so that background checks could be made before a person could buy a handgun. And some states impose waiting periods and mandatory counseling before an abortion. Pro-gun and pro-abortion supporters have argued that these are nothing more than covert tools to force choices on people.

- *How many people in fact opt out?* Where more than half of the people waive the rule, it cannot be said to mimic their choices. Since the default rule is sticky in that people tend to go along with it, we can also infer that it doesn't mimic people's choices where somewhat less than half of them opt out.
- *Who adopts the default rule?* Default rules adopted by the state might be paternalistic, while those adopted by private parties almost never are. In private contracting, whether for jobs, goods or services, the right to choose one's co-contractor will effectively police would-be paternalists. Employers who promote unwanted default rules would tend to drive their employees to seek jobs elsewhere.
- *Does the default rule economize on information costs?* A default rule which does not economize on people's information costs is more likely to be paternalistic. Pension plan decisions are difficult and technical, which is why we are happy to defer to our employer's pension department. Let them incur the costs of doing the spade work. By contrast, we know what kind of charities we prefer to support, and charitable giving decisions do not impose difficult informational problems. We can make such decision easily for ourselves.

If he disregards these reservations, the libertarian paternalist will seem less like a libertarian and a more like a paternalist. Indeed, the libertarian paternalist agenda, which regards people as poor judges of their own welfare and sees paternalism as a useful corrective, seems motivated primarily by a desire to nudge people in the right direction, often by switching the direction of existing default rules.

One example of the divergence between libertarian and paternalist defaults is provided by the Sunstein-Thaler proposal that we switch the presumption governing the rights of employees who are fired. The old common law default permitted employers to fire employees "for good cause or no cause, or even for bad cause."[18] This is known as the *employment at will* doctrine because the employee's job depends entirely upon the employer's unfettered will. In fact, the rule works both ways because the employee also has the right to leave the job for any reason and whenever he wants.

From the employee's perspective, the employment at will doctrine is mandatory and not presumptive. That is, the employee cannot waive his right to leave the job whenever he wants, as this would amount to a contact of slavery and violate the Thirteenth Amendment. He can walk whenever he wants, and he can't bargain that right away. He might be liable in damages for leaving the job, but he cannot be made to work against his will. From an employer's perspective, however, the employment at will doctrine is presumptive and not mandatory. The parties can bargain around it by stipulating that the employee will hold his job for a fixed period of time or (as in the case of tenured academics) indefinitely. In such cases, the employee may only be dismissed for cause when his poor job performance gives the employer good reason to fire him.

What the employment at will doctrine offers employers is flexibility in their business operations. Employees can be let go and new ones hired without the threat of litigation. The annoying quirks that disrupt an office, the surly manner that annoys co-workers and clients, the ineffectual work that never quite rises to the required level of incompetence and inattention, can harm a business without offering the employer a cause for termination that would satisfy a court—let alone the Alberta Human Rights Commission. Even when the misbehavior rises to the level of cause for dismissal, the employer will need a human resources bureaucracy and employment lawyers on retainer. Hiring an employee is thus less costly under employment at will default rules, with the result that more people will be hired. Because of this, it is by no means clear that employees are harmed by the contract at will doctrine. What the doctrine offers employees is a better chance of finding a job and a lower unemployment rate.

Nevertheless, the employment at will doctrine is under attack as relic of nineteenth-century laissez-faire ideology, and most states have recognized public policy exceptions to it. For example, employers can't ask employees to do something that contravenes public policy or federal law. Some states also impose a duty of good faith and fair dealing on employers who want to let people go. These exceptions appear to have depressed labor demand[19] and shifted jobs away from permanent to temporary hires (because temps lack any protection against dismissal).[20] Weakening the employment at will doctrine also gives litigation-minded employees an incentive to wait to be fired rather than to quit so that they are less likely to seek more productive jobs elsewhere. These burdens are likely to be felt most in the small and medium size firms that are most responsible for job creation because they are less able to shoulder the burden of litigation.

In spite of this, Sunstein and Thaler propose that the default regime shift from employment at will to a presumption that employees cannot be fired without good cause. To be sure, employers can bargain around the default rule, and many will do so. However, smaller firms are less likely to come up with standard form employment contracts that opt out of the new default regime. That's really the point of the proposed switch in default rules. If every firm opted out of the for-cause presumption in favor of the employment at will doctrine, the change in default rules wouldn't accomplish anything. The paternalist is therefore betting that the change will affect employee rights. Otherwise he wouldn't bother.

Libertarian paternalism might thus be a very different sort of thing than a set of libertarian default rules. The libertarian, but not the paternalist, would simply mimic the choices people would make if they had to put their mind to it. Moreover, there's another part to the libertarian agenda which distinguishes it from paternalism. As much as possible, the libertarian would seek to expand choice by turning mandatory rules into presumptive ones, with people given the right to opt out of default rules.

One example of this is the mandatory rules of marriage and divorce law. Social conservatives who think that marriage needs protection from the morals of the market-place sometimes say that "marriage is more than a contract: it is a covenant." It's not just a private agreement but a hallowed institution found in every society. But marriage is more than a covenant: it is a contract. Or rather it is less than a contract because in all but three states the parties cannot waive their right to a no-fault divorce. This runs counter to the way in which we tend to think about paternalism. We are apt to imagine the paternalist as a conservative who seeks to enforce a somewhat old-fashioned set of morals. Here, however, the paternalist mandates a divorce regime which social conservatives will find objectionable because it facilitates marriage breakups.

The right to seek a no-fault divorce narrows and does not expand our personal autonomy. True, it permits us to free ourselves without much difficulty from a marriage that we think has turned sour. However, questions of autonomy should be evaluated ex ante, at the time of the marriage, and not ex post at the time of divorce. Mandatory divorce "rights" fetter our choices by making it impossible to make a binding long term commitment to our spouse. The point of a promise is to renounce future options, and if that was thought to interfere with our autonomy, then we could never commit to any long term project.

Between 1969 and 1985, every state "liberalized" its divorce laws by moving to a no-fault regime. Before then, parties could not get a divorce without showing that the other party had committed a matrimonial fault such as adultery. The change was largely complete by 1979, when only two states required proof of fault before granting the divorce. During this period divorce rates almost doubled. This was unsurprising because the move to no-fault laws reduced the cost of divorce and sapped spousal incentives to invest in their marriage.[21]

Marriage and divorce laws are a good example of endogenous preferences. People feel differently about marriage when divorce becomes easy to get. They won't commit as closely to each other as they would in a regime where marriage is more permanent. To protect themselves, they'll invest less in the marriage and more in outside careers and friendships. They'll be less ready to buy a house or put a partner through medical school. They might also have fewer or no children. Children are "marriage specific" assets, valued more by couples who expect to stay together than by couples who don't. Not surprisingly, the birth rate to married couple fell after the divorce revolution. And all of these pathologies mutually reinforce one another, making a couple's emotional bonds to each other weaker.

The divorce revolution was celebrated at the time as progressive legislation that would benefit women. Before then, it was said that the requirement of a finding of matrimonial fault for a divorce trapped women in loveless marriages. Forty years later, however, no-fault divorce laws don't seem to have lived up to their billing. By removing the need to prove fault, no-fault divorce makes it easier and cheaper for an at-fault party to exit from the marriage, and this has led to an increase in divorce rates and has been a disaster for women and children. Children under sixteen who are living with only one biological parent are twice as likely to have a child in their teens, twice as likely to leave high school without a diploma, and 70 percent more likely to have a criminal conviction by the age of fifteen.[22]

Social conservatives are understandably concerned about how no-fault divorce has weakened marriage. However, no one has suggested a return to a mandatory fault regime, where no-fault divorces are banned. The move to no-fault divorce was from one mandatory regime to the other. Under a fault regime, the parties could not bargain at marriage for a right to a no-fault divorce. After the introduction of no-fault, the parties could not upon marriage elect to waive the right to a no-fault divorce. What conservatives now propose is to replace mandatory no-fault divorce rights with a default regime in which couples can opt out by waiving the right to a no-fault divorce through a "covenant marriage." Here the couple agrees to obtain premarital counseling and accept more limited grounds for divorce, typically spousal abuse, a felony with jail time, or adultery.

The adoption of covenant marriage legislation is a move from paternalism to a libertarian default regime. A mandatory marriage regime is relaxed and opt outs permitted. No-fault divorce is taken to be the default regime, with those who waive it given the right to elect the stricter fault regime of a covenant marriage. Not that many couples have done so, when given the choice. To date, about 1 to 3 percent of marrying couples elect the covenant marriage option in states where they are permitted to do so. Those who do so make divorce costlier for the person who wants out of the marriage. A husband who sought to abandon his wife would find himself paying her to secure her consent to a divorce, and we'd expect that this would shape his preferences. As fault becomes costlier, there will be less of it, and fewer divorces. Small faults will annoy less. Blemishes that seem oppressive when exit is costless will be far less troublesome when one realizes that the marriage will last. An expansion of free bargaining rights, in which divorce waivers are made enforceable, would therefore protect marriage and respect individual autonomy by expanding choices.

School choice offers another plausible vehicle for a libertarian default rule.[23] At present, the public school system is effectively mandatory for most parents. Private and parochial schools are in theory an option, but they are beyond the financial means for most parents as compared with public schools that don't charge tuition. The problem is that the public school system is broken in many cities. Children in the system have to attend their local school, which often does a very poor job in educating them. A libertarian default regime would then permit parents to opt out of the local public school and send their children to any school in the city, with local public schools as the default for those who don't want to change. A further liberalization would give parents the right to waive all public schools through vouchers to be spent on education at charter, private or parochial schools.

A further extension of libertarian default rules would take us into the domain of drug laws. A particularly troubling kind of paternalism limits the drugs available to the sick, especially those in pain or with little chance of recovery. The criminal prosecution of "pain doctors" for overprescribing painkillers has been said to result in defensive medicine in which painkillers are underprescribed. In addition, the ban on experimental drugs which have not received the approval of the Food and Drug Administration might make sense for most patients but not for the terminally ill for whom the new drug offers the only chance of recovery. The libertarian would at a minimum offer the terminally ill the right to opt out of default prohibitions against painkillers or experimental drugs.

More generally, a host of mandatory rules might be relaxed and opt out rights provided to the parties, through a natural extension of the logic of libertarian paternalism. Such laws include mandatory bankruptcy laws, which debtors might be permitted to waive (so as to permit them to promise not to seek bankruptcy protection); and mandatory securities laws, which shareholders might be permitted to waive (so as to permit small firms to waive compliance with costly prospectus requirements). Libertarian paternalism invites one to ask whether a purely libertarian default regime might serve the parties better than the paternalist's attempt to shape people's choices.

✎ The Bully Pulpit

Libertarian paternalism is a mild form of paternalism because it permits opt-outs. An even milder form of paternalism would rely on the "bully pulpit." That was Theodore Roosevelt's term for the moral and political suasion he could exercise as president by advocating a position. Current examples of this kind of paternalism are government ads advising people of the dangers of smoking or using drugs.

The Bully Pulpit does not impose penalties or monetary taxes on the disfavored activity. However, it does impose psychic taxes in the form of shame, fear and guilt, and thus is not cost-free. Its costs might even be more painful than real taxes and, therefore, deserve our scrutiny. The Bully Pulpit is especially troublesome when the paternalist is more likely to get it wrong than his subject. And as we know from experience, that happens often enough. Antitobacco ads might seem benign, but in the past, the Bully Pulpit was employed to stigmatize homosexuality and the moderate consumption of alcohol. A prominent example of the misuse of the Bully Pulpit today is government ads for state-run lotteries, where ticket purchasers are disproportionately poor people.

Even in an ostensibly benign cause, the Bully Pulpit can be excessive. For people who are made to feel guilt and continue with the activity in spite of this, the psychic tax amounts to a deadweight loss. It makes people feel worse, doesn't change their behavior, and brings in no tax revenues.[24]

Edward Glaeser notes a further problem with the Bully Pulpit.[25] In the hands of politicians or bureaucrats, it can be expected to lead to more intrusive forms of paternalism. A campaign against alcohol that employed the techniques of persuasion led to complete prohibition. And because it builds public support, the Bully Pulpit is less likely to encounter public opposition along the way. We would never have accepted the present restrictions on tobacco in 1962, when the campaign first began with the Surgeon General's report.

The fact that our preferences are in part endogenous would therefore seem to provide limited support for the paternalist. Laws may shape our preferences, but that does not tell us very much about whether or when a law might be adopted. As for libertarian paternalism, what is most attractive is the libertarianism, and what is most unattractive is the paternalism. The celebration of free choice argues for expanded autonomy rights, with mandatory laws converted into default ones. Finally, ostensibly innocuous strategies to shape people's preferences, such as the Bully Pulpit, also deserve our concern.

Perfectionism

Almost all the projects of social reformers of these
days are really *liberticide.*

John Stuart Mill, On Liberty

EIGHT

Private Perfectionism

It is better to be Socrates dissatisfied than a fool satisfied.

John Stuart Mill

IN PART II, we move from the soft paternalism that we saw in Part I to the enforcement of morals. Soft paternalism restricts a person's freedom but does so to satisfy a deeper set of his preferences, which might be moral or immoral, noble or base. In theory, the soft paternalist might promote morality by correcting the immoralist's judgment biases. "Thanks," says the killer. "That's just what I needed." Perfectionism is very different. It ignores our deepest wishes when these are deemed unworthy. Instead, it identifies a vision of the good and directs us to seek it, whether we want to or not. Until recently, those who sought to interfere with our choices based their arguments solely on grounds of soft paternalism or on Mill's harm-to-others principle. Recently, however, perfectionism has begun to make a comeback.

Perfectionism—the enforcement of morality—take two forms. The *private perfectionism* we examine in this chapter seeks to restrict a person's choices for his own benefit. Because it fetters immoral choices, it is a form of perfectionism; and because it does so to make the person better off, it is also a form of paternalism that in Chapter 1 we called hard paternalism. So, private perfectionism is simply another name for hard paternalism. Unlike soft paternalism, private perfectionism or hard paternalism enforces a moral code and does not seek to satisfy a person's deep preferences.

Private perfectionism is drawn by the lament of *The Parting Glass* and addresses the self-inflicted harm of the person who makes bad choices.

Oh, all the money that e'er I had,
I spent it in good company,
And all the harm that e'er I've done,
Alas, it was to none but me.

In Chapter 9, we identify a different kind of perfectionism called *social perfectionism*, which enforces morals for the benefit of third parties. Even as a person might corrupt himself through his actions, he might corrupt others by his example, and this might invite restrictions on people's choices. Here we fetter *A* to prevent him from harming *B*.

We can easily influence others by our bad example. Good behavior rubs off too. When toasted as the savior of Europe, after the Battle of Trafalgar, Pitt replied that England, not he, deserved the credit. "England has saved herself by her exertions; and will, as I trust, save Europe by her example." So we influence others, for good or for ill. The social perfectionist's laws which fetter a person's choice to prevent him from imposing moral harm on innocent third parties cannot be described as paternalistic because they do not seek to reform the individual for his own sake. Nevertheless, they are a means of enforcing morals and are a form of perfectionism.

It is important to keep the two kinds of perfectionism separate. Private perfectionism is a hard sell; social perfectionism an easier one. We don't care much for the rogue, but we might care about the innocent person he drags down to his level. So the private perfectionist might be tempted to appeal to the third party spillover effects that are the province of social perfectionists. But that's an illegitimate move. Private perfectionism concerns only the subject himself, and not those he might influence.

Nevertheless, the relation between the two forms of perfectionism is often close. For example, when "extreme boxing" is banned because it would corrupt spectators, we are talking of social perfectionism; where it is banned because it would corrupt (as well as injure) the boxers themselves, we are talking of private perfectionism. Both kinds of prohibitions assume that the state should promote personal virtue, and both are forms of perfectionism.[1]

⚉ Perfectionism

Perfectionism is an ill-chosen, almost pejorative term. Who would be so arrogant as to think he could reach perfection, let alone legislate to make someone else perfect? But our perfectionist doesn't really want to make men perfect. "Be ye perfect," said Christ; but he also said "My Kingdom is not of this world." He wasn't talking about the legal enforcement of morals. And when St. Thomas Aquinas summed up Christian theology, he distinctly argued that not every moral injunction should be legally enforced. There are separate realms of private and legal morality, and things such as prostitution should be left to the former, he thought. So a better term than perfectionism is legal moralism: that realm of morality that laws should enforce. But perfectionism is the generally accepted term, and so we seem to be stuck with it.

I don't propose to give content to what we should do to develop our nature on perfectionist lines. That's an interesting subject and one not free from controversy. Homeric virtues are, after all, very different from Aristotelian ones, and even more different from Christian ones. Because he was publicly shamed by Agamemnon, it was not unreasonable for Achilles to withdraw to his tent. At least that's how people in Homer's time might have understood Book 1 of *The Iliad*. But for Aristotle, several hundred years later, the greatsouled man would not bear grudges and sulk in his tent; and for Christians, Achilles displayed the cardinal sin of pride.

I'll skip those kinds of questions, however, because the question I pose is whether the perfectionist might fetter our choices, not what view of human nature he should hold. I'll assume that we all have an intuitive sense of the kinds of qualities he might have in mind and concentrate on whether we should give him that power over us. Much of the literature on the subject deals with what kind of person we should become, without paying much attention to the political question of how to get there. But, like Mill, I'll focus on the second question.

Because I won't try to define what perfectionism might entail, I don't have to come up with a list of virtues the perfectionist might espouse. It's enough that he might come up with a plausible list, even if people might quarrel about things at the edges. If the perfectionist were required to get everyone's assent for every item on the list, that would be an impossible task, and perfectionism would be a nonstarter. But I don't think that's necessary, any more than that the rights theorist must come up with a list of individual rights with which everyone will agree.

I also don't think that perfectionism must reform people's characters. It need not, in the phrase of Robert George, "make men moral." The perfectionist cannot force people to be moral, since moral choices are necessarily free choices. However, the perfectionist can force people to be good, since that's simply a matter of changing their behavior. Admittedly, that's easier to do if he reforms their character. When that happens, the perfectionist can ease off a bit. But reforming people's characters isn't necessary, strictly speaking. If all the perfectionist does is make hard drugs illegal, the drug addict might still have his craving. His preferences would not have changed a whit. What the perfectionist would have done, however, is changed the addict's behavior, if the prohibition is effective. That's enough to constitute perfectionism, if we believe that keeping hard drugs away from an addict is good for him, whether he likes it or not.

Oliver Wendell Holmes understood that laws must be made for the bad man more than for the good.

> You can see very plainly that a bad man has as much reason as a good one for wishing to avoid an encounter with the public force, and therefore you can see the practical importance of the distinction between morality and law. A man who cares nothing for an ethical rule which is believed and practiced by his neighbors is likely nevertheless to care a good deal to avoid being made to pay money, and will want to keep out of jail if he can.[2]

Aristotle also subscribed to the "bad man" theory of legislating. States exist to promote the moral goodness and virtue of their citizens, he thought. However, it is not enough to show people what virtue might require, or even to reward the virtuous man. While that might suffice for "the generous minded of our youth" something more is needed for "the many."

> For these do not by nature obey the sense of shame, but only fear, and do not abstain from bad acts because of their baseness but through fear of punishment; living by passion they pursue their own pleasures and the means to them, and avoid the opposite pains and have not even a conception of what is noble and truly pleasant, since they have never tasted it. What argument would remold such people? (NE 1179[b])

No argument, but instead the law's "compulsive power" must then be brought to bear. I therefore define perfectionism to include restrictions on immoral choices, even where that the perfectionist doesn't seek to change people's preferences.

𝕸 Neutralism

Amongst academics, perfectionism is very much a minority view today. Antiperfectionists or *neutralists* argue that the state should not take sides on questions of morality unless third parties are physically harmed. The most prominent modern political and legal philosophers, people such as John Rawls, Robert Nozick, and Ronald Dworkin, have all been neutralists,[3] and that also is the temper of our times. We each aspire to say that I did it my way.

The naïve neutralist might be a subjectivist (or moral relativist) who thinks that moral and aesthetic claims are meaningless, except as statements of personal preferences. That won't do, however, because the denial of all moral values is self-defeating. If values were wholly subjective and no one had standing to condemn another, we could not object to the perfectionist who sought to impose his moral views upon us. To take part in the debate about perfectionism, either for or against, one must first abandon relativism.

Not that there are many real subjectivists around. More often, subjectivism is a pose adopted to silence an opponent in a debate, "You're so judgmental," we say to the moralist, as though we aren't judging him ourselves. Most often, what bothers us is not the fact of judging but the content of the judgment. In the debate over abortion, affirmative action, and the other hot-button issues of the culture wars, the charge that an opponent is judgmental usually masks the belief that he is simply wrong.

That's not to say that the perfectionist's rules cannot in part be culturally bound. Her prescriptions might depend on the time and place in which he legislates. She might tolerate a more liberal divorce regime in the twentieth century than the nineteenth or in one state rather than another. She might also be slightly agnostic about the finer points of the laws she proposes. She might want to permit properly licensed people in her state to carry concealed weapons but remain curious about the effect of gun bans in other states. If crime rates were lower in the other states, she might be willing to change his mind. What she can't be is a complete relativist, however. She can't say "It's quite all right to murder a recent widow in your country, but in ours we call it murder." In that case, she would lack standing to enforce any moral code.

Though not a moral relativist, the neutralist must prize tolerance because he believes that the state should not legislate morality. However, what tolerance and intolerance might mean have changed over time. Today, tolerance is often taken to mean a nonjudgmental acceptance of all beliefs and behavior so that it becomes a synonym for a moral relativism where anything goes. By contrast, the older sense of tolerance was explicitly judgmental. Then we tolerated what we rejected, not what we accepted. We tolerated fools but did not embrace them; we tolerated pain but did not enjoy it. We tolerated other religions even though we thought them mistaken, and we tolerated other political beliefs even though we believed them wrong-headed. Crucially, we were unwilling to proscribe that which we tolerated. Otherwise, we'd have been intolerant. That's not to say that everything should be tolerated. It is not a virtue for a policeman to tolerate crime. Some things should be made illegal, and toleration makes one complicit in them.

We'll employ the older definitions of tolerance and intolerance. The neutralist might then condemn the wrongful or mistaken behavior he tolerates. He might accept that some actions are base, while permitting their practice because he believes that proscribing vice would be impracticable.[4] The neutralist might be tolerant without being a subjectivist.

Up till the nineteenth century, perfectionism was everywhere accepted. Plato believed that only philosophers had knowledge of the good and that, as the state should promote the good, it should be run by philosopher-kings. For Aristotle, the very purpose of the state was to make men moral. "Excellence must be the care of a state which is truly so called," he said. Otherwise, it is simply a collection of people and not a state.[5] Among the moderns the classical tradition was thoroughly perfectionist, from Aquinas in the thirteenth century to Rousseau and the American Founders in the eighteenth century.

In the nineteenth and twentieth centuries, however, neutralism became the dominant view. Benjamin Constant was the first to recognize this, in his 1816 distinction between the liberty of the ancients and that of the moderns.[6] The liberty of the ancients was the right to participate in the governance of the state. A person's private actions were subject to strict surveillance, and he was not given the liberty of free private opinions, especially in matters of religion. Nevertheless, he could go to the public square and debate a foreign treaty, the generalship of a war, and the conduct of his leaders; and for the ancients this made him free. In the modern state, said Constant, things are reversed. The right to participate in the affairs of the state has been effectively lost because states have become too large to permit the direct democracy of the public square. What we have gained, however, is individual independence, the right to our own opinions, to behave as we like as long as we don't harm others. That, today, is what liberty means.

Neutralism is also more consistent than perfectionism with modern egalitarian sentiments which ask us to respect everyone's conceptions of the good. For egalitarians, people are entitled to have their personal views of the good taken seriously by others even if they might disagree with them. Otherwise a person is "disrespected." This is Ronald Dworkin's theory of liberalism,[7] and as it requires an equal respect for different conceptions of the good life, it leaves little room for perfectionism.

Perfectionism is premodern in another way. On perfectionist theories, people have the moral responsibility to develop their nature and character through the practice of virtue. This wouldn't make sense to moderns who see moral duties as owed only to others, not to oneself. Phrasing the question in terms of duties to oneself begs the question, however, because perfectionists might also think it odd to speak of duties to oneself. What they would assert that a person who doesn't try to better himself can and will be blamed by others, whether or not his behavior rubs off on third parties.

Nevertheless, there has been a revival of perfectionist ideas from various directions. Perfectionists have emerged from a newly strengthened natural law tradition, and still others have expressed dissatisfaction with internal weaknesses in the neutralist position. The idea that morality has something to do with virtues that have intrinsic value has also been championed by Alasdair MacIntyre and a new school of virtue ethics. If the virtues have objective value, then it might not be unreasonable to suppose that the state might promote them. What was regarded as a closed issue thirty years ago is now very much an open one.

🌼 Neutralism: For and Against

Perfectionism can no longer be rejected out of hand, if ever it could. In what follows, we'll look at the debate between perfectionists and antiperfectionist neutralists, starting with a few preliminary objections to each of them. First, let us examine the neutralist's objections to private perfectionism on informational grounds: an individual will ordinarily have a better conception of what is good for him and of the conditions under which he will flourish than the state. "The strongest of all the arguments against the interference of the public with purely personal conduct," said Mill, "is that, when it does interfere, the odds are that it interferes wrongly, and in the wrong place."[8] This argues for neutralism because the individual is in a far better position to know what he needs to flourish. "With respect to his own feelings and circumstances the most ordinary man or woman has means of knowledge immeasurably surpassing those that can be possessed by anyone else."[9]

If deciding how to live was a technical question, like the choice of bathroom drains, we might delegate it to the expert. But living well is the most complex of arts and a set of mechanistic rules could never do justice to the suppleness needed to extract happiness from life. What instead is needed is the kind of flexibility that insulates a person from ridicule. Those who lack this are Henri Bergson's machine-men, who are the butt of our jokes.[10]

They follow a rigid plan and keep moving their feet even after they slip on the banana peel, and so we laugh at them.

If there were one simple program we each should follow, if the same set of ends should govern everyone's behavior, we could perhaps defer to the expert. However, what an individual must do in order to flourish must depend largely on his own particular attributes. The search for a single "good for man" is bound to prove elusive, and we should not expect everyone to seek it in precisely the same way. Those who think otherwise and, worse still, legislate on that basis can easily become figures of fun.

Bergson thought that both machine-men and machine-rules were deserving of ridicule. He told a story about a seaside border guard who sees a traveler drowning. The guard leaps into the water and, at great risk to himself, saves the man. He brings him in and they collapse on the shore. Whereupon the guard stands up and says, "Your passport, M'sieu?" A perfectionism that prescribes mechanistic rules that take no account of individual differences would be equally ridiculous and would resemble what Bergson described as a closed society in his *Two Sources of Morality and Religion*. Closed societies impose the top-down order of an ant colony, and are shot-through with mechanistic rules that leave little room for private choices. By contrast, the open society prized by Bergson (and later by Sir Karl Popper) is mobile, organic, and fluid, and lets the individual choose her best life-plan.

Apart from the informational problem, criminalizing vice can be expected to give rise to a black market. We don't eliminate drugs and prostitution but simply drive them underground. That was our experience with Prohibition in the 1920s, and today's War on Drugs is clearly less than an unqualified success. It turns ordinary citizens into lawbreakers and creates an enormous illegal industry. Legislating virtue also permits the police and prosecutors to harass citizens, and opens the door to political abuse. It caters to the prurient, the snoop, the busybody, and the blackmailer. For that reason, there cannot be many conservatives who would like to return to the days where homosexuality was a criminal offense, whatever their feelings about its morality.

But as telling as these objections are, they can be carried too far. The argument from personal flourishing suggests that an extensive perfectionism that would overrule minute personal choices is objectionable. However, this argument is less telling against a thin perfectionism which does not dictate a thick code of personal conduct. A moderate perfectionist would also refrain from enacting laws whose principle effect is to enrichen the bootlegger and drug dealer. Balance is everything, and to suggest that a tepid perfectionism would resemble an Iranian theocracy is mischievous.

The neutralist might also argue that states that seek to micromanage private virtue might be distracted from the more serious business of protecting life and limb or the less serious but still important business of fixing potholes. However, there is no logical reason why a state cannot do two things at once. It can operate a military and run a court system. It can collect taxes and send out welfare checks. And it can fix potholes and provide a mild dose of private perfectionism. Indeed, a state that is competent in one area is more likely to be competent in another.

Having examined three attacks on perfectionism, let us now consider and reject two arguments against neutralism. The first is the communitarian argument that neutralism weakens the sense of solidarity and community that is an essential good for every person. These concerns have become more acute of late, and scholars have recently bemoaned the loss in solidarity in America. Robert Putnam's *Bowling Alone* describes an America in which people have stopped participating in clubs and associations, and Alan Ehrenhalt's *Lost City* mourned a similar decline in civic participation.[11]

If we have lost our sense of solidarity with others, one reason might be the move to a more mobile information economy. In a modern information economy, people don't work at the same job all their lives as they might have done formerly. They must relocate, often to new cities, and bonds of friendship and affection suffer when this happens. But neutralism—the weakening of perfectionist laws—doesn't seem to have anything much to do with it—nor does the fact that America is a commercial society with a strong sense of individualism. If anything, communitarian bonds appear to be stronger in commercial societies than in precapitalist societies such as Banfield's Montegrano.

In an individualistic society, where one makes one's own way, such as the United States, a person must create his own self-protective networks, with the result that Americans are the world's greatest joiners, as Alexis de Tocqueville famously observed.[12] We'll join churches, the Rotary, professional organizations, much more than people in other countries. We'll also give more to charity, as we noted in Chapter 6. So there isn't much evidence that neutralism or the sense of individualism that might animate the neutralist weakens our sense of solidarity. And what philosophical critics of neutralism and individualism might forget is that the communitarian objection is really an empirical question, where the evidence points against them.

The second attack on neutralism is that it is self-defeating. It holds up personal autonomy as a basic good but prevents people from binding themselves as members of communities that reject autonomy as a good.[13]

Take the example of a person who enters a monastery that severely constrains his choices. Suppose that he finds joy and contentment in the monastic life and would be greatly saddened were he forced to leave it. Would we require him to do so to vindicate his autonomy rights? Would we force him to be free, like the members of Jean-Jacques Rousseau's civil state?[14]

The answer is no, of course. People who are forced to be free are less than free if they are prevented from making long-term commitments. People who can bind themselves to serve for a period of years in the army are freer than those who are not given this choice. People who are permitted to waive no-fault divorce laws by entering into a covenant marriage are freer than those who are legally barred from doing so. And the monk is freer if he is permitted to join a monastery. In extreme cases, such as the contract of slavery, the common law forces people to be free by refusing to enforce their agreements. That apart, however, freedom is enhanced when people are free to be forced.

🕮 Liberal Perfectionists

To evaluate perfectionism and neutralism properly, one must do more than attack straw men. Extreme versions of either position are easily criticized, but the criticism doesn't take one very far against the kind of moderate perfectionism or neutralism to which most people subscribe. That's something to underline because opponents often seem to talk past each other when it comes to legislating morals. Neutralists sometimes present pornographers as idealized martyrs for the First Amendment, as in the film *The People vs. Larry Flynt*, with every perfectionist painted as the Moral Majority's Jerry Falwell.

That doesn't describe most American perfectionists, who after all include nearly all of us. Nearly everyone has some version of the good they would enforce, whether this involves smoking, carbon emissions or racial prejudice. Moreover, most modern perfectionist theorists, such as Joseph Raz, are liberals who have modest goals and would employ modest means to achieve them.[15] Raz's brand of perfectionism would advance aesthetic and moral ideals through state-funded museums and public television, without criminalizing immoral acts that do not physically harm third parties.

When discussing perfectionism, the form of the interference with personal preferences crucially matters. Those who seek to shape behavior through hortatory laws that rely on expressive effects (and which do not empower an out-of-control human rights commission) tread lightly upon people's choices.

There is also an important difference between criminalizing vice on the one hand and on the other conditioning the receipt of welfare benefits on participation in a program with paternalistic ends, such as workfare. In workfare programs, people have to do something to improve their chances of getting a job if they are to continue to receive welfare. The goal in part is to reduce the welfare rolls, and in this workfare programs have proven to be a success. But the other goal of workfare programs is to break a culture of reliance on welfare and foster the kinds of habits that make people employable. That will reduce welfare rolls too, but it will also inculcate self-reliance and other virtues.

The tax treatment of charitable contributions is a particularly innocuous form of perfectionism. In the United States and most Western countries, moneys donated to registered charities may be deducted from income in calculating one's income taxes. However, some other countries, such as Russia, restrict charitable deductions or disallow them altogether. That's short sighted, for three reasons. First, the state doesn't have perfect knowledge of who deserves charitable support, and allowing the tax deduction permits the state to free ride on the knowledge of millions of donors. Second, much more money will flow to charities when people are permitted to choose to whom they give. And third, by encouraging charitable giving, the deduction fosters generosity, a goal that would rank high on any perfectionist's list of virtues.

Those who support a mild interference with personal preferences might then be called liberal perfectionists. Liberal perfectionists can respect personal autonomy and indeed must do so if they are liberals. They are necessarily constrained in the ways they might fetter our choices. As perfectionists, they believe that people should be encouraged to develop their nature to the highest degree possible; but as liberals, they believe that one of the elements of perfection is autonomy and that the ability to choose freely how we should flourish is an intrinsic good.

Is liberal perfectionism possible? If liberalism is inconsistent with any attempt to shape our preferences or choices, then liberal perfectionism is an oxymoron. There's another reason why liberalism perfectionism might seem to be a nonstarter. The perfectionist seems to want to legislate us into Heaven, but that's one thing he can never do. Because a moral or religious conversion requires private assent, it cannot be mandated; and this was Locke's argument for religious toleration: "The care of souls cannot belong to the civil magistrate, because his power consists only in outward force; but true and saving religion consists in the inward persuasion of the mind, without which nothing can be acceptable to God." Mill made a similar point when he said that we develop our character "only in making a choice."[16] "No life goes better by being led from the outside according to values the person doesn't endorse," argues Will Kymlicka. "My life only goes better if I'm leading it from the inside, according to my beliefs about value."[17]

The liberal perfectionist might respond to these challenges in three ways. First, he might foreswear any form of compulsion, and limit his perfectionism to educational measures and laws that influence people's choices without banning any of them. Second, he might favor laws that take certain choices off the table, but only in the most extreme of cases. And third, he might assert that illiberal restrictions that shape people's preferences might nevertheless result in subsequent autonomous choices, when the later choices reflect the changed preferences.

Persuasion, Not Compulsion

The liberal perfectionist might first reject any form of compulsion. He might allow the state to influence our choices, through education, museums and the like, and foreswear flat prohibitions on disfavored choices. In this way he might dodge the bullet. He'd still be a perfectionist, because he'd have a theory of the good which he'd try to promote. He'd also be a liberal, since he'd use only the most moderate of means to advance his goals. He wouldn't try to legislate anyone into Heaven, but might try to shape preferences in a nonintrusive manner.

One example of this are laws which, without prohibiting anything, promote what philosopher Robert George calls a "benign moral ecology."[18] Legislation that supports marriage (e.g., by removing the "marriage penalty" from the tax code) might thus result in a more moral and happier society without forcing anyone to do anything. Imposing a tax on vice or subsidizing virtue merely influences behavior by changing the calculation of costs and benefits.

The problem here is that very few people would dissent from this kind of perfectionism. Even John Stuart Mill thought that the state could "remonstrate" and "reason" with people.[19] It might impose "sin" taxes on the sale of alcohol, not to influence choices to be sure, but (what comes to the same thing) to raise needed revenue from a sale of something people might easily dispense with.[20] For that matter, libertarian Ludwig von Mises is said to have wanted to privatize everything except the Vienna State Opera. If I adhere to a broader definition, in which the perfectionist not only seeks to influence choices but also to restrict them, to proscribe immoral choices, it is because this is where the rubber meets the road. The only debate worthy of the name is one where there are really people on different sides of the issue; and if we take Mill to be a perfectionist, there's really no one on the other side. To sharpen the debate, then, I want to take a harder line and say that the perfectionist would in some cases be willing to restrict choices to enforce a moral vision. My question is whether he can do this and still claim he is a liberal.

Extreme Cases Only

My second claim is that he can do so, and indeed that most people who consider themselves liberals would support some restriction or other. The liberal perfectionist will prefer to see few such restrictions, but he need not object to all of them. Coercion generally does not promote perfection, but neither does unfettered choice in every case. The liberal perfectionist might support barriers in extreme cases, such as hard drugs, and still claim that he is a liberal, so long as he objects to more invasive restrictions on choice. He might respect a person's autonomy for 999 of the decisions he must make and reserve perfectionist fetters for the one grievous case in a thousand where he would expect the subject to stray, and where the perfectionist's choices would make him better off.

Hard drugs are a convenient peg upon which to hang the liberal perfectionist's prohibitions. Other examples might easily be added: public indecency, incest and desecrating graveyards. To suggest that there is no difference between this and the fanatic's religious persecution is fundamentally silly. A person might reserve flat prohibitions for the most extreme cases and still claim that he is a liberal. Otherwise, virtually no one would be a liberal, and the term would be devoid of interest.

Endogenous Preferences

Third, the liberal perfectionist might argue that restrictions that are illiberal in the first instance are consistent with autonomy rights when they effect a subsequent change in our preferences.[21] As we saw in Chapter 7's discussion of endogenous preferences, our desires are importantly shaped by the legal regime and a prohibition that runs contrary to what a person wants might in time reform his preferences so that they are no longer resented. A heroin addict might want the drug decriminalized so that he is free to enjoy it. However, if the prohibition is effective and he does stop using it, his craving might in time disappear. Presented with an opportunity to use it, he might then turn it down.

Where hard drugs are banned, the addict's decision not to use heroin is not autonomous before his preferences have changed. (If it helps, we can assume that every user is caught and that a sentence of capital punishment is imposed.) The addict wants his fix, but he's not free to have it. But what about the second decision, where he turns down the offer of heroin after his preferences have changed? That seems a free choice. The liberal perfectionist might even claim that the choice is freer because the addict is freed from his addiction.

Suppose that we question the person, after his preferences have changed, to evaluate whether his choice is free. He explains that he understands how dangerous the drug is. He knows that the momentary euphoria must be weighed against the ravages of drug addiction. He knows that were he to take up heroin again his job and his marriage would be destroyed. He understands just how painful that would be. And he knows this better than he did as an addict. He even knows that he might not have felt this way but for the criminal prohibition, and he's thankful for that. If autonomy means a rational choice made after a careful evaluation of costs and benefits, then his decision seems autonomous.[22]

Against this, it might be argued that no choice arrived at after the perfectionist's manipulation of our preferences could ever be free. However, this cannot mean that every choice that might be attributed to some past influence in our lives is unfree. Otherwise, an adult's decision not to use heroin would be unfree if his preference was shaped by an antidrug educational program when he was a child in school. Parental influences would also be suspect, and even Mill would turn out to be a perfectionist. So that can't be right.

Nor is it the case that every choice that is influenced by a prior violation of autonomy rights is unfree because that would take us into choices made by prior generations. Locke's argument for religious toleration is compelling, but the religion espoused by most Englishmen in Locke's time was the product not of tolerance but of Henry VIII's rupture with Rome 150 years before and of a set of civil penalties against Catholics that persisted to Locke's time—and of which Locke himself approved.

We'd then have to limit this objection to the person himself, where a prior illegitimate restriction changes his own preferences. Can we say that a decision founded on the new set of preferences is freely made? One answer to this might be that the prior restriction was not illegitimate because it was restricted to extreme cases such as antidrug laws. In that case, however, our third argument would collapse into the second one, and I want to say that even illegitimate restrictions might not deprive a subsequent decision of its autonomous quality where the person's preferences have changed. To do this, I have to make a distinction between moderate restrictive laws adopted in a democratic country and brainwashing.

To see this, consider the following laws, all of which will be regarded by some as trenching on individual rights.

- Laws restricting the kind of people to whom I might rent rooms in my house.
- Laws restricting abortion.
- Laws permitting abortion.
- Laws that give special benefits to married couples.
- Laws that prohibit same-sex marriages.

All of these laws might shape our preferences, in one direction or another. And if such laws are illegitimate, and if all decisions made on the basis of the preferences so changed are illegitimate, then many of our choices would not be worthy of respect. The libertarian's decision not to use soft drugs would be unfree if it had been shaped by what he regards as unjust legal prohibition, and so too the relaxation of his racial prejudices if they had been caused by what he regards as unjust civil rights laws. Let us suppose that Johanna:

1. Believes that the 1964 Civil Rights Act's antidiscrimination rules about renting rooms in one's house were unjust;
2. Would not have rented a room in her house in 1964 to anyone save a fellow Catalan Catholic; and
3. Would rent a room to people of different races and religions today because her prejudices have been relaxed as a consequence of the 1964 Act.

I should nevertheless like to say that Johanna's decision to rent to an African-American Protestant today is freely made. Like the former drug addict whose preferences have changed, Johanna can articulate sound reasons why she should rent to people of different races and religions. She might express great regret and embarrassment for her former views. If that's not a free choice, a theory which holds autonomy up as a primary good would have to acknowledge that we have far fewer free choices than we had thought. There would be no end to the doubts we might have about whether our decisions are free, even in a democratic society, and a theory which holds autonomy up as the highest good would paradoxically weaken it.

This does not justify an extensive regulation of our preferences. As we noted in the last chapter, the argument from endogenous preferences does not mean that every attempt to shape our preferences is legitimate or that none is. Theories of liberty and liberalism need not be completely theorized or provide us with a set of geometric theorems that neatly resolve every question. If the 1964 Act shaped our preferences, it did so in a positive way, one for which we may be sincerely thankful; and this does not commit us to a more extensive form of perfectionism.

Perhaps what is needed is hindsight. When a new law shapes our preferences, it is not always easy to say in advance how effective or painful the change will be. In 1964, some people might not unreasonably have thought that the Civil Rights bill was premature and that it would be bitterly resented for generations. (Of course, failure to pass the law would have been more deeply resented by another group of people.) That's not what happened, as it turned out. The law effected, or at least coincided, with a revolution in people's feelings about racial matters. Even people such as William F. Buckley who opposed the 1964 law came in time to regret their earlier views. That doesn't much help when it comes to deciding on new laws—but then it's always a lot easier to predict the past than the future.

This is not a confession of agnosticism. There are a good many policies whose likely effects are well understood. The economist can tell us with a great deal of confidence that price controls will lead to shortages when the price is set below market price. Nor should anyone have been very surprised when reducing the cost of marital fault led to increased divorce levels. But when it comes to social legislation such as the 1964 Civil Rights bill or same-sex marriage today, it is far more difficult to predict the future.

It is sometimes suggested that what is needed in such cases is practical judgment, which philosopher Michael Oakeshott likened to an art as opposed to a science.[23] The statesman, the man with the vision to see past his contemporaries, understands the swirling forces of history and knows how they will be reconciled after new laws are passed. And his learning cannot be reduced to the economist's technical knowledge. It cannot be written down in a book or circumscribed by a set of rules or principles.

That's a tempting dodge, which lends itself to paeans of praise for the sound legislator, rooted in the land, steeped in its traditions, and upholding the most admirable of principles, who knows just how things will turn out. He can't tell you how he knows—he just knows. The problem is that we recognize these people only in hindsight. Before then, they're just another voice, clamoring to be heard—as Churchill was, in his defense of Edward VIII during the Abdication Crisis.

ℳ Conservative Neutralists

The differences between perfectionists and neutralists might thus be slight. Liberal perfectionists who respect autonomy rights would reserve restrictive laws for the hardest of cases; and, this apart, their efforts to influence people (as opposed to banning certain choices) would very possibly have met with Mill's approval. For his part, the neutralist might be a conservative who objects to restrictive legislation on practical or prudential grounds. He might have as deep an appreciation for the importance of private virtue as the perfectionist but differ on whether virtue flourishes more strongly when it is legislated.

The conservative neutralist will have the same qualms about perfectionism that we saw in Chapter 6. More than left-liberals, the conservative is apt to question the paternalist's motives. He'll also be more likely to think the state's informational problem is insurmountable as it seeks to legislate for each of us without recognizing that we're all autonomous people with our own set of preferences. More than the left-liberal, the conservative is also willing to rely on social sanctions as a substitute for legal ones. And where the left-liberal concerns himself with distributional concerns and champions welfare schemes, the conservative is more interested in questions of private virtue, which he thinks develops only when people are free to choose for themselves. Finally, if the liberal rallies around words such as equality and justice, the conservative is drawn to freedom and liberty.

The conservative mistrusts reformers. "Reform, reform, reform," snorts the conservative. "Don't talk to me of reform. Things are bad enough already!" He might have a point. The horrifying example of twentieth-century schemes for enforcing morals through such creatures as New Soviet Man suggests that we should shrink from political theories that take human nature to be entirely malleable.

By nature a cynic, the conservative views political theorists with distaste and politicians with disgust. All in all, he thinks that Samuel Johnson summed it up well, in the lines he added to Goldsmith's *The Traveller*:

> *How small, of all that human hearts endure,*
> *That part which laws or kings can cause or cure!*

The conservative thinks that the state is unlikely to understand what people need to flourish. It is, after all, the conservative who wants to shrink down the size of the state. He doesn't trust the state to know how to run the Post Office, let alone our private lives. He is therefore inclined to agree with David Hume that "all plans of government, which suppose great reformation in the manners of mankind, are plainly imaginary."[24]

The conservative thinks that good governance relies more on the stock of private virtue than on grand social schemes. That's what the Founders believed and that's one reason why the conservative holds them in reverence. They thought that the government depends for its support on the virtue of its citizens and not that the virtue of the citizens depends on the support of the government. As such, the conservative is temperamentally suspicious of governmental schemes to legislate virtue, when this forecloses the self-help measures or bonding strategies people might employ on their own.

More than left-liberals, the conservative is comfortable with social sanctions as a substitute for the legal enforcement of morals. He thinks that Mill's fears about the deadening hand of social conventions were excessive in the Victorian era and are laughable in today's relaxed moral climate. By contrast, today's left-liberal is apt to see social norms as retrograde prejudices, to be attacked through civil rights laws that penalize any vestiges of racism and sexism.

The conservative is aware that, on a host of public issues from abortion to public schooling, he is apt to be in the minority. With conservative scholar Harvey Mansfield, he thinks that environmentalism is school prayer for left-liberals. If perfectionism seemed to cut the conservative's way in the past, that no longer is the case. Instead, the driver's seat is more likely to be occupied by the left-liberal, with his issues of class, race, and gender. That's not the conservative trilogy of duty, honor, country. The conservative still gets misty-eyed when he reads General MacArthur's West Point Farewell Speech, but he knows that he is increasingly alone in this.

> In my dreams I hear again the crash of guns, the rattle of musketry, the strange, mournful mutter of the battlefield. But in the evening of my memory I come back to West Point. Always there echoes and re-echoes: Duty, Honor, Country.

The conservative tends to bristle when he hears left-liberals talk about diversity. Too often, he thinks, diversity really means an enforced uniformity in political beliefs, where conservatives are systematically excluded. The diversity movement has been felt most strongly in university hiring policies, and it is no accident that academic faculties are overwhelmingly left-liberal. However, if "diversity" was something other than Orwellian double-speak, where war equals peace and uniformity equals diversity, then conservatives would "take diversity seriously," in the phrase of William Galston.[25] In so doing, they'd abandon perfectionism for a prudential neutralism.

Conservative neutralists see private perfectionists as closet statists who seek to expand the role of the government and weaken subsidiary institutions. In the debate about the Boy Scouts' policy of excluding homosexual scoutmasters, it was the perfectionist who sought to impose antidiscrimination requirements on a private organization, and the conservative neutralist who wished to limit state interference with individual choice.[26] So too, perfectionists such as Émile Combes who sought to ban private religious education in France were opposed by conservative neutralists. The conservative thinks that the perfectionist is often the enemy of the good.

The conservative neutralist will therefore want the state to stay out of the business of defining what gives value to life. He would legalize vice without celebrating it. He might prefer truth to falsehood, knowledge to ignorance, courage to cowardice, and kindness to spite. He might think beauty more valuable than ugliness, and deny that these terms are meaningless. But he might still not want the state to promote any one of these alternatives. Like Mill in *Utilitarianism*, he might have a discriminating moral and aesthetic sense; but like Mill in *On Liberty*, he might want the state to abstain from taking a position on any these issues.

The conservative neutralist is always on the side of subsidiary institutions as guardians of public virtue. Whether religious or not, he supports churches, synagogues, and faith-based institutions generally. He sees them as Edmund Burke saw his "little platoons," the private associations to which we look to reinforce social norms. The conservative will also think that opposition to faith-based groups comes from secularists with a partisan agenda who want top-down rules imposed by the state because they see themselves in control of its levers of power.

As a supporter of subsidiary institutions, the conservative, more than the left-liberal, supports the devolution of power from the federal to the state and local level. If mobility weakens our sense of solidarity, it also makes perfectionism less troubling because people can move to escape it. And the cheaper the move, the less we would worry about it. What we think of as Los Angeles is really a group of more than sixty cities, and moving from one to the other is relatively pain free. As a result, we wouldn't worry overmuch about restrictive laws one city might pass.

This is the idea behind laws in the United States and Canada that evaluate obscenity according to local community standards. What's obscene in Peoria might not be obscene in Las Vegas. Even if local standards are probably converging, differences between one community and another still remain, and when you settle in Frank Capra's wholesome Bedford Falls (*It's a Wonderful Life*), you wouldn't expect to see anything like Key West. The conservative doesn't hold up much hope for Key West, but he's rather fond of Bedford Falls.

In a federal country, such as the United States, migration across state lines also offers a means of escaping a burdensome, left-liberal perfectionism. That's not to say that moving is costless. However, where nearly half of Americans live in a different state than the one they were born in,[27] the question for many of us is not whether we will move, but where we will move to. In the area where I live, people have a choice between the District of Columbia, Virginia, and Maryland. With its relaxed gun laws, Virginia attracts more conservative people, while left-liberals might choose to settle in Montgomery County, Maryland. Not satisfied with a ban on smoking in restaurants, the Montgomery County city of Friendship Heights sought to ban smoking on the sidewalks. That wouldn't happen in Virginia.

Migration permits us to sort ourselves out by preferences. A conservative Virginian might think that there are a good many foolish laws in California; but he might ask himself why he should care if their effect is confined to that state. Were perfectionism imposed at the national level, and Virginians and Californians were required to conform to the same regime, a good many people in both states would be dissatisfied; but such complaints are fewer when the laws are passed at the state level, and people "vote with their feet" for the regime they prefer.[28] In a federal regime, we can also expect states to tailor perfectionist laws more closely to the local population. As the Supreme Court has noted, "a decentralized government . . . will be more sensitive to the diverse needs of a heterogeneous society."[29] That's an argument that is particularly telling for the conservative, who is apt to think that he's lost the debate at the national level.

Finally, the conservative, more than the left-liberal, is on the side of liberty and autonomy. With the exception of abortion and same-sex marriage, which the left-liberal frames as a questions of choice, the conservative is found among the supporters of free choice and free markets, and the left-liberal of equality and fairness. From free bargaining, to school choice and to free trade, the conservative aligns himself with personal autonomy and opposes the left-liberal in doing so. I do not want to say who is right in these quarrels, but only that neutralism is an eminently sensible position for conservatives.

Religious conservatives (and religious people are often conservative) are especially likely to prize free choices because they believe that God must be freely accepted into our hearts if He is to be accepted at all. This puts them on the side of freedom in a number of ways: for free will and against determinism, for the free exercise of religion and against state coercion, and for the free choices that mold our character and against a thoroughgoing perfectionism. They see the Earth as the place where we work out our salvation, which implies that we must be permitted to fail.

In conclusion, the space between American perfectionists and neutralists is much smaller than one would suppose, if all one did was listen to the shrill debate between partisans on both sides. Though perfectionism and neutralism mean very different things in theory, in practice they often converge.

NINE

Social Perfectionism

The most hateful of all names in an English ear is Nosey Parker.

George Orwell, England, Your England

SOFT AND HARD PATERNALISTS would override the subject's choices out of concern for the subject himself. But the subject's actions may have the third-party spillover effects that economists call externalities. What I do affects others, for good or for ill, and this may supply a reason to restrict my freedom. When my actions confer third party gains, we may speak of positive externalities, and when third parties are injured, we may speak of negative externalities.

% Coasian Bargains

Externalities might at first glance look like an insoluble problem. Why would I care what happens to third parties? Property and tort law supplies an answer. Where my behavior harms a third party, he might sue me for infringing his property rights (by dumping pollution on his back yard). Alternatively, he might sue me in tort or civil liability law (for harming his goods or himself). Even without legal incentives imposed from above, the third party might cure the problem by crafting a private bargain with me, as Ronald Coase showed in a brilliant 1960 article entitled *The Problem of Social Cost*.[1] Coase showed that:

1. Where there are no barriers to bargaining, all opportunities to reduce wasteful external costs will be exploited through private bargains;
2. This will be done without regard to who caused the harm; and
3. Without regard to whether the law affords a remedy in property or tort law.

To see this, let's suppose that my pollution spills over onto your land and bargaining is costless. Assume further that you value pollution-free land more than I value the right to pollute: you'd pay $100 to eliminate the pollution, and I derive a gain of only $10 from polluting. In that case, we'd eliminate the pollution whatever the legal regime might be. If I have the right to pollute, you'll pay me a figure between $10 and $100 not to do so. And if you have the right to sue me for pollution, I'll not pollute because I'd have to pay you $100 in damages and derive a gain of only $10. Same result either way, whatever the legal regime.

Suppose next that I value the right to pollute more than you value pollution-free land: You'd pay no more than $10 to eliminate the pollution, and I derive a gain of $100 from polluting. Once again, the legal regime wouldn't change what we do. If I have the right to pollute, you wouldn't be able to pay me enough to make me stop. And if you could sue me for polluting, I'd prefer to pay damages and keep on polluting because that's worth more to me than the damages award. What determines whether I continue to pollute is the dollars and cents issue of whether it is value increasing to do so and not which way the legal regime cuts.

Coase presented his paper at a workshop of about twenty eminent economists, all of whom thought Coase was wrong at the beginning of the talk, and all of whom agreed with Coase at the end. That's the stuff of a Nobel prize, which Coase won in 1991. The Coase Theorem effected a revolution in legal theory. Formerly, lawyers thought that people simply did what the legal regimes of property and tort law told them to do. But after Coase showed how private agreements were more fundamental still, Coasian bargains were thought the bedrock or private ordering. In its extreme form, the Coase Theorem was taken to assert that the legal regime is or should be irrelevant. But that's not what Coase himself thought. The interesting question, said Coase, is not how parties behave when they can bargain over everything but what happens when they can't do so. What happens when there are barriers to bargaining, either because the costs of bargaining (called *transaction costs*) are too high or because the bargains aren't enforceable at law?*

It's all very easy to assume that third parties will cut a deal when there is only one or a few of them. But what happens when there are thousands

---

* When a contract violates public policy, it might be unenforceable in court and performance of the contract might even be a crime, as in the case of a contract to murder another. In such cases, a private Coasian bargain is unlikely to cure the externalities problem—for good reason.

of them? To reach an agreement, they'd all have to bear the costs of finding each other, identifying and pricing the harm, and then bargaining with the polluter (and there might be dozens of them). Add to this the free rider problem, where a third party decides not to bear the bargaining costs or pay to cure the problem because he'd prefer to let the other fellow to do this. The free rider would know that his contribution to the bargain wouldn't much change the amount of pollution. He'd also know that he couldn't be excluded from enjoying the benefits of reduced pollution, even if he doesn't contribute to the bargain. He'd therefore be strongly tempted to drop out of the agreement. And if one third party thinks this, all might do so, with the result that the agreement would unravel.

In sum, we simply wouldn't expect Coasian agreements to cure mass pollution problems. In such cases, the legal regime, which looked irrelevant when everything was solved through a Coasian bargain, now looks relevant. It shapes what we do. In the presence of nontrivial transaction costs, we'd expect to find less pollution if polluters can be sued.

✹ Moral Externalities

We are accustomed to think of externalities as physical things, like the sludge which seeps downriver from the polluting plant. But externalities might also be moral in nature. I am better off when I live in a society composed of honest, trustworthy people. Because I can trust them, I find it easier to reach an agreement with them. I can also rely on them to pitch in at times of crisis, without asking for a reward for doing so. They are also the kind of people who provide models of good behavior that others might emulate. As individuals, such people possess the high *human capital* of good character and trustworthiness. These are of value not only to the individual but also to those around her, and economists call the spillover benefits such people confer on others *social capital*.

Because social capital is so important, many people will agree with communitarian philosopher Charles Taylor that the state should seek to inculcate a set of social virtues. It is important for an individual:

> that certain activities and institutions flourish in society. It is even of importance to him what the moral tone of the whole society is ... because freedom and individual diversity can only flourish in a society where there is a general recognition of their worth.[2]

In the last chapter, we described a private perfectionism that interferes with a person's choice in order to promote his moral welfare. Here we ask whether the state should promote social capital by fettering a person's freedom in order to benefit those he might influence, and this I call *social perfectionism*.

The kinds of externalities that diminish social capital cannot be made the subject of a Coasian bargain. I can pay a neighbor to stop releasing pollution onto my yard, but I can't pay anyone to act morally. I'd never be able to police him, and in any event we're talking about the behavior of an entire society, and not just one person. The problem was described by Walter Berns:

> Consider the case of the parent who wants to convince his children of the impropriety of the use of the four-letter verb meaning to copulate. At the present time the task confronting him is only slightly less formidable than that faced by the parent who would teach his children that the world is flat. Just as the latter will have to face a body of scientific evidence to the contrary, the former will have to overcome the power of common usage and the idea of propriety it implies. . . . The parent will fail in his effort to educate because he will be on his own, trying to teach a lesson his society no longer wants taught—by the law, by the language, or by the schools.[3]

As we noted, social perfectionism is an easier sell than private perfectionism, which is why we need to keep the two separate. Private perfectionism seeks to reform the scoundrel, and he's not a very likeable character. Truth is, we don't much care what happens to Grille. We are, however, more willing to help those he might corrupt. These were the knights whom Acrasia ensnared in the Bower of Bliss and whom Guyon freed. Innocent third parties are more sympathetic, and there are a lot more of them. Besides, we respect their autonomy more when we seek to shield them from improper influences than the private perfectionist does when he impeaches a subject's choices "for his own good."

However, not every spillover effect rises to a level of concern, and there are at least five arguments for ignoring social externalities:

- *The Ubiquity of Social Harms.* The concern for spillover benefits and costs of goods and bads can make one forget just how ubiquitous they are. External goods include such things as the passerby's pleasure when he sees a classically designed building. There are a vast number of such benefits, and to suppose that recipients have an obligation of financial support is absurd.[4] Similarly, not every external bad imposes a duty upon its creator. We do not impose aesthetic taxes on concrete-slab buildings. We'd go mad if we tried to tote up all such gains and costs in a social welfare balance sheet.

- *Excessive Perfectionism*. Recall that a Coasian bargain wouldn't eliminate all pollution but only the level of pollution where the costs exceed the benefits of polluting. We don't want to pay $100 to ban pollution that imposes a cost of only $10. Similarly, we wouldn't want to ban social ills when the cure would be worse than the disease.
- *Laws of General Application*. The paternalist who seeks to curb our choices in the name of physical or moral externalities does so in the guise of a legislator. That is, he cannot fine-tune rules to catch the idiosyncratic case of every externality but must instead impose laws of general application. Some weak soul somewhere always might be offended by generally innocuous behavior, but that doesn't give the paternalist an excuse to ban it. The standard for obscenity is based on the reaction of the ordinary person and not the prim and easily shocked puritan.
- *Private Solutions to the Problem*. We should not assume that spillover public goods cannot be produced without government subsidies or that spillover bads require legal prohibitions. This would ignore the enormous nonprofit industry that operates schools and universities, runs hospitals, supports medical research, and does the numberless little things that a government could never hope to emulate successfully. People are also constrained from immoral behavior by the social sanctions this might attract, and as Mill noted, this might permit us to dispense with legal sanctions. What matters is whether, at the margin, spillover goods are undersupplied and spillover bads oversupplied and not whether there are third-party effects.*
- *Perfectionist Overreaching*. Finally, the social perfectionist must persuade us that he won't abuse the power we give him by fettering basic freedoms. This is so large a subject that we will devote the next three sections to it.

✿ The Harm-to-Others Principle

Though Mill strongly resisted social perfectionism, the concern for third party moral harms would seem consistent with John Stuart Mill's harm-to-others principle. If it isn't, it's because Mill's principle is really two principles in one.

---

* More technically, the efficient amount of public goods is produced when the (marginal) cost of one more unit of good would exceed the additional (marginal) benefit.

First, it is a theory of antipaternalism because it conclusively presumes that people are the best judges of their own welfare: the state should never interfere with our choices with the goal of making us more moral so long as third parties aren't harmed. Second, the harm-to-others principle is a theory about what counts as a third-party harm: physical harms do, moral harms don't. This strikes one as a paradox. A harm is a harm, and once one admits their existence, moral harms would seem to matter as much as any other kind of harm. Ignoring them would seem no more reasonable than crafting an exception in the Securities and Exchange Act for red-headed men.

Disputes about harms are really over questions of fact and not moral philosophy. People might have different opinions about whether there are moral externalities, but it really comes down to what the data shows. When illegitimacy rates are high, what happens to teenage delinquency? What about crime rates and pervasive drug use? If there's a correlation between two social pathologies, which way does causation run? Here, as elsewhere, what matters is the empirical evidence, and the philosophical problem aspires to the condition of economics, could the problem of missing data be solved.

The neutralist can't win the debate by assuming away moral externalities. The costs of such externalities might be high or low, but they won't be zero unless no one through his behavior could ever influence another. A parent who sincerely believes this would be indifferent about whom his child chooses as a friend, and we should all be quite unaffected by our companions, whether we find them in a church or a prison yard. That's absurd, and Mill rejected this easy way out. "I fully admit," he said, "that the mischief which a person does to himself may seriously affect, both through their sympathies and their interests, those nearly connected with him and, in a minor degree, society at large."[5]

In discounting moral externalities, Mill also foreswore an appeal to individual rights. A rights theorist might claim that third-party moral harms could never justify fettering my choices because this would violate my rights. I get to do what I want, without a veto imposed by someone whose feelings are hurt or character altered. Let the other fellow look after himself. But that's not how Mill saw it. As a utilitarian, Mill judged acts and rules according to their consequences that includes third-party spillover consequences. The test of whether a right makes sense is always whether it produces greater utility (or makes people happier), without regard to the abstract boundaries of rights theories. Indeed, Mill explicitly rejected "any advantage which could be derived ... from the idea of abstract right, as a thing independent of utility."[6]

If moral externalities make people worse off, then, rights theories could not get in the way of restrictions on choice.

We'd therefore expect that Mill would sharply disagree with rights theorists on the subject of moral externalities. But that's not what happened. Instead, there was a complete overlap in their views. While admitting that moral spillover effects exist, Mill thought they should always be ignored. Otherwise, he said, we'd be down the garden path to oppression because almost anything might count as a third-party moral cost. To keep the harm principle within reasonable bounds, Mill's prudential neutralism would require a physical harm before interfering with choices. That means we'd have to put up with real moral externalities that do impose spillover effects. But this, said Mill, is an "inconvenience . . . which society can afford to bear, for the sake of the greater good of human freedom."[7]

All this looks rather like another Mill Problem, where Mill seems to contradict himself: Mill rejected the idea of abstract rights, but ended up in the same place anyway. Indeed, Mill reserved his harshest criticism for laws which address moral externalities, and which seek to benefit not the subject, but those he affects. This "monstrous" principle is without limits. "There is no violation of liberty which it would not justify; it acknowledges no right to any freedom whatever, except perhaps to that of holding opinions in secret."[8]

So is Mill inconsistent? I think not. A utilitarian who evaluates rules according to their consequences rather than abstract rights might nevertheless embrace a prudential theory of rights if (a) enforcing the right results in greater overall utility; and (b) any relaxation of the right, even in the most extreme circumstances, is bound to result in diminished utility because of judicial or administrative error. Take the most serious case of a moral externality where the spillover effects are greatest. Even here, a utilitarian might without inconsistency ask us to ignore third-party costs because he thinks that the perfectionist could not be trusted to limit herself to this case but must inevitably fetter other choices and turn into a tyrant. And that's just what Mill said.

The fear that the perfectionist will overreach and impose excessive restrictions on our choices suggests an answer to another Mill Problem. Mill had an objective theory of happiness, which he defended in his *Utilitarianism*. There he wrote that not all pleasures are equally valuable, that some goods have intrinsic merit by virtue of the deeper pleasures they afford, pleasures that the ill-educated might not fully appreciate until they have experienced them. People "should be forever stimulating each other to increased exercise of their higher faculties . . . toward wise instead of foolish, elevating instead of degrading, objects and contemplations."⁹ But then why shouldn't the state nudge people toward these higher pleasures? We know that *On Liberty* trumps *Utilitarianism*, that the stimulation to which Mill refers should never, in his view, be enforced by legal barriers; but we're left to wonder why the libertarian should win every trick. Mill's answer, once again, is that the perfectionist would abuse his power and fetter too many of our choices.

So much for the two Mill Problems, then. But that's not the end of the matter because the problem of possible overreaching by the perfectionist remains and requires an answer. Can the social perfectionist respond to this charge, then? I believe he can, with an empirical and not a philosophical answer. The neutralist's claim is that any attempt to legislate social norms will lead to a moral tyranny. And this claim is asserted so often, and so confidently, that the neutralist is apt to forget that it is really an empirical claim. If meaningful, it amounts to a prediction that relaxing Mill's assumption of zero spillover effects with their attendant social costs will result in oppression. But that doesn't begin to describe the experience of Western countries, with their perfectionist legislation in criminal and family law. Not every power is taken to the limit.

The American neutralist is apt to assume that any attempt to enforce morals, and indeed any departure from his country's constitutional protections will lead to oppression, as though there were no middle ground between the United States and Iran. This betrays a blind ignorance of the liberties the English and citizens of other Western countries enjoy. In some respects, America better respects liberty than other countries, in other respects less; and even where there are differences, Western countries tend to end up in the same place.

Compare the criminal laws of the United States and England, for example. Criminal evidence and procedural law in the United States is shaped by constitutional guarantees in the Bill of Rights and is considerably more solicitous of the defendant than in England. It is easier for an English Crown prosecutor to obtain a conviction because English evidentiary rules are less stringent than those of the United States and because Crown prosecutors may appeal an acquittal if they believe that a jury has acted irresponsibly. That couldn't happen in America. On the other hand, criminal sentencing law is much harsher in the United States than in England. We have capital punishment in the United States and far longer prison terms. So it might be a wash. The rational criminal who compares the costs and benefits of his crime will measure the costs by looking to both the probability and the consequences of conviction, and the calculus might be the same in the two countries.* The criminal is less likely to be convicted in America, but when they get you here, they really get you. Criticizing America for its harsh sentencing laws without taking its pro-defense evidentiary and procedural laws into account would be as unfair as criticizing England for its pro-prosecutor evidentiary and procedural laws without taking its mild sentencing laws into account.

That's not to say that departures from freedom in the name of social externalities in England and America are never troubling. Curbs on free speech, of the kind we saw in the last chapter, in the name of multicultural sensitivities are particularly worrisome, as they seem to justify precisely the sort of unbounded restrictions on our freedom that Mill had in mind. When the only standard for a free speech ban is whether some group feels itself offended, then almost no speech is safe. Nearly every form of political expression might be thought to hurt the feelings of some group, somewhere.

Social perfectionism is an empirical more than a philosophical problem and cannot be resolved by an appeal to first principles, whether found in the neutralist's libertarian ideals or in the social perfectionist's multicultural sensitivities. What is needed, instead, is a comparison of the costs and benefits of interfering with individual choices. That's not an exact science, and first hunches will have to be corrected in light of subsequent experience. The project of liberty and the tension between it and social perfectionism remains a challenge to be addressed by looking at the consequences of legal policies.

In what follows, we'll look at one possible consequence from a classic debate about social perfectionism fifty years ago.

🕊 The Disintegration Thesis

Laws that sought to reform morals were greatly relaxed in the last half of the last century, especially with respect to sexual preferences. Until recently, private homosexual acts were crimes in both the United States and England. In the United States in 1986, the Supreme Court upheld a state law that criminalized sodomy;[10] however, in 2003 the Court reversed itself and held that such laws are unconstitutional.[11] In England, sodomy laws were repealed

---

* This assumes that the rational criminal has no preferences as to risk. If he is a risk avoider, he will pay more attention to the probability of conviction than to the sentence on conviction; and this means that the English regime might deter more criminals, all other things being equal.

even earlier, after the 1957 Wolfenden Report recommended that private homosexual acts between consenting adults should no longer be a criminal offence. The Report distinguished between law and morals and stated that "it is not the duty of the law to concern itself with immorality as such."[12] The law should protect public order and decency and provide safeguards against the corruption of others but has no place in the bedrooms of the nation. That might not sound like a ringing endorsement of Mill. However, given public attitudes to homosexuality at the time, Mill's harm-to-others principle, including his rejection of moral harms, clearly inspired the Report.

The Report sparked a well-known debate between Patrick Devlin and legal philosopher H.L.A. Hart that became part of the syllabus of every course on legal philosophy. Lord Devlin was a High Court judge of liberal sympathies but he criticized the Report in *The Enforcement of Morals* and was roundly criticized in turn by Hart in *Law, Liberty, and Morality*, and the two little books remain leading statements of their respective positions.[13] They were a turning point in our beliefs about legislating morality because we all thought that Hart had trounced Devlin and put paid to any idea that the law should concern itself with the enforcement of morals. One hundred years after *On Liberty*, Mill had finally triumphed.

Lord Devlin was a common lawyer and not a natural lawyer. He did not object to homosexuality because he thought it was objectively wrong. At least, he did not think that it was the business of the law to criminalize behavior just because it was objectively wrong, and in this he agreed with the Wolfenden Report. Nevertheless, he thought that the Report had missed something—moral externalities. Mill had conceded that the example of an immoral fellow subject might injure us. If so, said Devlin, the state has a prima facie right to penalize such behavior. "A nation of debauchees would not in 1940 have responded satisfactorily to Winston Churchill's call to blood and toil and sweat and tears."[14] We are bound together in the moral enterprise of good governance, and a state might disintegrate if it fails to enforce its moral code.

Devlin was in short a social perfectionist. He thought that a state might enforce through its laws the social norms that are constitutive of its society, the norms that preserve both the society and the state. For the state, this is a matter of self-protection, like the laws against treason. The norms are enforced, not because they are right, but because they are necessary if the state is to survive, and in evaluating these norms the judge should look not to the moralist but to 'the man on the Clapham omnibus,' the sensible ordinary citizen with his common sense morality. It does not matter whether what he believes is right or wrong, so long as he deeply believes the act is wrong.

In response, Hart defended the decriminalization of homosexuality and, like Mill, denied that moral externalities should play any part in the design of the law. The very idea that homosexuality gives rise to moral externalities was "absurd" and not entitled to any more respect "than the Emperor Justinian's statement that homosexuality was the cause of earthquakes." More broadly, no reputable historian had seen any connection between sexual transgressions and the survival of a society. Devlin himself was "confused and confusing" and "not very perspicuous."[15]

Though Hart was thought to have won the debate fifty years ago, today it is less clear. In particular, Hart's denial of social externalities in sexual matters now seems very dated. Divorce is something other than the morally neutral personal choice we thought it was. A good deal of evidence shows that it harms children and that stepparents do not appear to makes things any better for them. Similarly, the children of unwed mothers are more likely to fall afoul of the law and become unwed parents themselves.[16] From today's perspective, it is Hart who looks naïve and Devlin who appears the realist.

This is not to say that the state should trench on individual liberties. No one today would want to ban no-fault divorces. At most, the social conservative would want to provide the opt-out for covenant marriages we saw in Chapter 7. Devlin himself would limit his social perfectionism to cases "beyond the limits of tolerance. It is not nearly enough to say that a majority dislikes a practice; there must be a real feeling of reprobation." And this, thought Devlin, was how the ordinary Englishman viewed homosexuality in 1959. What he felt was more than reprobation—it was a deeply felt disgust which signaled that the bounds of toleration had been exceeded. "Not everything is to be tolerated. No society can do without intolerance, indignation, and disgust."[17] And if that is the feeling homosexuality inspired for most people, he thought, the state cannot be denied the right to proscribe it.

Is Devlin's social perfectionism necessarily illiberal? Can it respect individual liberty? Devlin thought it could. Perfectionism should be reserved for the hardest cases, he said. Beyond that, "there must be toleration of the maximum individual freedom that is consistent with the integrity of society."[18] And this, thought Devlin, the common law did. He lived, he believed, in a liberal society, at least a society that respected individual freedom as much as any contemporary society; and had he been pressed, he might have said that he did not think that the England of 1959 had any lessons to take from other countries at the time on the subject of liberty.

Devlin's theory about societal disintegration rested on a slippery slope argument about moral externalities. A slippery slope argument asserts that an otherwise benign change will prove dangerous because it opens the door to excesses. For Devlin, tolerating behavior that is or might be harmless might be perilous because it might lead us to tolerate clearly harmful behavior. But neutralists such as Mill also rely on a slippery slope argument: proscribing admittedly harmful behavior might be dangerous because it could lead us to proscribe harmless behavior. As between the two slippery slope theories, it is by no means clear that the neutralist has the better argument or that it is impossible to strike a proper balance between the competing claims of social perfectionism and liberty.

Before Devlin's argument from repugnance can provide an argument for social perfectionism, however, four things must be shown:

- We must believe that emotions can have a moral status, that there are good and bad emotions.
- We must have reason to think that our feelings of repugnance usefully reinforce valuable social norms.
- We must have some evidence that the proposed change would weaken our sense of repugnance.
- We must believe that this weakening would lead to a disintegration of the social fabric.

Do Emotions Have a Moral Status?

Devlin was not the first to think that emotions, such as the sense of repugnance, have a moral status. Though rationalists might object to the idea of moral emotions or moral sentiments, most of us, and many philosophers and moralists, see them as central to our moral life. Aristotle noted that being moral is not simply a matter of right action; it also involves having the right sentiments. We can and do blame those whose feelings are inadequate, who cannot feel friendship, love, patriotism, anger, or joy when these are called for.[19] We blame people for bad feelings and for the absence of feelings. We dislike people who don't feel gratitude for gifts received or empathy for another's suffering. In part this is because we bear a responsibility for shaping our feelings. But we also blame people for their feelings even when they can't change them because they are constitutive of people's identities and moral personhood.

People who aren't shocked by immoral behavior pose a danger to society. A jury that hears evidence of a chilling murder without being outraged is far less likely to convict than a more passionate jury. At present, our rules of criminal procedure are designed to minimize a jury's emotional response to a crime, with the goal of producing a wholly rational and unemotional verdict. In capital cases, the trial and sentencing often take place years after the crime, when jurors are less emotional, and perhaps in a different city if it is thought that the defendant "can't get a fair trial" in the city where the crime occurred. No one wants a lynch mob as a jury, but if criminal procedure laws succeeded in producing a jury without affect, without any feeling, far more criminals would escape justice. That is precisely why criminal defense lawyers want to stretch out a trial so long that no one cares any longer. A perfectly rational criminal justice system, from which any emotion is excluded, is apt to regard crimes with indifference, as though they were committed 100 years ago.

Mill's friend, James Fitzjames Stephen, understood this. Stephen was the most eminent criminal lawyer of his day and, like Mill, was a utilitarian, though of a decidedly conservative cast of mind. While Stephen authored a high rational criminal code,* he also recognized that "the custom of looking upon certain courses of conduct with aversion [is] the essence of morality."[20] When we lose our sense of moral outrage, we learn to tolerate the intolerable.

Do Our Emotions Point Us in the Right Direction?

If our emotions have a moral status, the next question is whether our feelings of repugnance usefully buttress valuable social norms. The point is that moral sentiments can and do mislead. Many things that inspired disgust in the past, such as interracial marriages, now are entirely accepted, and today we feel disgust at people who continue to harbor such prejudices. For most of us, that is true of homosexuality as well. Homosexual acts no longer inspire the visceral distaste that most people felt fifty years ago. Were he alive today, Devlin would doubtless oppose their criminalization, and he was even willing to concede that attitudes were shifting in his day.

We cannot judge Devlin's concern about homosexuality from the morally elevated perch of today's America, without recognizing that some of the things we find disgusting today might seem quite ordinary in fifty years hence and that some things we placidly accept today might seem disgusting then.

---

* Which, rejected in England, was adopted in Canada.

But that poses the question whether moral sentiments ever provide a reliable guide for our actions. They are not infallible, to be sure. In truth, there are no infallible guides. We cannot say that moral sentiments never did betray the heart that loved her, as Wordsworth said of nature. Nothing on earth does that and particularly not nature.

That's not the standard, however. The test is not whether moral sentiments are always reliable but whether our unaided conscience with its feelings of shame, guilt, and repugnance outperforms or supplements other criteria, notably rules of reason. On the argument from repugnance, then, our emotions might sometimes provide a better moral guide than reason, and this was Edmund Burke's great theme in his *Reflections on the French Revolution*. The English, said Burke, "are generally men of untaught feelings" so that "instead of casting away all our old prejudices, we cherish them to a considerable degree, and, to take more shame to ourselves, we cherish them because they are prejudices." Because of our prejudices, we feel revulsion at things the rationalist might accept, such as the excesses of the French Revolution. In Goya's celebrated drawing, the sleep of reason brings forth monsters. But the sleep of emotions such as pity can be even more murderous.

Lionel Trilling portrayed the primacy of our emotions as moral guides in *The Middle of the Journey*, his 1947 novel of postwar politics. Rationalism is represented by the Crooms, sensible, intellectual marxisants, and raw emotion by Gifford Maxim, a character inspired by Whittaker Chambers. Maxim is everything the Crooms are not: sentimental, religious and anticommunist. The climax of the novel is built around Duck, a brutish handyman whom the Crooms idealize as a member of the working class. Duck has a lovely daughter, who flubs a poem she was to recite in public. Embarrassed, Duck strikes her twice, hard, and the girl falls dead. The child had a weak heart. Duck did not know this. He was not a murderer. But he was an evil person. Understanding all, Arthur Croom is prepared to hire Duck again. When questioned by Maxim, Arthur explains that his wife believes as he does. It wasn't Duck's fault.

"Nancy means," Arthur said when Nancy did not immediately speak, "that social causes, environment, education or lack of education, economic pressure, the character-pattern imposed by society, in this case a disorganized society, all go to explain and account for any given individual's actions."

Maxim was annoyed by Arthur's indifference. "Is that what you mean, Nancy?'

"Yes," she said. "We can't say he's to blame personally, individually. "But," she said with great unhappiness, "I can't stand the idea of having him around me."[21]

Here is a simple question. When we are confronted with a novel issue and our reason is silent on the matter, should we allow a sense of repugnance to inform our decisions? Might our feelings be coded with information that we ignore at our peril? That is the claim of Leon Kass, the former chair of the President's Council on Bioethics.

In crucial cases . . . repugnance is the emotional expression of deep wisdom, beyond reason's power to fully articulate it. Can anyone really give an argument fully adequate to the horror which is father-daughter incest (even with consent), or having sex with animals, or mutilating a corpse, or eating human flesh, or raping or murdering another human being? Would anyone's failure to give full rational justification for his revulsion at those practices make that revulsion ethically suspect? Not at all.[22]

The hard questions come where our repugnance points one way and our reason seems to point another way, as in the debate about embryonic stem cell research, but happily I do not have to take sides on that contentious issue.

Would the Proposed Change Weaken our Sense of Repugnance?

Let us assume, therefore, that our emotions have a moral status and that a sense of repugnance usefully reinforces valuable social norms. Even then, the social perfectionist would have no reason for concern unless he felt that a relaxation of legal or social norms threatened our sense of repugnance. However, there is little evidence that this has happened. If anything, our politics and popular culture have become more ill tempered since then. Fifty years ago, there was nothing like today's angry cable news shows and indignant talk radio hosts. The principle difference, however, is that other things outrage us today, such as racism and sexism.

Would Losing a Sense of Repugnance Lead to the Disintegration of Society?

Finally, even if we grant that Devlin was correct in thinking that a society had to have a common code of morality, he was wrong to think that a change in our moral views would lead to the disintegration of society. In one sense, Devlin was right because the idea that a society is constituted in part by its moral code is unexceptional. English society in 1959 had particular views about sexual deviance, and these views along with an ensemble of beliefs and practices about culture, government, and history made up what was meant by England.

When social norms change, we might therefore mourn the passing of a society because a distinctive way of living dies with it. In the same way, the disappearance of a language makes the world a less diverse place, which is thought to be regrettable. There is an important difference, however. Though new languages do not arise to take the place of disappearing old ones, a new society emerges out of the ashes of the old. And before we can regret the passing of an old society, we have to assume that the new society that replaces it was a step backward. That's far from clear, however. We are a very different society from that of Devlin's day, even as Devlin's society was very different from that of the Edwardians. We are in some respects a better society today than we were fifty years ago, in some respects worse, and we can't pick and choose. Nor would many of us want to go backward in time.

The Duty of Respect and Public Reasons

Let us finally consider an objection to social perfectionism from a theoretical direction. The objection from the *duty of respect* sees social (and private) perfectionism as incompatible with egalitarian duties of respect for differences in a diverse society. Because people have very different sets of beliefs about the good, only *public reasons*—principles to which people of different faiths and beliefs would subscribe on abstract theories of justice—provide a basis for legislative action.

The objection from a duty of respect would be unpersuasive if it came down to subjectivism or moral relativism. A subjectivist ethic of egalitarian respect that shields everyone from criticism is destructive of moral discourse and every ethic, including that of respect. If the murderer is beyond criticism, so is the perfectionist. If it has any traction, therefore, the objection from public reason must be more limited; and this is the kind of neutralism Ronald Dworkin advances.[23]

Dworkin rules out of order any argument for perfectionism founded upon a particular conception of the good life. This is especially the case for a perfectionism grounded in traditional religious belief, as this in his view would amount to establishing a religion. Those who object on religious grounds to abortion would be silenced, while secularists who support abortion would have the right to speak. All faith-based views about the good would be excluded from the political deliberation, leaving only the kinds of public reasons that people of any or no religion can accept.

This argument involves several difficulties. Dworkin assumes that the set of neutral public reasons to which everyone would subscribe is always the same—a hard core of fundamental beliefs, in truth, justice, and the American way, which both the religious believer and nonbeliever, conservative and left-liberal, would accept as foundational. For Americans, there probably is a large overlap in basic beliefs, but that's not to say that the overlap must be complete. There might even be no overlap whatsoever, as between some people. Religious believers might see democratic principles as rooted in a conception of life as a gift of God, while nonbelievers might have a rigorously secular political philosophy. The two might end up on the same page when it comes to practical politics without sharing any foundational beliefs.

Does the fact the believers and nonbelievers might agree about practical politics and (for that matter) constitutional principles rescue Dworkin's duty of respect? The nonbeliever might tell the religious believer "what's important is that the political and legal implications of your foundational beliefs coincide with my foundational beliefs. Let's forget about how you got there." However, this move seems illegitimate. The religious believer's crushing response would be "I get to decide what my foundational principles are. They are not at all what you believe, and you can't take any comfort in the accident that we end up with similar ideas about practical politics. How I get there matters to me."

Nor would we expect that people will have the same political beliefs, whether foundational or not. As we noted in the last chapter, there is a broad overlap in our political beliefs, for most Americans in any event. Inevitably, however, there are also stark differences over the place of religion in the public square, abortion, voting rights, efficiency as a political norm, the role of the courts, and a host of core constitutional norms. We live with these disagreements in the knowledge that our side won't always win. Most of us learn to tolerate what we might consider the folly of others regarding such issues as school prayer, free trade, and federalism. We might even concede that we're far from infallible and that there is something to be said for experimenting with what seem like bad ideas, as these sometimes turn out to be good ones. In addition, the process of verifying that an idea is bad is of value in itself because it underlines the message about the idea's badness and inculcates respect for the democratic process. We can be tolerant in just this way without being a moral relativist or an agnostic about what constitutes a good life and a good society.

Not everyone is tolerant, however, and the intolerant will refuse to acknowledge any possibility that they might be wrong. Such people are inclined to think, when political issues don't turn out they way they'd like, that we should prorogue the electorate and elect a new electorate in its place. The conservative might want to limit the franchise to people like himself, sound people who understand economics and whose ownership of property gives them a stake in the community, people who are unlikely to support harebrained ideas such as rent control or massive wealth transfers from rich to poor. That would tilt our politics to the right, even as the duty of respect would tilt our politics to the left. On Dworkin's duty or respect, religious conservatives are told that their views on subjects which deeply disturb them, such as abortion, cannot aspire to the condition of public reasons. They are made to feel that there is even something a little churlish about voicing their ideas publicly. Like the conservative's attempt to narrow the franchise, the duty of respect therefore invites a certain cynicism, particularly when those who seek to purge the electorate pride themselves on their tolerance.

In the hands of some people, the duty of respect might thus be opportunistic and employed to advance a partisan agenda. The person who dislikes religious-based schools and restrictions on abortion and who latches onto the duty of respect is just such an opportunist. Where every issue breaks just his way, one might be skeptical of his claim to philosophical detachment and sympathize with Natural Law theorists Robert George and Christopher Wolfe when they argue that the objection:

> almost always has the effect of making the liberal position the winner in morally charged political controversies. It does this in effect by ruling out of bounds substantive moral argument on behalf of nonliberal positions.[24]

More recently, Dworkin has seemed more willing to cut the religious voter some slack:

> Liberals must try to show religious conservatives that their ambition to fuse religion and politics . . . is an error because it contradicts very basic principles that are also part of their faith. Conservatives must try to show liberals that they are wrong in that judgment.[25]

Nevertheless, Dworkin thinks that the left-liberal would win this debate. The core of Western religions is that people cannot come to God under compulsion. If their faith is to count, they must accept God willingly. A law which compelled belief in Catholicism would then be self-defeating, according to the current principles of that religion. However, this does not take us very far when it comes to such matters as abortion. A ban on abortion does not compel belief in Catholicism any more than a ban on capital punishment (which the Church also opposes, though not so definitively). Nor would a ban on abortion interfere with the practice of any other religion, except possibly religions that command women to have abortions—of which none come to mind.*

The left-liberal might respond that a law which criminalizes abortion imposes one religion's definition of when life begins and that this amounts to the establishment of an official religion. However, this seems wrong on two counts. First, the religious conservative might respond that she believes that life begins at conception, not because her church teaches so but simply because she thinks that life begins at conception. And who can say that she is insincere in this? Second, she might respond with a *tu quoque*: if courts decide that life begins not at conception but at a latter time, and this coincides with the views of another church, why wouldn't this establish the doctrines of that other church? If the mere overlap of views is enough to condemn one view, why not the other? That's not to say that the conservative is entitled to impose her views on others, as against the will of a majority, but only that she should be permitted to participate in the debate.

Other difficulties arise with the duty of respect. When political issues are debated, the neutralist would silence those whose political principles are inescapably founded on religious principles; but he'd require them to obey the legislation enacted by the Rump Parliament from which they were excluded.

---

* Where the mother's life is in danger, the Jewish religion imposes just such a command; but in such cases, Catholicism would not ban an abortion.

There would be two classes of people: the refined sort who inhabit faculty common rooms and who are permitted into the public square where issues are decided; and those who are barred from the public square and who simply fall into line and meekly comply with the rules enacted for them. If that's neutralism, it's a very hypocritical kind of neutralism, one which more closely resembles paternalism. Like a child, the religious voter is required to observe laws for which she could not vote.

We can turn this around and argue that those who are bound to follow the laws should also be permitted onto the public square to debate them. That was the point of the Twenty-Sixth Amendment, which gave everyone over eighteen the right to vote. The amendment was passed in the middle of the Vietnam War, when eighteen-year-olds were drafted into the military, and the slogan "old enough to fight, old enough to vote" was found to be compelling. Similarly, Americans who enlisted in the military during World War II out of simple patriotism or even religious convictions were obviously entitled to vote their beliefs.

George Orwell understood this. "What has kept England on its feet?" he asked in 1941. It wasn't abstract principles of social justice. Rather, it was:

> chiefly the atavistic emotion of patriotism, the ingrained feeling of the English-speaking people that they are superior to foreigners. For the last twenty years the main object of English left-wing intellectuals has been to break this feeling down, and if they had succeeded, we might be watching the S.S. men patrolling the London streets at this moment.[26]

Patriotism is one of those emotions that can't be brought into the public square, on public reason theories. Indeed, all emotions, including patriotism, are to be left at the gate, with only calm, rational deliberation permitted to be heard. Orwell's point was that that's not reason enough to send men into battle. And if those who are sent into battle fight out of patriotism, they should be permitted to voice their patriotism in the public square when the question of war is raised.

The same is true of religious motivations. When calling upon our fathers and grandfathers to fight, nearly seventy years ago, their leaders did not hesitate to appeal to religious sentiments. In his Fourth Inaugural Address, President Roosevelt concluded "we pray to Him now for the vision to see our way clearly—to see the way that leads to a better life for ourselves and for all our fellow men—to the achievement of His will to peace on earth." And at the darkest hour, on June 18, 1940, Winston Churchill spoke to the House of Commons:

> What General Weygand called the Battle of France is over. I expect that the Battle of Britain is about to begin. Upon this battle depends the survival of Christian civilization. Upon it depends our own British life, and the long continuity of our institutions and our Empire. . . . Let us therefore brace ourselves to our duties, and so bear ourselves that, if the British Empire and its Commonwealth last for a thousand years, men will still say, "This was their finest hour."

Having made such appeals, could either Roosevelt or Churchill deny the right to participate in the public debate to those who saw the war as a "Crusade in Europe"? Or could those who approve of the appeals made then now wish to exclude those who vote their religious beliefs today?

The neutralist might respond that as prosecution of the war against Germany was justified on the thin set of public reasons permitted in the public debate, those who fought out of religious conviction might also have been permitted to vote their sentiments. They were on the correct side, whether they understood this or not. But once again, this comes down to paternalism. An elite set of superior, rational voters watches over decisions made by an inferior set of passionate voters and vetoes them if they violate what the rational voter thinks the right result.

The neutralist might deny the charge of paternalism and reply that his public reasons are accessible to all men. Faced with a passionate voter, the neutralist would explain that sentiment provides a poor guide to political debate and appeal to the rational principles which everyone can understand. The difficulty here is that, while everyone can understand the thin principles of public reason, that is not what moves voters, as a matter of fact. That's not why Orwell's simple patriots defended their country or responded to Churchill's call to defend Christian civilization. So once again we are left with an uncomfortable distinction between two classes of voters.

As this seems uncomfortably paternalistic, the neutralist might reply that while he might deplore the votes of a passionate majority, he would not deprive them of their right to vote. In that case, however, the public reason objection would lose all traction. The neutralist would be confined to a rhetorical point where he seeks to rule out of order certain kinds of political speech but is powerless against a majority of citizens who vote their passions.

He would put up his hand to silence those with whom he disagrees. But this blocking technique wouldn't be successful because they would continue to assert the right to vote their beliefs.

There is also no reason why political debate should confine itself to public reasons. For example, it would be perfectly rational for a nonbeliever to vote for a party aligned to a particular religion if she concludes that their views are likely to promote the best overall results. The middle-of-the-road non-Christian in Germany might thus vote for the Christian Democratic Party, which in fact solicits their votes.

Take further the example of one who (a) opposes the establishment of any religion as his country's official religion; and (b) wants the state to support parochial schools to promote competition in K-12 education. Not merely is it possible to hold these beliefs simultaneously, but a very large number of Americans do so. The problem is that very few countries offer both these options. America not only bars the establishment of any religion but also prevents the states from subsidizing parochial schools. In many U.S. cities, parents are offered a choice between a free but broken public school system, and a good but expensive private or parochial school. In England the reverse holds. There is an established Anglican church but non-Anglican parochial schools are subsidized by the state. If one had to choose, not a few Americans might prefer the English regime—and think it more liberal than the American one.

John Rawls advanced a theory of public reason neutralism which, oddly enough, resembled Devlin's disintegration thesis. For Rawls, "a just and stable society of free and equal citizens who still remain profoundly divided by reasonable religious, philosophical, and moral doctrines" cannot endure unless everyone within it can give their free and willing support to a common definition of justice.[27] As one might expect, Rawls' disintegration thesis suffers from the same difficulties as that of Devlin. Devlin's moral consensus concerning homosexuality has fallen apart, and our society did not disintegrate. Similarly, a society doesn't disintegrate because people hold different ideas about what justice might entail. What is essential is a common acceptance of the state's constitutional principles. We might have different views about whether the Electoral College in U.S. elections commends itself as a matter of justice. What we can't do is disagree about the role of the Supreme Court as the arbiter of constitutional questions. If we accept that, it doesn't much matter how we feel about constitutional details, as the experience of the 2000 election showed. Who now cares about the Electoral College?

Countries, especially in the West, are not held together by a philosophical consensus about justice. In particular, America is so very diverse that the search for common principles of justice is bound to be elusive. What we are left with is the thinnest set of principles with which Americans would agree. But that's not why we obey the law. We do so because we are bound to do so, and because it is right to be bound when the state is just.

This might seem to concede too much to the neutralist. If the duty to obey the law assumes that the state is just, might we look to abstract principles of justice to define when a state is just? But that won't work either. States are just in different ways, and there may be little overlap between them. The constitutional regimes of England and America are dissimilar and in both cases have changed a great deal in the last 100 years. Yet people who live or lived in those countries are or were morally bound to obey their laws, as the states all are or were just in their various ways.

Clearly the neutralist can't banish all religious voters from the public square, and Rawls sought to provide a breathing space for the reasonable pluralism of a diverse country such as America. For ordinary political questions, said Rawls, people might vote or voice their views according to the comprehensive worldview provided by their religion or political beliefs. They won't be able persuade those who disagree with them that these views are correct, but that doesn't matter for the general kinds of questions that arise in politics: what to do about social security, whether to enter into a free trade agreement, or how to vote as between the major political parties. But then Rawls distinguished among these questions and a thin set of constitutional essentials and principles of basic justice, formed through an overlapping consensus by people of very different political views. The idiosyncratic beliefs of Catholic, Muslims, and vegetarians are ignored, and what remains is a small core of rational principles to which all might subscribe.

Even here, however, Rawls argued that his ideal of public reason should govern when citizens engage in any kind of advocacy in the public forum.[28] This entails what Rawls called reciprocity, which is the idea that the only ideas which can be advanced in the public square are those that both speaker and listener would regard as reasonable, even though they have different comprehensive world views. For example, a Catholic could not advance a faith-based argument for abortion restrictions, since non-Catholics would not accept this. But a Catholic might argue for universal suffrage because both he and his non-Catholic listener might think that a general right to vote is a matter of basic justice on neutral, nondenominational grounds.

As a prudential matter, most Americans would concede this point. A Catholic politician will not ground his political arguments on purely religious grounds, unless he wants to commit political suicide. Instead, he'll frame his arguments to appeal across denominational boundaries. But this doesn't prevent him from advancing goals where the teachings of his religion and those of neutral nonsectarian principles overlap. In particular, he might support a social perfectionism which appeals to public reasons based on neutral, nonreligious principles. If immoral contracts impose public harm, as the social perfectionist asserts, the question of moral externalities rests, not on a private or religious conception of human nature, but rather on a humble calculation of costs and benefits. A harm is a harm, and there is in principle no reason to distinguish among species of ills so long as their deleterious effects are conceded.

The empirical dispute between neutralists and social perfectionists is on prominent display in the controversy surrounding same-sex marriages. Neutralists argue that same-sex marriages either would not impose social costs or that any such costs would be exceeded by the social benefits of more stable same-sex relationships. For their part, conservatives argue that legalizing homosexual marriages would devalue marriage for heterosexuals and would result in a costly decline in marriage rates and in the number of children born into married families.

If we could stipulate or with certainty predict what the consequences of legalizing same-sex marriages would be and fairly consider the costs, one side or the other would be largely bereft of arguments. The social perfectionist would have little to fall back on if same-sex marriages did not affect heterosexual marriages after all.* He might seek support from natural law theories, but it would be an odd natural law that had no social consequences of any kind. Similarly, the neutralist who promotes an institution which is truly harmful faces an uphill battle. If same-sex marriages imposed enormous costs on society and the corresponding benefits were trivial, would we really want to change our marriage laws? Even if the neutralist falls back on a theory of abstract rights, he'd still have to explain why a right which leaves us worse off should command our respect.

This is not to say that examining the costs of a vexed social proposal such as same-sex marriage comes down to bean counting. Rather, it is simply to say that consequences matter and that a person who disregards the evidence one way or the other would fail to persuade most of us. It also argues for prudence in the introduction of new rights or institutions. We might, without contradiction, welcome same-sex marriages in Canada and resist them

---

* Of course, the private perfectionist might oppose same-sex marriages because he believes that homosexual acts are immoral.

in Virginia. We might be unwilling to experiment in our backyard, while happily looking to the results of the same experiment somewhere else. Let others take the risk. If the change is benign, we can always follow suit later.

Finally, the perfectionist might throw back the neutralist challenge and argue that, shorn of religious principles, there isn't much left to the duty of respect or public reasons. The duty of respect founders unless it can be shown that everyone has an equal right to participate in the public debate. But just why should we sign on to equality rights? When the Founders said that "we hold these truths to be self-evident, that all men are created equal," they weren't stating an empirical proposition. Rather, they believed that people "were endowed by their Creator with certain unalienable rights." From that perspective, equality rights make sense. For the religious believer, everyone has a soul, and that implies a right to be treated with equal respect. I won't enter into the debate whether equality rights are derived from religious premises except to note that this is a tenable view;[29] and that, if correct, this would deliver a crushing blow to public reason neutralism.

TEN

An Extension: Nationalism

Something we were withholding made us weak. Until we found out
that it was ourselves.

Robert Frost, The Gift Outright

IN THIS CHAPTER, I LOOK at an often-overlooked social externality: nationalism.
By nationalism, I mean the simple patriotism that makes men willing to sacrifice for their country, including the ultimate sacrifice that some people
make in wartime.* In addition, I mean the patriotism to one's country and
not to one's state or province in a federal country. When offered the command of the Union forces in 1861, Robert E. Lee declined because he could
not fight against his country—Virginia. That was a time when some still
referred to the United States in the plural ("the United States are . . . " not "the
United States is . . ."). If we don't do that any longer, the war in which Lee
fought had something to do with the change in number.

By nationalism, I also mean something different from the communitarianism I described in Chapter 8. There I described the sense in which a person
is weakened when she does not sense that she belongs to some group greater
than herself. That was what Frost meant, in the poem he recited at the
Kennedy Inauguration, and which I have quoted above. We are made smaller
when we withdraw into ourselves. When I refer to nationalism, however,
I refer to the way in which the group (and not its members) is weakened
when people do not feel they belong to it, as the United States was weakened
when Lee withdrew his loyalty to it.

Nationalism is nevertheless a social externality, indeed one of the most
important in our lives. As an externality, it depends for its existence upon a

---

* Many writers distinguish between nationalism and patriotism. I don't, at least not when
patriotism takes the form of support for one's nation.

shared sense of membership in a national community. It is not enough that I feel this sense of membership. My fellow citizens must also do so. Otherwise, the nation could not exist. The state might exist, but not the nation. And if joint membership in the nation benefits its members, then promoting a sense of nationalism is part of the work of social perfectionism.

In what follows, I argue that the kind of nationalism felt in Western democracies—which I call liberal nationalism[1]—is benign because it is rooted in adherence to liberal principles of liberty, equality, and democracy. This is particularly true of the United States, which has no unifying monarchy and is fast losing a common culture. Instead, the core nationalist symbol for Americans is the idea of constitutionally protected liberties as defined in the Bill of Rights and the Declaration of Independence. I also argue that this helps to understand how courts interpret the constitution.

🏵 Liberal Nationalism

The genius of American nationalism is liberal nationalism, in which the core icon is not blood or earth but a constitutional ideal of liberty. In other countries, dynastic houses and cultural icons serve as a focal point for nationalist or patriotic sentiments. By contrast, America does entirely without the former and increasingly without the latter. Nationalism itself is a rather suspect doctrine, "the political doctrine that dares not speak its name," in Michael Lind's ironic phrase.[2] Yet Americans are highly patriotic, and America is not without its national symbols. Of these, the most important is perhaps the sense that America has a special mission to promote liberty. The American conception of freedom is highly legalistic and focuses upon the liberties guaranteed all Americans by the Constitution. The freedoms promised by the Declaration of Independence and guaranteed by the Bill of Rights have assumed the status of what historian Pauline Maier calls "American Scripture."[3]

This reverses the way in which nationalist symbols operate in most other countries. Ernest Gellner argued that the growth of European nationalism was a response to the wound of modernity, with the dislocation and alienation that resulted on the shift from an agricultural to an industrial economy during the Industrial Revolution. Nationalism united a fractured society, wrote Gellner, with "Gesellschaft using the idiom of Gemeinschaft"—a legal society using the idiom of a common set of beliefs, aspirations and longings. Through a sense of belonging to their nation, people saw themselves as

German or French, sharing an emotional bond with other members of their nation and not merely as people who happen by reason of their residence to be citizens of a particular state and governed by its laws. Oliver Goldsmith's deserted village was reinvented in an organic nation-state and "a mobile anonymous society simulat[ed] a closed cosy community."[4] In America, however, when a constitutional icon takes the place of the fatherland, gemeinschaft uses the idiom of gesellschaft, and the sentimental bonds are formed by its laws.

It needn't have turned out that way. Even after the Civil War, the focal points of American nationalism were a common language, culture, and history—not a set of national constitutional protections that constrained state legislators. Had that definition of what it meant to an American persisted, the argument that I am advancing would not be persuasive. But it did not persist. The civil rights revolution and the new waves of immigration from the 1960s on have weakened the common culture, and the diversity movement in our schools has downgraded the study of a common American history, especially the idea that some value might attach to it. What is left, as an icon of national sentiment, is a common set of constitutional principles that constitute what it is to be an American.

This did not happen all at once. World War II had played a large role, with its call for national service in a military that purposely united soldiers from different states in the same units, dissolving regional barriers as never before. The country's war aims were also identified with national goals through President Franklin D. Roosevelt's Four Freedoms (particularly as portrayed by Norman Rockwell in the *Saturday Evening Post* in the middle of the war). This helps to explain the success of the judicial revolution in the 1950s and 1960s, in which the Supreme Court held that many of the rights in the Bill of Rights restricted state legislatures as well as Congress. Before the judicial revolution, the popular revolution took place in the hearts of the American people, as John Adams said of the American Revolution.

The importance of constitutional liberties as a nationalist icon has so frequently been noted that the point might seem banal. "[T]he American Constitution is unlike any other," said historian Hans Kohn. "[I]t represents the lifeblood of the American nation, its supreme symbol and manifestation."[5] Other countries had their common cultures or religions. What America had was an idea. Robert Penn Warren wrote, "To be American is not . . . a matter of blood; it is a matter of an idea—and [American] history is the image of that idea."[6] And what was the idea? Not simply liberty or liberty under law, for those were also English ideas. The special American contribution, which defined the nation itself, was the idea of constitutionally protected liberty. This was Wendell Willkie's idea of America in his 1943 bestseller *One World*:

> Our nation is composed of no one race, faith, or cultural heritage. It is a grouping of some thirty peoples possessing varying religious concepts, philosophies, and historical backgrounds. They are linked together by their confidence in our democratic institutions as expressed in the Declaration of Independence and guaranteed by the Constitution. . . .[7]

The same idea has been repeated in countless stump speeches and high school debates, and according to pollsters continues to define this country.[8] American constitutional scholars, particularly those who had lived through World War II, have voiced it. They had been asked to make enormous sacrifices when their country was threatened, and their patriotic sentiments remained strong. Thus Charles Black asked, "Can we really bear to say, even (and above all) to ourselves, that the unity of this Union is a unity only in governmental power and economic exchange, but is not a moral union in the observance of human rights?" And, answering his question, he argued:

> Ours is a nation that founded its very right to exist on the ground of its commitment to the securing of nobly envisioned human rights in very wide comprehension—a country that now bases its claim to the world's regard on a questing devotion to the securing of human rights.[9]

Objections to Liberal Nationalism

In this section, I consider two objections to liberal nationalism, one (roughly) from the left; and the other from the right. The objection from the left is that liberal principles are universally valid, and indeed the Declaration of Independence asserts this. If so, how can the views expressed in the Declaration be appropriated to define a particular nation's identity? The objection from the right is that what defines Americans is a common culture and not a set of constitutional liberties. I will argue that neither objection is persuasive.

The Objection from Universalism

Americans seem to be amongst the most nationalistic people in the world, and this was particularly true immediately after September 11, 2001. Since then, the passion of the moment has cooled, and the prosecution of an unpopular war in Iraq has led many Americans to wonder whether their form of nationalism is entirely benign. The desire to protect our country can lead us to magnify threats to it and inspire a preemption doctrine in which we strike the first blow against dictators who lack the means to inflict serious harm against us. It can also lead to an America-first policy that erects trade barriers against third world countries that desperately need to export if they are to emerge from poverty.

There is obviously some truth to all of this. Nevertheless, what might be called the objection from *universalism* can also be overstated. This objection assumes that remote and universal ties always outweigh local ones and that loyalty to one's country always comes at the cost of loyalty to more encompassing groups, such as humanity in general. One kind of solidarity waxes, the other wanes. But the alternative to national or local bonds is often not universal bonds, but no bonds at all.

William Goodwin once asked himself what he would do if he had a choice between two people to save from a fire, where he could rescue only one. It was either his father or the Abbé Fénelon, a celebrated French dramatist and liberal. The choice was clear to Godwin. The author of *Télémaque* was of greater value to human happiness than his father, and Fénelon would be saved. "The life of Fenelon would still be more valuable . . . and justice, pure, unadulterated justice, would still have preferred that which was most valuable."[10] Nevertheless, there is something heartless in his choice. We learn to love more encompassing groups only by holding those close to us dearer still. If we don't, our profession of love for humanity at large must be suspect.

Solidarity—the love of family and of those closest to us—is one of the most basic of human goods and so too is the love of one's country. It is more than an efficient insurance contract that permits us to exploit opportunities for gain with fewer of Coase's transaction costs. We trust our fellow citizens more than strangers and can more easily understand them, all this because we are members of the same nation. Solidarity is also an ultimate good, desirable for its own sake, which if ignored drains life and the ideals of the content that gives them meaning. In particular, the nation is a crucial nexus of solidarity because it is the nation that commands our allegiance in times of war. When we were attacked on 9-11, we all knew that America was attacked, and not just New York City and Arlington, Virginia.

Solidarity cannot exist without rivalry. I root for the local high school and against the other team. I choose one religion in preference to another. If I don't, I am simply irreligious. It is a mistake to think that only the most encompassing communities count and that local allegiances are suspect.

What this ignores, in a world of natural rivalries, is that we cannot take the side of one community without taking sides against another.

All loyalty is local, then. Universal principles and allegiances cannot displace the loyalty to one's town, one's nation, or one's country. In addition, there is a special reason why American nationalism merits the support of its citizens. Wedded as it is to liberal principles, American nationalism has a self-protective mechanism that other kinds of nationalism lack. American nationalism cannot easily be made to justify illiberal and oppressive measures because these would be inconsistent with the idea of what it is to be an American.

In World War I, Max Weber argued that Germany should win because it defended *Kultur*, while Émile Durkheim supported France in the name of *civilisation*. In a sense, both were right because both were patriots and patriotism can be admirable. But it is different when nationalism is erected upon a foundation of liberal ideals, as in the America of today.* Such ideals impose a duty of respect for opposing viewpoints and foster a climate of dialogue and rational deliberation. They also promote economic ties between democratic states, which further reduces the chance of conflict. One application of this is Thomas Friedman's (now slightly dated) Golden Arches theory of conflict prevention: no two countries with McDonald's restaurants have ever gone to war with each other.[11]

Nevertheless, if liberal democracies tend not to fight each other, might they feel less constrained when it comes to attacking less than liberal regimes? That is the thesis of Robert Kagan in *Dangerous Nation*, and from the War of 1812 to the Iraq War, one doesn't lack for examples.[12] Even here, however, liberal principles, stronger now than in the past, constrain how Americans prosecute their wars, as compared with other countries. Patriotic symbols such as the Bill of Rights or the Declaration of Independence contain their own internal barriers to an adventuresome foreign policy when a war is seen as depriving the enemy of his freedom or independence. A free press will also bring to light abuses, such as those that occurred at the Abu Ghraib prison in Iraq. The debate about the limits of presidential power will also take place in federal courts when prosecution of the war trenches on constitutional rights.[13]

Linking nationalism to liberalism might therefore serve to limit the former's excesses. But why even bother if liberalism is the more fundamental

---

* With its bans on teaching German and its "liberty cabbage," American nationalism was only a little less jingoistic than European nationalism during World War I.

good? Why not support liberty directly, rather than employ nationalism as a crutch to inculcate a respect for constitutional norms? This is doubtless what Robert Goodin and Philip Pettit had in mind when they excluded nationalism from the topics to be covered in their collection of essays on political philosophy. "Nationalism . . . does not figure, on the grounds that it hardly counts as a principled way of thinking about things."[14]

There is an easy answer to this objection, if nationalism is the powerful sentiment that I take it to be. When national sentiments are strong, then the respect accorded to liberal principles is strengthened when they piggyback onto a national symbol. I believe more strongly in freedom of religion if its denial is a betrayal of my country.

The nationalist might also advance a theory of rights particular to his own country. Unlike a universalist theory, where the content of rights is determined through an abstract deliberation about the duties owed to all men without regard to their nationality, a particularist theory of rights need not claim that its stock of rights is appropriate in every state or society and might defend a conception of rights for his state only.[15] The particularist might see his country's charter as uniquely appropriate for his own country and not readily exportable. Or he might think that it is an optimal set of rights for everyone but reserve judgment about prescribing for citizens of other countries.

The metaphor of a race is instructive. To say that the particularist thinks a particular runner deserves to win does not mean that he would wish to call off the race and simply hand his favorite the prize. He might want the race to be run in any event, not merely because it is enjoyable, but also because it provides new information about who is the best runner. In the same way, the particularist might think that the Bill of Rights represents the perfection of legal reasoning but still seek the verification that comes from the laboratory of international competition in the provision of constitutional protections.

The Cultural Objection

The cultural objection to liberal nationalism is that what makes people Americans is participation in a common culture and not adherence to constitutional principles. This objection is heard most frequently by conservatives opposed to U.S. immigration policies, whose effect is to favor immigrants from Latin America over those from Europe.

Nothing, in principle, is objectionable about the desire to preserve a homogenous culture. In most countries, a common cultural heritage provides a central national symbol. In his pioneering studies of nationalism, Ernest Gellner made even stronger claims about the need for common cultural bonds. "[A] high culture pervades the whole of society, defines it, and needs to be sustained by that polity. *That* is the secret of nationalism."[16] What Gellner had in mind was not folk culture but *Kultur*, the high culture of a national art and literature.

The importance of cultural bonds in European nations is generally conceded. Taking *Beowulf* from a literature curriculum would uniquely weaken national sentiments in England. In addition, the desire to preserve a national identity, in Québec, France, or Israel may be consistent with democratic and liberal principles.[17] A nation that seeks to preserve its language might thus adopt a measured policy of favoring immigrants who speak the language, while still asserting a devotion to liberal principles.

Conservatives such as Peter Brimelow have argued that, like the countries of Europe, America has a national culture that it should promote through more restrictive immigration policies.[18] I do not want to take sides in this debate except to say that, as a factual matter, I believe that Brimelow is wrong. At one time in the past, America possibly had the kind of cultural identity that Brimelow admires. Had it remained a relatively homogenous nation, it might have been justified in screening for a like group of homogenous immigrants, as Michael Walzer has argued.[19] However, America has become a pluralist society, and any attempt to screen immigrants on the basis of national origin would unjustly privilege one class of natives over another.

What remains, as a defining touchstone of the American identity, are the constitutional rights of the liberal nationalist. And if constitutional liberties are a core national symbol and if the cultural screening of immigrants is inconsistent with the understanding Americans have of their country, then Brimelow's defense of nationalism would perversely weaken national sentiments. One could not exclude aliens on cultural grounds without weakening that which it means for Americans to be American.

🎄 Fostering Nationalism

Let us assume, therefore, that American nationalism is benign, that it is a good that deserves to be fostered. How then should one do so, as a matter of public policy? In what follows, I argue that, apart from such obvious devices as Fourth of July parades, the courts play a most important role in promoting a sense of nationalism. I also examine what a nationalist perspective implies when it comes to constitutional interpretation.

John Adams understood the importance of national symbols, in a famous letter to his wife.

> The Second Day of July 1776, will be the most memorable Epocha, in the History of America.—I am apt to believe that it will be celebrated, by succeeding Generations, as the great anniversary Festival. It ought to be commemorated, as the Day of Deliverance by solemn Acts of Devotion to God Almighty. It ought to be solemnized with Pomp and Parade, with Shews, Games, Sports, Guns, Bells, Bonfires and Illuminations from one End of this Continent to the other from this Time forward forever more.[20]

Adams got the date wrong (or do we?), but that apart he was spot on. No nation, not even the French, celebrates its founding with quite the spirit of Americans, and when they do so, it is organic and organized from below. What matters to us is the local parade, led by veterans, reenactors, school board candidates, and middle school bands, and not a grand défilé on Constitution Avenue.

In no other country do patriotic symbols matter so much. Where else would people pay attention to whether a politician wears a lapel pin of his country's flag? We don't even notice our patriotism, the ubiquity of Old Glories, though they strike visitors from every other country. When an American politician concludes a speech with "God Bless America," we pay attention to the prayer's subject, but the object is just as important. A Google search reveals more than 4,000,000 hits for "God Bless America," 480,000 for "God Bless England." As for "God Bless Canada," there were only 330,000 hits (many ironic), and almost twice as many for "God Bless Canada, eh?"

Plainly, the sense of American nationalism seems able to stand on its own two feet. However, this is not to say that it cannot be weakened by policymakers or that Americans are indifferent to national icons or to decisions that seem to weaken them. An obvious example is the response to highly unpopular court decisions that held that asking students to recite the Pledge of Allegiance (with the words "under God") violates the First Amendment's prohibition against establishing a religion. Such decisions have been overturned on procedural grounds,[21] but the litigation continues and has sparked a strong popular outcry.

Americans are comfortable with techniques to promote nationalism that employ the means that Mill would generally have permitted, such as public symbols and education in schools. But that leaves legislative and judicial policies, as seen in the debate over the Pledge of Allegiance. Nationalism cannot be commanded, but it can be influenced, either to strengthen or weaken a sense of nationalism. And of such strategies, I will concentrate upon judicial policies because a patriotic electorate is more likely to police legislative statutes that weaken the sense of nationalism. By contrast, an independent federal bench can make unpopular decisions just because it is independent, and no one would wish to change this. Judicial decisions are also read closely by lawyers, newspaper editors, and other influential members of the community.

The Supreme Court has adopted a nationalist perspective when the county is at war, relaxing civil liberties that it enforces more strictly during times of peace.[22] During the Civil War, the Court acquiesced in Lincoln's claim that the War Power authorized him to suspend the writ of Habeas Corpus. In *Ex parte Merryman*,[23] Chief Justice Taney (who had delivered the majority opinion in the *Dred Scott* case) held that the suspension was unconstitutional, but Lincoln chose to ignore the decision. He delivered his response in a July 4, 1861, message to Congress. "Are all the laws, but [the right of Habeas Corpus], to go unexecuted, and the government itself go to pieces, lest that one be violated?"[24] And thereafter the courts were essentially silent as hundreds of citizens were interned or expelled from the country. One of them, Clement Vallandigham, ran as the 1863 Democratic nominee for governor of Ohio from his exile in Canada. Much the same thing happened during World War II, when the Supreme Court upheld the internment of Japanese-Americans.[25] "Though the Constitution protects against invasions of individual rights," noted Justice Goldberg in another case, "it is not a suicide pact."[26]

Nevertheless, one of the most ringing judicial endorsements of American civil liberties came in the middle of World War II, in *West Virginia Board of Education v. Barnette*, where the Supreme Court held that a Jehovah's Witness could not be compelled to salute the flag. "If there is any fixed star in our constitutional constellation," said Justice Jackson, "it is that no official, high or petty, can prescribe what shall be orthodox in politics, nationalism, religion, or other matters of opinion or force citizens to confess by word or act their faith therein."[27] This too was more a vindication than a denial of American symbols because the defense of liberty is the greatest of American symbols.

Such cases feature a clash of symbols in which an abstract fundamental symbol—the Bill of Rights—takes priority over a concrete and less central

icon—the flag or the Pledge of Allegiance. Behind this clash are more fundamental differences in outlook between the rationalist and the romantic,
Whig and Tory, and Protestant and Catholic. From one perspective, the
destruction of images might look like mere iconoclasm, but what this misses
is the struggle between competing icons.

Seeing constitutional freedoms as a national American symbol assists in
understanding other Supreme Court decisions that have been faulted for
offering insufficient protection to nationalist symbols.[28] In *Texas v. Johnson*,[29]
a Texas statute that criminalized flag burning was found to violate First
Amendment guarantees of free speech. However, it is a mistake to think that
the Court was insensitive to national symbols, for First Amendment rights,
stated in the broadest possible fashion, are themselves a symbol of the nation.
"If there is a bedrock principle underlying the First Amendment," said the
Court, "it is that the government may not prohibit the expression of an idea
simply because society finds the idea itself offensive or disagreeable."

🕮 The Bill of Rights

A nationalist perspective suggests that basic liberties should enjoy constitutional protection at the national level and not be left for the states to legislate. But for the argument from nationalism, a strong case could be made for
limiting national constitutional liberties to a thin set of rights or for empow-
ering states to opt out of the Bill of Rights. Nationalism concerns also suggest
a need for caution before removing contentious issues from political deliberation by turning them into constitutional rights.

But for nationalism concerns, a persuasive case may be made for letting
each state set its own policies with respect to such matters as free speech,
gun control, and religious expression. This might happen through a return to
the constitutional vision that prevailed prior to twentieth-century decisions
that held that the Bill of Rights applied to the states and limited what they
could enact. Many Americans would find this a regrettable step backward to
a Jim Crow era of states' rights that has been consigned to the dustbin of history. However, other countries have maintained a liberal tradition without
an American-style set of substantive national civil rights.

Of all countries, Canada affords the most useful comparison for the
American constitutional lawyer. With America, Canada shares a common
border and legal heritage, and both have federal systems of government. Yet
the two countries are leagues apart when it comes to constitutional liberties.

Prior to the Canadian *Charter of Rights*, the responsibility for civil rights was assigned to the provinces under s. 92(13) of the British North America Act. Even after the Charter was enacted in 1982, its rights were made subject "to such reasonable limits prescribed by law as can be demonstrably justified in a free and democratic society,"[30] a clause designed to exclude what were perceived as the excesses of American judicial activism. In addition, the Charter's Notwithstanding Clause (section 33) permits a province to declare that a piece of legislation is valid even though it contravenes the Charter's Fundamental Freedoms and Equality Rights. By countenancing an opt-out of its rights, the Canadian Charter more closely resembles the Nullification doctrine and John C. Calhoun's constitution than the modern American version.

Much can be said for the Canadian system, which has proven more popular than the American model when new constitutions are adopted in other countries. On abstract Public Choice principles, the devolutionary Canadian regime would appear superior to the centralized American one. First, diverse laws would permit Americans to settle in jurisdictions whose policies match their preferences, as we saw in Chapter 8. The diversity of options, as between different states, would mean that, more than today, migrants could sort themselves out by voting with their feet. Gun lovers could settle in Virginia, opponents in Maryland.

Second, state competition in the provision of basic rights might usefully signal which set of rights is superior, as was suggested in Frederick Jackson Turner's Frontier Thesis.[31] Turner described a process in which western states, with fewer geographical advantages, competed for people through liberal laws and democratic institutions. Faced with the loss of valuable natives, eastern states responded by adopting similar legal regimes; and the process, said Turner, reached back into the Old World, which liberalized its laws to reduce emigration by valuable subjects. This is a race to the top, won by states that offer the most desirable set of laws.

Given the opportunity to do so, states could be expected to compete for valuable migrants through their civil rights laws. States that indulge in a taste for discrimination would likely be punished on migration markets and states with superior laws rewarded, as they were in Turner's time. This might yield valuable information about constitutional rights. Once one abandons the assumption that the best set of rights can be determined through abstract ratiocination by an academic clerisy, it becomes important to look for evidence as to optimal laws. Locational choices made by citizens who vote with their feet provide one of the best sources of evidence about the relative merit of differential state laws, and this evidence is lost when rights are nationalized.

The third reason why basic liberties should be a state law matter, on Public Choice theories, is that legislative authority should be assigned to the level of government that captures all of the benefits and bears all of the costs of its laws.[32] Therefore, the power to raise an army to defend the country should be assigned to the national government. As for basic civil rights, the benefits and burdens would be felt primarily by in-state residents. Whether Virginia subsidizes parochial schools will matter a great deal to Virginia parents and much less to Californians. Thus the arguments for assigning the responsibility for enacting such laws to the state level would appear as strong here as they are for basic contract and property law.

Nevertheless, one cost of the devolution of basic rights—the weakening of nationalist bonds—has almost entirely been forgotten. Nationalism is a social good whose benefits spill across state lines to reach national borders. When constitutional rights are a national symbol, and where there are substantial regional differences in civil rights law, this may impose the costs of weakened nationalist sentiments.

Lincoln understood this for he felt the strains that slavery placed upon the loyalty sentiments of abolitionist Whigs in antebellum America. In a letter to James Speed he wrote:

> I confess that I hate to see the poor creatures hunted down, and caught, and carried back to their stripes, and unrewarded toils; but I bite my lip and keep quiet. In 1841 you and I had together a tedious low-water trip, on a Steam Boat from Louisville to St. Louis. You may remember, as I well do, that from Louisville to the mouth of the Ohio there were, on board, ten or a dozen slaves, shackled together with irons. That sight was a continual torment to me; and I see something like it every time I touch the Ohio, or any other slave-border. It is hardly fair for you to assume, that I have no interest in a thing which has, and continually exercises, the power of making me miserable. You ought rather to appreciate how much the great body of the Northern people do crucify their feelings, in order to maintain their loyalty to the Constitution and the Union.[33]

When the differences in civil rights are profound, as Lincoln famously noted, the nation is a house divided that cannot stand. But even where the differences are less great, the sense of common nationhood might weaken when devolution results in a checkerboard of basic rights, and the vision of a national icon is blurred. Like Canadian provinces, American states would likely refrain from effecting broad changes in basic rights because liberal norms are deeply embedded in every region of the country. However, the threat to a national symbol argues for prudence in the devolution of constitutional rights.

State differences in basic civil rights would be particularly troubling where they amount to barriers from moving from one state to another. In Canada, Québec's language legislation that makes Anglophone migrants from Ontario send their children to French-language schools is just such as barrier and has frayed the already weak sense of Canadian national identity. Given the relative importance of Canada in the world, that might not be a great tragedy. Czechoslovakia split apart, and no one much took notice. But if something similar happened in the United States, if the sense of American identity dissolved, that would be an event of global significance.

A nationalist understanding of civil rights, where constitutional liberties are defined by the central government, nevertheless suggests the need for caution before turning contentious political questions into constitutional rights. More than most countries, America withdraws issues from the political arena and assigns them to the courts, and this might reasonably be thought to tax the competence of the bench. Courts are not well equipped to deal with essentially political questions, such as how to run school boards or deal with global warming. Turning political questions into judicial ones also undermines the way in which political debate reaffirms the value of deliberative democracy—which political philosopher Jeremy Waldron calls the "dignity of legislation."[34] A nationalist perspective suggests another reason for prudence in transferring issues out of the political arena.

In politics, there are winners and losers, and there is nothing particularly dishonorable about being a loser. In constitutional debates before the courts, however, the loser's argument is fundamentally illegitimate. Because constitutional rights are a national symbol, there is something un-American about taking the wrong side on a constitutional question such as abortion, and this may weaken nationalist sentiments. Losers find themselves marginalized, their deepest beliefs dismissed as irrelevant or un-American. Though an outsider (as a Canadian), Charles Taylor sympathized with their frustration:

> I suspect that a good part of the anger comes not from the measures themselves, but from what they see as the attitudes lying behind these measures. That is because they identify the "liberal" philosophy which has dictated these measures as in its very essence dismissive, and even

sometimes contemptuous of what their lives are centered on. They are not only being asked to make a sacrifice, they are being told that they are barbarians even to see this as a sacrifice.[35]

This is something all sides should care about if nationalism is valuable in itself and argues for prudence before constitutionalizing a political issue.

A nationalist understanding of basic rights therefore transcends ideological categories. The argument from nationalism suggests that basic rights should be set at the national and not the state level, and this will please left-liberals. But a nationalist perspective also argues for a thinner set of constitutional rights, in which courts leave political issues to be dealt with by Congress, and this will please conservatives.

Nationalist principles were deeply ingrained in a previous generation of constitutional scholars who were more likely to have served in their country's armed forces. In the modem academy, the nationalist voice is stilled, and the liberal nationalism of George Washington, Alexander Hamilton, Abraham Lincoln, and Theodore Roosevelt forgotten. On the left, nationalism conflicts with preferred modes of discourse, which are abstract and universalist, and is seen as burdened with the questionable political baggage of slavery and racism. The left-liberal is more of an internationalist that a nationalist. On the right, the economist's emphasis on quantitative methods, which ignore things that can't be counted, darkens windows that open only to qualitative judgment. Not everything that counts can be counted, said Albert Einstein, but this warning is often ignored by economists. Matthew Arnold made a similar point. There are many things we do not understand, he observed, unless we understand that they are beautiful. So too, in the study of constitutional law and our country's history, there are things we do not understand unless we understand that they are loved.

ELEVEN

Conclusion

> What more is necessary to make us a happy and a prosperous
> people? Still one thing more, fellow-citizens—a wise and frugal
> Government, which shall restrain men from injuring one another
> [and] shall leave them otherwise free to regulate their own pursuits
> of industry and improvement. . . .
>
> *Thomas Jefferson, First Inaugural Address*

I BEGAN THIS BOOK with a definition of liberalism. I said that a liberal is one who believes that people's preferences are prima facie worthy of respect. Unless we can find a reason to fetter their choices, people should be free to do what they want. The onus is always upon the paternalist or perfectionist to tell us why people's freedom should be curtailed.

So defined, a liberal would resist a paternalism or perfectionism that takes all choices away from people. But that leaves a wide area where the liberal might consent to fetters on choices. I examined different arguments for doing just that, for interfering with people's preferences, without ruling all such barriers out of order. Both sides of the debate, paternalist and antipaternalist, perfectionist and antiperfectionist, have much to commend them. That might sound like a paradox, but my point is that balance is needed.

A soft paternalism would restrict choices where these would be inconsistent with a person's deepest preferences. We might simply be mistaken in our choices as a consequence of mental errors, preferring x but choosing not-x because judgment biases mislead us. If so, this might provide an argument for paternalistic nudges in the direction of x, and over the last few years a vast literature was erected on this narrow foundation. Today, this kind of cognitive paternalism seems excessive. Our hunches are better adapted to the environment in which we live than the paternalist gave them credit. Then too, the paternalist is often more likely to be misled by judgment biases than the subject for whom he legislates. The net effect of the judgment bias literature might thus be more antipaternalist than paternalist in its direction.

Weakness of the will might provide a more persuasive justification for paternalism, with legal barriers supplementing the self-control strategies a person might employ to avoid temptation. Those who don't want to use hard drugs will find it easier to do so if they don't hang around drug users and easier still if hard drugs are made illegal. As a response to weakness of the will, however, this is a strategy of last resort because our own efforts at self-control will ordinarily suffice and because the argument from weakness of the will might easily permit the paternalist to overreach and ban pleasures that we should be permitted to enjoy.

Paternalism might in theory economize on the cost of producing information needed in order to make a decision. Before we enter into a bargain, we need to know something about the product or services we are buying, and this will impose information costs. As the parties have the incentive to reduce such costs, they will ordinarily not need the help of a paternalistic judge. In extreme cases, however, such as contracts of slavery, judicial policing of unfair terms might free the parties from oppressive bargains and reduce information production costs. We wouldn't have to read every contract carefully to make sure that a trap isn't being laid for us. The paternalist might also usefully ban extreme strategies employed to reveal information about oneself, such as dueling.

Happiness is a hot topic amongst social scientists these days, in large measure because of counterintuitive findings that more money doesn't necessarily produce more happiness. That might be thought to argue for paternalistic fetters on the acquisitive instinct. However, the happiness literature is ambiguous when it comes to policy recommendations. Rich countries are happier than poor countries and rich people are happier than poor people. Moreover, the subjective measures of happiness social scientists use ignore other of life's goods, which those who strive to get ahead are more likely to attain—a justified sense of self-worth, a feeling of accomplishment.

Our preferences are importantly shaped by outside forces, such as family and friends, and this also includes the laws which paternalists might enact. This must give the antipaternalist pause because it is problematical to argue that laws should not interfere with preferences when preferences are themselves shaped by laws. However, this argues for very limited interference with preferences. Much depends on just how the paternalist would interfere with our choices for paternalism is easiest to accept when people can waive or opt out of the restrictions. The "libertarian paternalist" would eschew nonwaivable mandatory fetters but instead would adopt waivable default rules that nudge us toward his social goals. The logic of libertarian paternalism argues for a broad relaxation of mandatory rules, turning them into waivable default rules, and on net, this would likely mean less, not more paternalism.

Soft paternalism is a relatively easy sell because it doesn't overrule preferences so much as direct people toward choices which reflect their deepest preferences. Perfectionism is a harder sell because it ignores people's preferences and enforces a code of morality. I distinguish between a private perfectionism that bans immoral choices with the goal of making the subject better off and a social perfectionism which doesn't worry about the subject but only the people he might influence for ill by his immoral behavior. Many of us will find social perfectionism more appealing than private perfectionism because we'll care less about the rogue than the people he influences.

In theory, paternalism and antipaternalism, like perfectionism and anti-perfectionism, are radically different. In practice, however, nearly all of us tend to converge to a middle ground. The liberal perfectionist will propose only the mildest interference with personal preferences, while the conservative neutralist will find prudential reasons why the legislator should not seek to enforce morals.

And so I conclude, without a grand theory or a key to unlock every door. I have defended a moderate, even a liberal kind of paternalism and perfectionism, one which avoids hard edges and to which most of us subscribe. I am even a little embarrassed to see that I resemble the Mild Young Men of Stephen Potter's *One-Upsmanship*. Potter had tired of John Osborne and the Angry Young Men of the 1950s, and one-upped them with a set of the mildest people he could find. Like Potter's curates and solicitors, I say "But I see value in that, too!"

The kind of liberalism I defend is mild in just that way. It isn't angry and it's anything but dogmatic. Having begun with one definition of liberalism, then, I find I am ending with another, more familiar one. The kind of liberalism I have in mind is the one to which nearly everyone subscribes, and which we all saw in each other after 9-11. We all knew then, what most of us have now forgotten, that we were really on the same side, that we shared a common inheritance, of Voltaire and Aquinas, that we did not have to choose one and reject the other, that we could be on the side of liberty as well as of reasonable limits on liberty.

We also knew that our liberalism is not capable of precise definition, any more than kindness and charity. It embraces different, even inconsistent, impulses, and holds them in equilibrated tension. That was Lionel Trilling's point, in *The Middle of the Journey*, where the liberal who speaks for Trilling resists the extreme solutions of communism and Dostoyevskian conservatism. He might not have neat answers, but he knows that liberty resists neatness and dogma. Liberty, the ordered liberty of Western legal systems, with their mixture of freedom and responsibility, is supple, like any principle that seeks to teach people how to live. It is not even a theory but more like an attitude of openness to the many different experiences which life affords for happiness and goodness.

Until now, we have taken the perspective of the subject who resists interference with his preferences. Our paternalists and perfectionists were seen as little better than officious intermeddlers who purport to steer us straight without really knowing us very well. But let us now see ourselves as the paternalist or perfectionist, well intentioned for the most part, not omniscient, bumbling at times, and animated by the most sincere concern for our subjects. More than concern, we feel kindness and have charity for them. We know how costly and valuable a human life is, and how dear a thing it is to see a person flourish. Would we then, possessing the power to make our subjects follow our commands, regulate their lives minutely? Would we not withdraw and let them live their lives unaided by us, except where they seem about to inflict the most grievous harm on themselves or others? Like Spenser, would we not let a Grille fail, that he might learn to grow and succeed? If so, our paternalists and perfectionists would meet with their subjects, not as antagonists but as friends, reconciled in the joint project of living the most rewarding of all possible lives.

Notes

※ Preface

1 Harold Demsetz, *Information and Efficiency: Another Viewpoint*, 12 J. L. & Econ. 1 (1969).

※ Chapter 1 Paternalism and Perfectionism

1 http://firstamendmentcenter.org.analysis.aspx?id=8954.
2 William A. Galston, *Liberal Pluralism: The Implications of Value Pluralism for Political Theory and Practice* 3, 28 (Cambridge: Cambridge U.P., 2002). Isaiah Berlin's liberalism, especially his idea of negative liberty, was founded on the idea that state interference with personal preferences was presumptively unjustified, and this too was the idea that informed the liberalism of John Stuart Mill. See Isaiah Berlin, *Two Concepts of Liberty,* in Liberty: Four Essays on Liberty lvi (Oxford: Oxford U.P., 1969); John Stuart Mill, On Liberty (Indianapolis: Hackett, 1978).
3 Ronald Dworkin, A Matter of Principle 181 (Cambridge: Harvard U.P., 1985).
4 H.L.A. Hart, *Legal and Moral Obligation*, in Essays in Moral Philosophy 82, 102 (A.I. Melden ed.) (Seattle: U. Washington P., 1958).
5 Robert Nozick, Anarchy, State, and Utopia 42–45 (New York: Basic Books, 1974).
6 Mill, On Liberty at 9.
7 George Sher, Beyond Neutrality: Perfectionism and Politics (Cambridge: Cambridge U.P., 1997).
8 Derek Parfit, Reasons and Persons 46 (Oxford: Oxford U.P., 1984).
9 See Gerald Dworkin, *Paternalism: Some Second Thoughts,* in Rolf Sartorius (ed.), Paternalism 105, 107 (Minneapolis: U. Minnesota P., 1983).
10 Sher, Beyond Neutrality at 15.
11 Patrick Devlin, The Enforcement of Morals 19, 16 (London: Oxford U.P., 1965).

※ Chapter 2 Hierarchic Paternalism

1 Quoted in C. R. Margolin, *Salvation versus Liberation: The Movement for Children's Rights in a Historical Context*, 25 Social Problems 441, 441 (1978). For statements of child liberationism, see John Holt, Escape from Childhood: The Needs and Rights

of Children (Cambridge: Holt, 1995); Howard Cohen, Equal Rights for Children (Totowa: Littlefield, Adams, 1980).

2 Robert Young, *In the Interests of Children and Adolescents*, in Whose Child: Children's Rights, Parental Authority, and State Power 177, 182–84 (William Allen and Hugh LaFollette ed.) (Totowa, N.J.: Rowman and Littlefield, 1980).

3 Ivan Illich, Celebration of Awareness (Harmondsworth: Penguin, 1973); Allison James and Alan Prout, Constructing and Reconstructing Childhood (Basingstoke: Falmer, 1990).

4 Richard Farson, Birthrights (New York: Macmillan, 1974).

5 Onora O'Neill, *Children's Rights and Children's Lives*, 98 Ethics 445, 450 (1988). See also Will Kymlicka, Contemporary Political Philosophy: An Introduction 285 (Oxford: Oxford U.P., 1990); Jeremy Waldron, Liberal Rights: Collected Papers 374 (New York: Cambridge U.P., 1993).

6 Martin Guggenheim, What's Wrong with Children's Rights 14 (Cambridge: Harvard U.P., 2005).

7 www.pbs.org/frontline/shows/fostercare/inside/guggenheim.html (interview with Martin Guggenheim).

8 Don Butler, *Jaws Drop as Quebec Judge Backs Girl Grounded by Dad*, Ottawa Citizen, June 18, 2008.

9 For an argument that the Amish violate children's rights by not preparing them to live outside their communities, see Amy Gutmann, *Children, Paternalism, and Education: A Liberal Argument*, 9 Phil. Pub. Aff. 338, 342–43 (1980). The right of the Amish to take their children from high school was upheld by the Supreme Court in Wisconsin v. Yoder, 406 U.S. 205 (1972).

10 Aldrich v. Bailey, 132 N.Y. 85, 87–88 (1892).

11 For an argument that involuntary committal policies should be expanded and that dangerously ill patients are too frequently released from mental hospitals, see E. Fuller Torrey, The Insanity Offense: How America's Failure to Treat the Seriously Mentally Ill Endangers Its Citizens (New York: W.W. Norton, 2008).

12 Faber v. Sweet Style Mfg. Corp., 242 N.Y.S.2d 763 (Sup. Ct., Trial Term, 1963).

13 Williamson v. Matthews, 379 So.2d 1245 (Ala. Sup. Ct, 1980).

14 Quoted in W.J. Cash, The Mind of the South 81 (New York: Vintage, 1991). See Elizabeth Fox-Genovese and Eugene D. Genovese, The Mind of the Master Class: History and Faith in the Slaveholders' Worldview 329–82 (Cambridge: Cambridge U.P., 2005).

15 Cash, Mind of the South at 83.

16 George Fitzhugh, Sociology of the South: Or the Failure of Free Society 48, electronic edition at http://docsouth.unc.edu/southlit/fitzhughsoc/fitzhugh.html.

17 George Fitzhugh, Cannibals All! Or, Slaves without Masters 17–21 (Cambridge: Belknap Press (1960); Wilfred Carsel, *The Slaveholders' Indictment of Northern Wage Slavery*, 6 Journal of Southern History 504–520 (1940).

18 Fitzhugh, Sociology of the South at 24.

19 John C. Calhoun, Union and Liberty: The Political Philosophy of John C. Calhoun 467 (Indianapolis: Liberty Fund, 1992); Margaret L. Coit, John C. Calhoun: American Patriot 300–02 (Houghton Mifflin, 1950).

20 George Fitzhugh, Cannibals All at 69.

21 *Id.* at 188. Lincoln was a careful reader of Fitzhugh, whom he saw as a formidable if infuriating opponent. For Lincoln's rejection of mud sill theories, see Abraham Lincoln: Speeches and Writings 1859–65 96–99 (New York: Library of America, 1989) (address to the Wisconsin State Agricultural Society).

22 Eugene D. Genovese, Roll, Jordan, Roll: The World the Slaves Made 5 (New York: Vintage, 1976).

23 See C. Vann Woodward, The Strange Career of Jim Crow 31–59 (Oxford: Oxford U.P., 3d rev. ed. 2002); William J. Cooper, The Conservative Regime: South Carolina 1877–90 84–115 (Baton Rouge: LSU Press, 1991).

24 David E. Bernstein, Only One Place of Redress: African Americans, Labor Regulations, & the Courts from Reconstruction to the New Deal (Durham, N.C.: Duke U.P., 2001); Jennifer Roback, *Southern Labor Law in the Jim Crow Era: Exploitative or Competitive*, 61 U. Chicago L. Rev. 1161 (1984).

25 http://cepa.newschool.edu/het/texts/carlyle/negroquest/htm. See David M. Levy, How the Dismal Science Got its Name: Classical Economics and the Ur-Text of Racial Politics (Ann Arbor: U. Michigan Press, 2001).

26 Wendy McElroy, Individualist Feminism of the Nineteenth Century: Collected Writings and Biographical Profiles (New York: McFarland, 2001); Wendy McElroy, Freedom, Feminism and the State (Oakland: Independent Institute, 2d ed., 1991).

27 On the distinction between equity and gender feminism, see Christina Hoff Sommers, Who Stole Feminism? How Women Have Betrayed Women (New York: Touchstone/Simon & Schuster, 1995).

28 Alison M. Jagger, Feminist Politics and Human Nature 148 (Totowa, N.J.: Rowman and Littlefield, 1988). See also Ann Scales, *The Emergence of a Feminist Jurisprudence: An Essay*, 95 Yale L.J. 1373 (1986).

29 Frances Olsen, From False Paternalism to False Equality: Judicial Assaults on Feminist Community, Illinois 1869–95, 84 Mich. L. Rev. 1518, 1522 (1986).

30 Quoted in A.N. Wilson, The Victorians 311 (New York: W.W. Norton, 2003).

31 Arthur Leff, *Unconscionability and the Code—The Emperors' New Clause*, 115 U. Pa. L. Rev. 485, 557 (1967).

𝄢 Chapter 3 Cognitive Paternalism

1 Elke U. Weber, *Perception Matters: Psychophysics for Economists*, in The Psychology of Economic Decisions 163, 166–67 (Isabelle Brocas & Juan D. Carrillo, eds.) (Oxford: Oxford U.P., 2004); Steven Pinker, How the Mind Works ch. 4 (New York: Norton, 1997).

2 P.S. Laplace, A Philosophical Essay on Probabilities (F.W. Truscott & F.L. Emory, trans.) (New York: Dover, 1951) [1814].

3 G.E. Hinton, *Mapping Part-whole Hierarchies into Connectionist Networks*, 46 Artificial Intelligence 47 (1990).

4 Mario Bunge, Intuition and Science (Englewood Cliffs N.J.: Prentice Hall, 1962); Roger Frantz, *Intuition in Behavioral Economics*, in Handbook of Contemporary Behavioral Economics 50, 52–53 (Morris Altman (ed.) (Armonk N.Y.: M.E. Sharp, 2006).

5 Paul M. Slovic, Melissa Finucane, Ellen Peters, & Donald McGregror, *The Affect Heuristic*, in Heuristics and Biases: The Psychology of Intuitive Judgment 397 (Thomas Gilovich, Dale Griffin, & Daniel Kahneman eds.) (Cambridge: Cambridge U.P., 2002).

6 Anthony Damasio, Descartes' Error 193–94, 169 (New York: Putnam, 1994).

7 Robert Boyd & Peter J. Richardson, *Norms and Bounded Rationality*, in Bounded Rationality: The Adaptive Toolbox 281 (Gerd Gigerenzer & Reinhard Selten eds.) (Cambridge: MIT Press, 2001).

8 For an overview, see Matthew Rabin, *Psychology and Economics*, 36 J. Econ. Lit. 11 (1998).

9 Amos Tversky & Daniel Kahneman, *Availability: A Heuristic for Judging Frequency and Probability*, in Judgment Under Uncertainty: Heuristics and Biases 163 (Daniel Kahneman, Paul Slovic, & Amos Tversky eds.) (Cambridge: Cambridge U.P., 1982).

10 Amos Tversky & Daniel Kahneman, *Introduction*, in Judgment Under Uncertainty at 14.

11 Thomas Gilovich, Robert Vallone, & Amos Tversky, *The Hot Hand in Basketball: On the Misperception of Random Sequences*, 17 Cog. Psych. 295 (1985).

12 Daniel Kahneman, Jack L. Knetch, & Richard H. Thaler, *Experimental Tests of the Endowment Effect and the Coase Theorem*, 98 J. Pol. Econ. 1325 (1990); Jack L. Knetsch & Fang-Fang Tang, *The Context, or Reference, Dependence of Economic Values*, in Handbook of Contemporary Behavioral Economics at 423. Endowment effects might be an example of "prospect theory," which posits that people are risk averse as to gains but risk loving as to losses.

13 For further examples, see Gerd Gigerenzer, Rationality for Mortals: How People Cope with Uncertainty 14–15 (Oxford: Oxford U.P., 2008).

14 Charles R. Plott & Kathryn Zeiler, *Exchange Asymmetries Incorrectly Interpreted as Evidence of Endowment Effect Theory and Prospect Theory?*, 97 Am. Econ. Rev. 1449 (2007); Charles R. Plott & Kathryn Zeiler, *The Willingness to Pay—Willingness to Accept Gap, the 'Endowment Effect,' Subject Misconceptions, and Experimental Procedures for Eliciting Valuations*, 95 Am. Econ. Rev. 530 (2005).

15 Vernon L. Smith & James M. Walker, *Monetary Rewards and Decision Cost in Experimental Economics*, 31 Econ. Inquiry 245 (1993); Amos Tversky & Ward Edwards, *Information versus Reward in Binary Choices*, 71 J. Exp. Psych. 680 (1966).

16 For evidence of learning in repeated experiments, see David S. Brookshire & Don L. Coursey, *Measuring the Value of a Public Good: An Empirical Comparison of Elicitation Procedure*, 77 Am. Econ. Rev. 554 (1987); Colin F. Camerer, *Progress in Behavioral Game Theory*, 11 J. Econ. Persp. 167 (1997).

17 R.M. Hogarth, *Beyond Discrete Biases: Functional and Dysfunctional Aspects of Judgmental Heuristics*, 90 Psych. Bul. 197 (1981).

18 Maya Bar-Hillel, *On the Subjective Probability of Compound Events*, 9 J. Org. Behav. Hum. Performance 396 (1973).

19 William Edwards, *Conservatism in Human Information Processing*, in Formal Representation of Human Judgment 32, 53–88 (Benjamin Kleinmuntz ed.) (New York: Wiley, 1968).

20 Dan M. Kahan, *Two Conceptions of Emotion in Risk Regulation*, 156 U. Penn. L. Rev. 741 (2008).

21 Catherine M. Sharkey, *Unintended Consequences of Medical Malpractice Caps*, 80 N.Y.U. L. Rev 391 (2005).

22 See David M. Grether, *Individual Behavior and Market Performance*, 76 Am. J. Agric. Econ. 1079 (1994); Richard A. Epstein, *Behavioral Economics, Human Error and Market Corrections*, 73 U. Chi. L. Rev. 111 (2006).

23 Andrei Shleifer, Inefficient Markets: An Introduction to Behavioral Finance 112–53 (Oxford: Clarendon, 2000); Richard H. Thaler (ed.), Advances in Behavioral Finance I and II (New York: Russell Sage, 1993 and 2005).

24 John A. List, *Neoclassical Theory Versus Prospect Theory: Evidence from the Marketplace*, 72 Econometrica 615 (2004); John A. List, *Does Market Experience Eliminate Market Anomalies?*, 118 Q.J. Econ. 41 (2001); Vernon L. Smith, *Theory, Experiment and Economics*, 3 J. Econ. Persp. 151 (1989).

25 Russell Korobkin, *The Problems with Heuristics for the Law*," in Heuristics and the Law 45, 58 (Gerd Gigerenzer and Christoph Engel eds.) (Cambridge: MIT Press, 2006).

26 Thomas H. Jackson, The Logic and Limits of Bankruptcy Law 238–39 (Cambridge: Harvard U.P., 1986).

27 Jeffrey Stake, *The Uneasy Case for Adverse Possession*, 89 Geo. L.J. 2419 (2001).

28 Jeffrey Rachlinski & Forest Jourden, *Remedies and the Psychology of Ownership*, 51 Vand. L. Rev. 1541, 1574 (1998). For other problems, see Russell Korobkin, *The Endowment Effect and Legal Analysis*, 97 Nw. U. L. Rev. 1227, 1256–66 (2003).

29 Gigerenzer, Rationality for Mortals at 7–8.

30 *Id.* at 24–27; Gigerenzer, *Bounded and Rational, in* Contemporary Debates in Cognitive Science 124 (R.J. Stainton ed.) (Oxford: Blackwell, 2006).

31 Gerd Gigerenzer, Rationality for Mortals at 21–23.

32 Daniel Kahneman & Dale T. Miller, *Norm Theory: Comparing Reality to its Alternatives*, 93 Psych. Rev. 136 (1986).

33 Christoph Engel and Gerd Gigerenzer, *Law and Heuristics: An Interdisciplinary Venture,* in Heuristics and the Law 1, 5.

34 Leda Cosmides & John Tooby, *Better than Rational: Evolutionary Psychology and the Invisible Hand*, 84 Am. Econ. Rev. Papers and Proceedings 327 (1994).

35 Leslie A. Real, *Animal Choice Behavior and the Evolution of Cognitive Architecture*, 253 Science 980 (August 30, 1991).

36 Evelyn Waugh, Officers and Gentlemen 86 (Boston: Little, Brown, 1979).

37 Christine Jolls, Cass Sunstein, & Richard Thaler, *A Behavioral Approach to Law & Economics*, 50 Stan. L. Rev. 1471, 1529–30 (1998); Donald C. Langevoort, *Behavioral Theories of Judgment and Decision Making in Legal Scholarship: A Literature Review*, 51 Vand. L. Rev. 1499, 1508–10 (1998); Mark Kelman, Yuval Rottenstreich, & Amos Tversky, *Context-Dependence in Legal Decision Making*, 25 J. Legal Stud. 287 (1996).

38 Hal R. Arkes & Cindy A. Schipani, *Medical Malpractice v. the Business Judgment Rule: Differences in Hindsight Bias*, 73 Or. L. Rev. 587 (1994).

39 Jeffrey J. Rachlinski, *A Positive Psychological Theory of Judging in Hindsight*, 65 U. Chi. L. Rev. 571 (1998).

40 Jolls et al., *A Behavioral Approach to Law & Economics* at 1520–22. Timur Kuran & Cass Sunstein, *Availability Cascades and Risk Regulation*, 51 Stan. L. Rev. 683 (1999).

🕮 Chapter 4 Akrasia

1 On weakness of the will, see generally Jon Elster, Ulysses and the Sirens (Cambridge: Cambridge U.P., rev. ed. 1984); Alfred R. Mele, Irrationality: An Essay on Akrasia, Self-deception, and Self-control (New York: Oxford U.P., 1987).

2 Nichomachean Ethics VII.7 (trans. Roger Crisp) (Cambridge: Cambridge U.P., 2000).

3 The overpowering desire might be short lived, like the "itches" described in George Ainslie, Breakdown of Will 51–54 (Cambridge; Cambridge U.P., 2001). Ainslie labels longer term obsessive desires, such as avarice, as compulsions. Because they are so strong, itches and compulsions do not lend themselves readily to paternalistic fetters.

4 Racine, Phèdre, *Préface*, in Théâtre-Poésie 817 (Paris: Pléiade, 1999).

5 *Id.* at 819. On Jansenism's righteous sinner, see Blaise Pascal, II Œuvres complètes, Pensée 220 (Paris: Pléiade, 2000); Leszek Kolakowski, God Owes Us Nothing: A Brief Remark on Pascal's Religion and on the Spirit of Jansenism 9–14 (Chicago: U. Chicago P., 1995).

6 Racine, Phèdre, at 819.

7 Sainte-Beuve, III Port Royal 575–76 (Paris: Pléiade, 1955).

8 Summa Theologica II.1., Q. 6, art. 7.

9 Jean De La Bruyère, Les charactères 11.9 (Paris: P.U.F., 1994).

10 La Rochefoucauld, Maxim 192 (Paris: Livre de poche, 1994).

11 Anna Kemeny, *Driven to Excel: A Portrait of Canada's Workaholics*, Canadian Social Trends 2 (Spring 2002); Lelslie-Ann Keown, *Time Escapes Me: Workaholics and Time Perception*, 28 Canadian Social Trends (Summer 2007). See generally, Daniel S. Hamermesh & Joel B. Slemrod, *The Economics of Workaholism: We Should Not Have Worked on this Paper*, 8 B.E. J. Econ. Analysis & Policy (2008).

12 For a review of the psychologist's understanding of addiction, see Jon Elster, Strong Feeling chs. 3, 5 (Cambridge: MIT Press, 1999).

13 Gary S. Becker, *An Empirical Analysis of Cigarette Addiction*, 84 Am. Econ. Rev. 396–418 (1994), reprinted *in Accounting for Tastes* 85 (Gary S. Becker ed.) (Cambridge: Harvard U.P., 1996); Philip J. Cook & George Tauchen, *The Effect of Liquor Taxes on Heavy Drinking*, 13 Bell J. Econ. 379–90 (1982).

14 Philip J. Cook, Paying the Tab: The Costs and Benefits of Alcohol Control 65–71 (Princeton: Princeton U.P., 2007).

15 See Alfred R. Mele, Self-Deception Unmasked (Princeton: Princeton U.P., 2001); Alfred R. Mele, Motivation and Agency (New York: Oxford U.P., 2003); Annette Barnes, Seeing Through Self-Deception (Cambridge: Cambridge U.P., 1997).

16 Shelley E. Taylor & Jonathon D. Brown, *Illusion and Well-Being: A Social Psychological Perspective on Mental Health*, 103 Psych. Bul. 193 (1988).

17 Robert Trivers, The Elements of a Scientific Theory of Self-Deception, mimeo 2003.

18 Raphael Demos, *Lying to Oneself,* 57 J. Phil. 588 (1960); Donald Davidson, *Deception and Division,* in The Multiple Self 79 (Jon Elster ed.) (Cambridge: Cambridge U.P., 1986).

19 Alfred R. Mele, Irrationality 123 (New York: Oxford U.P., 1987).

20 Pascal, Pensée 397, II Œuvres complètes at 680. See Jon Elster, Ulysses and the Sirens 47 ff.

21 Pascal, Pensée 171; *id.* at 604.

22 Pascal, Pensée 43.

23 Amélie Rorty, Where *Does the Akratic Break Take Place?,* 58 Aust. J. Phil. 333 (1980).

24 Epistle to the Galatians 5:17.

25 St. Augustine, Confessions, Book VIII., Chaps. v., vii., xi.

26 Susan Cheever, My Name Is Bill: Bill Wilson—His Life and the Creation of Alcoholics Anonymous 118 (New York: Simon and Shuster, 2004).

27 Richard Herrnstein & Drazen Prelec, *A Theory of Addiction,* in Choice over Time 331 (George Lowenstein & Jon Elster eds.) (New York: Russell Sage Foundation, 1992).

28 Milton Friedman, A Theory of the Consumption Function (Princeton: Princeton U.P., 1957). See also Franco Modigliani & Richard Brumberg, *Utility Analysis and the Consumption Function: An Interpretation of Cross-section Data,* in Post-Keynesian Economics 388 (Kenneth K. Kurihara ed.) (New Brunswick N.J.: Rutgers U.P., 1954).

29 537 A.2d 1227 (N.J. Sup. Ct., 1987).

30 Reinhart Selten, *What is Bounded Rationality?,* in Gigerenzer and Selten 13, 32–33. See also Richard H. Thaler, *Some Empirical Evidence on Dynamic Inconsistency,* 8 Econ. Letters 201 (1981).

31 Richard H. Thaler, The Winner's Curse: Paradoxes and Anomalies of Economic Life 99–100 (Princeton: Princeton U.P., 1992).

32 The manner in which hyperbolic discounting tests are framed might also determine the results, with people simply preferring the most salient outcomes. Ariel Rubenstein, *'Economics and Psychology'? The Case of Hyperbolic Discounting,* 44 Int. Econ. Rev. 1207 (2003).

33 Aristotle, Nicomachean Ethics VII.3. See also Donald Davidson, *How Is Weakness of the Will Possible,* in Moral Concepts 93 (Joel Feinberg ed.) (Oxford: Clarendon Press, 1970).

34 The example is "Uncle Al" in Eric A. Finkelstein & Laurie Zuckerman, The Fattening of America: How the Economy Makes Us Fat and What to Do about It (Hoboken N.J.: Wiley, 2008). This makes it difficult to design an empirical test of akrasia. If people are assumed to reveal their preferences through their actual choices, then they're never weak-willed. What they choose is by definition what they truly desire. However, if the revealed preferences assumption is relaxed and we admit the possibility that people might not choose wisely, we might test for akrasia by examining the ex post subjective well-being of obese people. See Alois

Stutzer & Bruno S. Frey, *What Happiness Research Can Tell Us about Self-Control Problems and Utility Misprediction,* in Economics and Psychology: A Promising New Cross-Disciplinary Field 169 (Bruno S. Frey & Alois Stutzer, eds.) (Cambridge: MIT Press, 2007).

35 Jon Elster, *Ulysses and the Sirens: A Theory of Imperfect Rationality,* 16 Social Sc. Information 469 (1977).

36 George Loewenstein, *Anticipation and the Value of Delayed Consumption,* 97 Econ. J. 666 (1987), reprinted in George Loewenstein, Exotic Preferences 388 (Oxford: Oxford U.P., 2007).

37 Derek Parfit, *Personal Identity,* 80 Phil. Rev. 3 (1971).

38 Gary S. Becker & Kevin Murphy, *A Theory of Rational Addiction,* 96 J. Pol. Econ. 675–700 (1988).

39 Elster, Strong Feelings at 5.

40 Athanasios Orphanides & David Zervos, *Rational Addiction with Learning and Regret,* 103 J. Pol. Econ. 739 (1995). See also Elster, Strong Feelings at 171–73.

41 Jon Elster, Ulysses and the Sirens: Studies in Rationality and Irrationality (New York: Cambridge U.P., 1979); Thomas Schelling, *The Intimate Contest for Self-Command,* 60 Public Interest 94 (1980), reprinted in Thomas C. Schelling, Choice and Consequence 57 (Cambridge: Harvard U.P., 1984).

42 George Ainslie, *The Dangers of Willpower,* in Getting Hooked: Rationality and Addiction 65, 75 (Jon Elster & Ole-Jørgen Skog eds.), (Cambridge: Cambridge U.P., 1999).

43 Kay Redfield Jamison, An Unquiet Mind: A Memoir of Moods and Madness (New York: Vintage, 1996).

44 Thomas H. Jackson, The Logic and Limits of Bankruptcy Law 234–37 (Cambridge: Harvard U.P., 1986).

45 Ainslie, The Dangers of Willpower at 74.

46 *Id.* at 70.

47 Mill, On Liberty at 56.

⅏ Chapter 5 Information Costs

1 Anthony Kronman, *Mistake, Information, Disclosure and the Law of Contracts,* 7 J. Leg. Stud. 1. (1978).

2 Richard Hare, *What Is Wrong with Slavery?,* 8 Phil. & Pub. Aff. 103 (1979).

3 92 Eng. Rep. 270 (1705).

4 Isaiah Berlin, *Two Concepts of Liberty,* in Liberty: Four Essays on Liberty 118 (Oxford: Oxford U.P., 1969).

5 Sheena S. Iyengar & Mark R. Lepper, *When Choice Is Demotivating: Can One Desire Too Much of a Good Thing?,* 79 J. Personality and Soc. Psych. 995 (2000).

6 James B. Twitchell, *Lead Us Into Temptation: The Triumph of American Materialism* 46 (New York: Columbia U. P. 1999).

7 F.A. Hayek, *The Use of Knowledge in Society,* 35 Am. Econ. Rev. 519 (1945).

8 George Akerlof, *The Market for 'Lemons': Quality Uncertainty and the Market Mechanism,* 84 Q.J. Econ. 488 (1970).

9 Thomas Hobbes, Leviathan 14.18.

10 Michael A. Spence, *Job Market Signaling*, 87 Q.J. Econ. 355 (1973).

11 Ruth Benedict, The Chrysanthemum and the Sword: Patterns of Japanese Culture (New York: Mariner Books, 1989).

12 Joanne Freeman, Affairs of Honor: National Politics in the New Republic (New Haven: Yale U.P., 2001).

13 James Bowman, Honor: A History 74 (New York: Encounter Books, 2006)

🏵 Chapter 6 Happiness

1 Tibor Scitovsky, *My Own Criticism of* The Joyless Economy, 10 Critical Rev. 595, 599 (1996).

2 Arthur Brooks, *How to Succeed in Life . . . By really Trying*, The American 27 (May–June 2008).

3 Richard A. Easterlin, *Does Economic Growth Improve the Human Lot*, in Nations and Households in Economic Growth: Essays in Honor of Morris Abramowitz (Paul A. David & Melvin W. Reder eds.) (New York: Academic Press, 1974).

4 John F. Desmond, *Flannery O'Connor and Simone Weil*, 8 Logos 102 (2005).

5 See Will Wilkinson, *In Pursuit of Happiness Research: Is It Reliable? What Does It Imply for Policy?*, 590 Policy Analysis (Cato, April 11, 2007).

6 William Pavot, *Further Validation of the Satisfaction with Life Scale: Evidence for the Convergence of Well-Being Measures*, 57 J. Pers. Assessment 149 (1991); Jonathan Shedler, Martin Mayman, & Monica Manis, *The Illusion of Mental Health*, 48 Am. Psych. 1117 (1993). See generally, Robert H. Frank, Does Absolute Income Matter, in Economics and Happiness: Framing the Analysis 65–66 (Luigino Bruni & Pier Luigi Porta eds.) (Oxford: Oxford U.P., 2005).

7 See generally Bruno S. Frey, Happiness: A Revolution in Economics ch. 2, (Cambridge: MIT Press, 2008).

8 Frey & Stutzer, Happiness and Economics; Richard A. Easterlin, *Income and Happiness: Towards a Unified Theory*, 111 Econ. J. 465 (2001).

9 Ed Diener, Marissa Diener, & Carol Diener, *Factors Predicting the Subjective Well-being of Nations*, 69 J. Personality & Soc. Pscyh. 851 (1995); Frey & Stutzer, Happiness and Economics at 19.

10 Diener, Diener, & Diener, Factors Predicting the Subjective Well-being of Nations. But see Richard Layard, *Rethinking Public Economics*, in Bruni and Porta 147, 149. The correlation between wealth and happiness is not linear and declines as income increases as predicted by economic theories of diminishing marginal utility. Frey, Happiness at 29.

11 The best evidence to date finds that lottery winners do experience an increase in happiness. Jonathan Gardner & Andrew J. Oswald, Does Money Buy Happiness: A Longitudinal Study Using Data from Windfalls (Coventry: Warwick University, 2001, mimeo); J. Garner & A. Oswald, *Money and Mental Well-Being: A Longitudinal Study of Medium-Sized Lottery Wins*, 26 J. Health Econ. 49 (2007). See Frey, Happiness at 30.

12 For a review of the literature, see Daniel Kahneman, *Objective Happiness*, in Well-Being: The Foundations of Hedonic Psychology 3 (Daniel Kahneman, Ed Diener, & Norbert Schwarz eds.) (New York: Russell Sage, 2003).

13 Barry Schwartz, The Paradox of Choice: Why More Is Less (New York: Harper & Collins, 2004); Robert E. Lane. The Loss of Happiness in Market Democracies (New Haven: Yale U.P., 2000); Bruno Frey & Alois Stutzer, *What Can Economists Learn from Happiness Research*, 40 J. Econ. Lit. 402 (2002); but see Rafael Di Tella & Robert MacCulloch, *Gross National Happiness as an Answer to the Eastelin Paradox?*, 86 J. Devel. Econ. 22 (2008) (biggest contributor to happiness in a 1975–97 sample was the increase in income).

14 Jan Ott, *Did the Market Depress Happiness in the U.S.?*, 2 J. Happiness Studies 433 (2001).

15 David Lykken & Auke Tellegen, *Happiness is a Stochastic Phenomenon*, 7 Psych. Sc. 186, 189 (1966).

16 David Lykken, Happiness: The Nature and Nurture of Joy and Contentment (New York: St. Martin's Press, 2000).

17 Richard Easterlin, *Explaining Happiness*, 100 Proc. Nat'l Academy Sc. 11176 (2003).

18 Tibor Scitovsky, The Joyless Economy: An Inquiry into Human Satisfaction and Consumer Dissatisfaction (New York: Oxford U.P., 1976).

19 Lane, The Loss of Happiness in Market Democracies at 8–9.

20 Sara J. Solnick & David Hemenway, *Is More Always Better?, A Survey on Positional Concerns*, 37 J. Econ. Beh. & Org. 373 (1998).

21 Sentences et Maximes Morales, no. 576.

22 Tertullian, *Of Spectacles*, in I Translations of the Writings of the Fathers: The Writings of Tertullian 8–35 (Alexander Roberts & James Donaldson, eds.) (Edinburgh: Clark, 1869).

23 Robert Frank, Luxury Fever: Why Money Fails To Satisfy in an Era of Excess (New York: Free Press, 1999).

24 Richard Laylard, Happiness: Lessons from a New Science 228 (New York: Penguin, 2005).

25 Richard A. Easterlin, *Building a Better Theory of Well-Being*, in Bruni & Porta 29, 31–31. See also Thomas Mehnert, Herbert H. Kraus, Rosemary Nadler, & Mary Boyd, *Correlates of Life Satisfaction for Those with Disabling Conditions*, 35 Rehabilitative Psych. 1 (1990).

26 Easterlin, *Building a Better Theory of Well-Being* 29, 46 at Table 1.7 (1).

27 On married vs. nonmarried, see Arthur C. Brooks, Gross National Happiness 60–65 (New York: Basic, 2008); on religious vs. nonreligious, see Brooks, *id.* at 41–55; on charitable vs. noncharitable, see Brooks, *id.* at 175–92.

28 Heather P. Lacey, Dylan M. Smith, & Peter A. Ubel, *Hope To Die Before I Get Old: Mispredicting Happiness Across the Adult Lifespan*, 7 J. Happiness Stud. 167 (2006). See generally Michael Argyle, *Causes and Correlates of Happiness*, in Kahneman, Diener & Schwartz, Well-Being at 353.

29 Gary S. Becker & Kevin Murphy, Social Economics: Market Behavior in a Social Environment 124 (Cambridge: Harvard U.P., 2000).

30 Edward C. Banfield, The Moral Basis of a Backward Society 116 (Glencoe, IL: Free Press, 1958).

31 Max Weber, The Protestant Ethic and the Spirit of Capitalism 57 (trans. Talcott Parsons) (New York: Scribner's, 1958).

32 Diener, Diener, & Diener, Factors Predicting the Subjective Well-being of Nations.

33 *Id.*

34 Ruut Veenhoven, *Wellbeing in the Welfare State*, 2 J. Comp. Policy Anal. 91 (2000); Wim Kalmijn & Ruut Veenhoven, *Measuring Inequality of Happiness in Nations: In Search for Proper Statistics*, 6 J. Happiness Stud. 357 (2005). But see Karen E. Dynan & Enrichetta Ravina, *Increasing Income Inequality, External Habits, and Self-Reported Happiness*, 97 Am. Econ. Rev. P. & P. (May 2007) (people's happiness levels depends in part on how well their group is doing relative to average incomes in their area).

35 Ruut Veenhoven, *Freedom and Happiness: A Comparative Study of Forty-four Nations in the Early 1990s*, in Culture and Subjective Well-Being 257 (Ed Diener & Eunkook Suh eds.) (Cambridge: MIT Press, 2000).

36 Carol Graham & Stephan Pettinato, *Happiness, Markets, and Democracy: Latin America in Comparative Perspective*, 2 J. Happiness Studies 237 (2001). For a review of the strong correlation between happiness levels at the national level and democratic institutions, see Frey, Happiness at ch. 6.

37 Ellen J. Langer & Judith Rodin, *The Effects of Choice and Enhanced Personal Responsibility for the Aged*, 34 J. Personality and Soc. Psych. 191 (1976).

38 Arthur C. Brooks, Who Really Cares: The Surprising Truth about Compassionate Conservatism 120–21 (New York: Basic, 2006).

39 Seymour Martin Lipset & Gary Marks, It Didn't Happen Here: Why Socialism Failed in the United States (New York: W.W. Norton, 2001). See Frey, Happiness at 57–58.

40 Carol D. Ryff, *Happiness is Everything, Or Is It? Explorations of the Meaning of Psychological Well-Being*, 57 J. Personality and Soc. Psych. 1069 (1989); Carol D. Ryff & Corey L.M. Keyes, The Structure of Psychological Well-Being Revisited, 69 J. Personality and Soc. Psych. 719 (1995).

41 *Supra* note 23.

42 C.S. Lewis, Surprised by Joy 18 (San Diego: Harcourt, 1955).

43 Charles Baudelaire, II Œuvres 233 (Paris: Pléiade, 1976).

44 Rudolph Otto, The Idea of the Holy 12–13 (London: Oxford U.P., 1958).

45 Frey & Stutzer at 59–60.

Ⅶ Chapter 7 Endogenous Preferences

1 Cass R. Sunstein, *On the Expressive Function of Law*, 144 U. Pa. L. Rev. 2021 (1996).

2 R. v. Drybones, [1970] S.C.R. 282.

3 Human Rights, Citizenship and Multiculturalism Act, R.S.A. Chapter H-14.

4 Mark Steyn, *It's all very odd, 'that's for sure,'* Macleans, January 17, 2008.

5 Yurchak v. Frank Cairo Enterprises Ltd. (July 5, 2006).

6 Halter v. Ceda-Reactor Limited (May 16, 2005).

7 Mill, On Liberty at 80.

8 *Id.* at 67, 58, 56.

9 Gallup poll quoted in Eric J. Johnson & Daniel G. Goldstein, *Do Defaults Save Lives?*, 302 Science 1338 (2003).

10 Brigette Madrian & Dennis Shea, *The Power of Suggestion: Inertia in 401(k) Participation and Savings Behavior*, 116 Q.J. Econ. 1149 (2001).

11 Eric Johnson, Steven Bellman, & Gerald L. Lohse, *Defaults, Framing and Privacy: Why Opting In-Opting Out*, 13 Marketing Letters 5 (2002).

12 Eric J. Johnson, J. Hershey, J. Meszaros, & H. Kunreuther, *Framing, Probability Distortions, and Insurance Decisions*, 7 J. Risk & Uncertainty 35 (1993).

13 Dan Ariely, George Lowenstein, & Drazen Prelec, *Tom Sawyer and the Construction of Value*, 60 J. Econ. Beh. & Org. 1 (2006).

14 Timothy D. Wilson & Jonathan W. Schooler, *Thinking Too Much: Introspection Can Reduce the Quality of Preferences and Decisions*, 60 J. Personality and Soc. Psych. 181 (1991).

15 Cass R. Sunstein & Richard H. Thaler, *Libertarian Paternalism is Not an Oxymoron*, 70 U. Chi. L. Rev. 1159 (2003); Richard H. Thaler & Cass R. Sunstein, Nudge: Improving Decisions About Health, Wealth, and Happiness (New Haven: Yale U.P., 2008). See also Colin Camerer, Samuel Issacharoff, George Loewenstein, Ted O'Donoghue, & Matthew Rabin, *Regulation for Conservatives: Behavioral Economics and the Case for Asymmetric Paternalism*, 151 U. Pa. L. Rev. 1211 (2003).

16 See Gregory Mitchell, *Libertarian Paternalism Is an Oxymoron*, 99 Nw. U. L. Rev. 1245 (2005); Christine Jolls & Cass R. Sunstein, Debiasing through Law, 35 J. Legal Stud. 199 (2006).

17 James J. Choi, David Laibson, Brigitte Madrian, & Andrew Metrick, *Optimal Defaults and Active Decisions*, NBER Working Paper No. 11074 (January 2005).

18 Payne v. Western & Atlantic Railroad, 81 Tenn. 507, 518 (1884), overruled on other grounds, Hutton v. Watters, 132 Tenn. 527, 179 S.W. 134 (1915). See generally, Richard A. Epstein, *In Defense of the Contract at Will*, 51 U. Chi. L. Rev. 947 (1984).

19 James N. Dertouzos & Lynn A. Karoly, *Employment Effects of Worker Protection: Evidence from the United States*, 23 Cornell Intern. and Ind. and Labor Rel. Rep. (Ithaca, N.Y.: ILR Press, 1993); but see T.J. Miles, *Common Law Exceptions to Employment at Will and U.S. Labor Markets*, 16 J. L., Econ. & Org. 74 (1998).

20 David H. Autor, *Outsourcing at Will: Unjust Dismissal Doctrine and the Growth of Temporary Help Employment*, NBER Working Paper No. W7557 (February 2000).

21 Margaret F. Brinig & F.H. Buckley, *No-fault Laws and At-fault People*, 18 Int. Rev. Law & Econ. 325 (1998).

22 Paul R. Amato, Laura S. Loomis, & Alan Booth, *Parental Divorce, Marital Conflict, and Offspring Well-being during Early Childhood*, 73 Social Forces 895 (1995).

23 A point conceded by Thaler & Sunstein in Nudge at 199 ff.

24 George Loewenstein & Ted O'Donoghue, *"We Can Do This the Easy Way or the Hard Way": Negative Emotions, Self Regulation, and the Law*, 73 U. Chi. L. Rev. 183 (2006).

25 Edward L. Glaeser, Paternalism and Psychology, 73 U. Chi. L. Rev. 133 (2006).

🎜 Chapter 8 Private Perfectionism

1 For recent statements of perfectionism, see Robert P. George, Making Men Moral (Oxford: Clarendon, 1993); Thomas Hurka, Perfectionism (New York: Oxford U.P., 1993); George Sher, Beyond Neutrality.

2 Oliver Wendell Holmes, Jr., *The Path of the Law*, 10 Harv. L. Rev. 457, 459 (1897).

3 The most prominent modern neutralists are John Rawls, Robert Nozick, and Ronald Dworkin. See John Rawls, A Theory of Justice 94 (Cambridge: Harvard U.P., 1971); Robert Nozick, Anarchy, State, and Utopia (New York: Basic Books, 1974); Ronald Dworkin, *Liberalism*, in A Matter of Principle 196 (Cambridge: Harvard U.P., 1985).

4 Steven Wall, Liberalism, Perfectionism and Restraint ch. 4 (Cambridge: Cambridge U.P., 1998); Steven Wall, *The Structure of Perfectionist Toleration*, in Perfectionism and Neutrality (Steven Wall & George Klosko eds.) (Cambridge: Cambridge U.P., 2003).

5 Aristotle, Politics iii.5.1280^b (trans. Stephen Everson) (Cambridge: Cambridge U.P., 1996).

6 Benjamin Constant, *The Liberty of the Ancients Compared with that of the Moderns*, in Constant: Political Writings 309 (Cambridge: Cambridge U.P., 1998).

7 Dworkin, A Matter of Principle at 191–92.

8 Mill, On Liberty at 81.

9 *Id.* at 74.

10 Henri Bergson, Le rire (Paris: P.U.F., 1940).

11 Robert Putnam, Bowling Alone (New York: Simon & Schuster, 2001); Alan Ehrenhalt, The Lost City: The Forgotten Virtues of Community in America (New York: Basic Books, 1996).

12 Alexis de Tocqueville, Democracy in America 2, 114 (New York: Vintage, 1990).

13 For this criticism of autonomy-based liberalism, see John Gray, Isaiah Berlin ch. 6 (Princeton: Princeton U.P., 1996).

14 Jean-Jacques Rousseau, *The Social Contract*, in The Social Contract 167, 184 (Ernest Barker ed.) (Oxford: Oxford U.P., 1960).

15 Joseph Raz, The Morality of Freedom 420–23 (Oxford: Clarendon, 1986).

16 Mill, On Liberty at 56.

17 Will Kymlicka, Liberalism, Community, and Culture 12 (Oxford: Oxford U.P., 1989).

18 Robert F. George, Making Men Moral 37 (Oxford: Clarendon, 1993).

19 Mill, On Liberty at 9.

20 *Id.* at 99–100.

21 Sher, Beyond Neutrality at 61 ff.

22 *Id.* at 63.

23 Michael Oakeshott, *Rationalism in Politics*, in Rationalism in Politics and Other Essays 5, 11–17 (Michael Oakeshott, ed.) (Indianapolis: Liberty Fund, 1991).

24 David Hume, *Idea of a Perfect Commonwealth*, in Essays, Moral, Political, and Literary 512, 514 (Eugene F. Miller, ed.) (Indianapolis: Liberty Fund, 1987).

25 Galston, Liberalism Pluralism at 26.

26 Boy Scouts of America v. Dale, 120 S. Ct. 2446 (2000).

27 About 40% of Americans were born in another state than the one they live in. Kristin A. Hansen, 1990 Selected Place of Birth and Migration Statistics for States, Bureau of the Census CPH-L-121, at Table 1. Another 10% are foreign born.

28 Charles M. Tiebout, *A Pure Theory of Local Expenditures*, 64 J. Pol. Econ. 416 (1956).

29 Gregory v. Ashcroft, 111 S. Ct. 2395, 2399 (1991). See further Albert Breton, The Economic Theory of Representative Government 114 (Toronto: U. of Toronto P., 1974).

𝍦 Chapter 9 Social Perfectionism

1 Ronald Coase, *The Problem of Social Cost*, 3 J. Law & Econ. 1 (1960).

2 Charles Taylor, *Atomism,* in Philosophy and the Human Sciences: Philosophical Papers 207 (Charles Taylor, ed.) (Cambridge: Cambridge U.P., 1985).

3 Walter Berns, *Pornography vs. Democracy: The Case for Censorship*, 22 Pub. Interest 19–20 (1971).

4 Richard Arneson, *The Principle of Fairness and Free-Rider Problems,* 92 Ethics 616, 621 (1982).

5 Mill, On Liberty at 79.

6 *Id.* at 10.

7 *Id.* at 80.

8 *Id.* at 87.

9 *Id.* at 74.

10 Bowers v. Hardwick, 478 U.S. 186 (1986).

11 Lawrence v. Texas, 539 U.S. 558 (2003).

12 Report of the Committee on Homosexual Offences and Prostitution para. 257, Cmd. 247 (1957).

13 Patrick Devlin, The Enforcement of Morals; H.L.A. Hart, Law, Liberty, and Morality (London, Oxford U.P., 1962).

14 Devlin, The Enforcement of Morals at 111.

15 Hart at 29, 50–52.

16 See David Popenoe, Life Without Father 52–78 (Cambridge: Harvard U.P. 1999); Sara McLanahan & Irwin Garfinkel, *Single Mothers, the Underclass, and Social Policy,* 501 Annals, AAPSS 92, 98–99 (1989); Irwin Garfinkel & Sara S. McLanahan, Single Mothers and Their Children: A New American Dilemma (Washington, D.C.: Urban Institute, 1986).

17 Devlin, The Enforcement of Morals at 17.

18 *Id.* at 16.

19 See Robert C. Solomon, *The Virtues of a Passionate Life: Erotic Love and 'The Will to Power,'* in Virtue and Vice 91 (Ellen Frankel Paul, Fred D. Miller, & Jeffrey Paul, eds.) (Cambridge: Cambridge, 1998); Robert C. Solomon, The Joy of Philosophy: Thinking Thin *versus* the Passionate Life 65 ff. (New York: Oxford U.P., 1999).

20 James Fitzjames Stephen, Liberty, Equality, Fraternity 13 (Indianapolis: Liberty Fund, 1993).

21 Lionel Trilling, The Middle of the Journey 298 (New York: Charles Scribner, 1975).

22 Leon R. Kass, *The Wisdom of Repugnance*, in The Ethics of Human Cloning 3, 18 (Leon R. Kass & James Q. Wilson eds.) (Washington, D.C.: AEI Press, 1998).

23 Dworkin, A Matter of Principle at 191–92; Ronald Dworkin, Life's Dominion: An Argument about Abortion, Euthanasia, and Individual Freedom 161–67 (New York: Knopf, 1993).

24 Robert George and Christopher Wolfe, *Introduction*, in Natural Law and Public Reason 2 (Washington, D.C.: Georgetown University Press, 2000).

25 Ronald Dworkin, Is Democracy Possible Here? Principles for a New Political Debate 65 (Princeton: Princeton U.P., 2006).

26 George Orwell, *Wells, Hitler and the World State*, in The Penguin Essays of George Orwell 194, 196 (Penguin Books, 1984).

27 John Rawls, Political Liberalism 47 (New York: Columbia U.P., 1993).

28 *Id.* at 215.

29 John Dunn, The Political Thought of John Locke (Cambridge: Cambridge U.P., 1968); Jeremy Waldron, God, Locke and Equality: Christian Foundations of Locke's Political Thought (Cambridge: Cambridge U.P., 2002); Hugh Heclo, *Christianity and Democracy in America,* in Christianity and Democracy in America (Cambridge: Harvard U.P., 2007). For arguments that the Founders were influenced by their religious beliefs, see Daniel Dreisbach, Thomas Jefferson and the Wall of Separation between Church and State (New York: NYU Press, 2003); Philip Hamburger, Separation of Church and State (Cambridge: Harvard U.P., 2004). Nonreligious explanations for equality rights, notably those suggested by John Rawls, have also been advanced, but I need not enquire which theory is more persuasive.

🎔 Chapter 10 An Extension: Nationalism

1 The term is Yael Tamir's. See Yael Tamir, Liberal Nationalism (Princeton: Princeton U.P., 1993).

2 Michael Lind, The Next American Nation: The New Nationalism and the Fourth American Revolution 6 (New York: Free Press, 1996).

3 Pauline Maier, American Scripture: Making the Declaration of Independence (New York: Knopf, 1997).

4 Ernest Gellner, Nationalism 74 (New York: NYU Press, 1997).

5 Hans Kohn, American Nationalism: An Interpretive Essay 8 (New York: Macmillan, 1957) See also Yehoshua Arieli, Individualism and Nationalism in American Ideology 17–24 (1966); Michael Kammen, A Machine that Would Go of Itself: The Constitution in American Culture (New York: Knopf, 1986).

6 Robert Penn Warren, The Legacy of the Civil War: Meditations on the Centennial 78 (Lincoln: U. of Nebraska P., 1961).

7 Wendell L. Willkie, One World 215–16 (New York: Simon and Schuster, 1943).

8 Ernest C. Ladd, The Ladd Report 149–51 (New York: Free Press, 1999).

9 Charles L. Black, Jr., A New Birth of Freedom: Human Rights, Named and Unnamed 156, 1 (New Haven: Yale U.P., 1997).

10 William Godwin, Enquiry Concerning Political Justice, Book 2, Chapter 2 at http://www.efm.bris.ac.uk/het/godwin/pj.htm.

11 Thomas L. Friedman, The Lexus and the Olive Tree: Understanding Globalization (New York: Farrar, Straus and Giroux, 2000).

12 Robert Kagan, Dangerous Nation: America's Foreign Policy from Its Earliest Days to the Dawn of the Twentieth Century (New York: Vintage, 2007). As for the Iraq War, Kagan's point would apply to those who believed we were bringing democracy to the Arab world but not to those who believed that the war was fought for self-protection.

13 Boumedienne v. Bush, 553 U.S. (2008).

14 Robert E. Goodin & Philip Pettit, Introduction, in A Companion to Contemporary Political Philosophy 1, 3 (Oxford: Blackwell, 1993).

15 Michael Walzer defends this understanding of fidelity to national rights in Spheres of Justice: A Defense of Pluralism and Equality 313–14 (New York: Basic Books, 1983).

16 Ernest Gellner, Nations and Nationalism 18 (Ithaca: Cornell U.P., 1983).

17 Will Kymlicka, Liberalism, Community and Culture (New York: Oxford U.P., 1989).

18 Peter Brimelow, Alien Nation: Common Sense about America's Immigration Disaster (New York: Random House, 1995). Though the prescription might vary, the desire to preserve America's cultural heritage as the cement of national unity cuts across traditional political lines. Arthur M. Schlesinger Jr., The Disuniting of America: Reflections on a Multicultural Society (New York: W.W. Norton, 1998).

19 Walzer, Spheres of Justice at 40. I gloss over the fact that this kind of nationalism excluded Native- and African-Americans and that each new wave of immigrants aroused nativist fears about whether they could be assimilated.

20 Letter, John Adams to Abigail Adams, July 3, 1776, in The American Revolution: Writings from the War of Independence 126, 127 (New York: Library of America, 2001).

21 Newdow v. United States Congress, 542 U.S. 1 (2004).

22 Richard A. Posner, Not a Suicide Pact: The Constitution in a Time of National Emergency (Oxford: Oxford U.P., 2006). "Like any brittle thing, a Constitution that will not bend will break." Id. at 1. It is too early to say how the assertion of judicial competence in Boumedienne, supra note 13, will change this, but it is not irrelevant that that decision came almost seven years after 9–11. Plainly, the Court felt that a national emergency cannot last forever.

23 17 F. Cas. 144 (1861).

24 Special Message to Congress, in Lincoln: Speeches and Writings 1859–1865 246, 253 (New York: Library of America, 1989).

25 Korematsu v. United States, 323 U.S. 214 (1944).

26 Kennedy v. Mendoza-Martinez, 372 U.S. 144, 159 (1963).

27 319 U.S. 624 (1943).

28 Eric Rasmusen, The Economics of Desecration: Flag Burning and Related Activities, 27 J. Legal Stud. 245 (1998).

29 491 U.S. 397 (1989).

30 Canadian Charter of Rights and Freedoms, s. 1, Constitution Act, S. Can. 1982, enacted as Canada Act, 1982, 31 Eliz. II, c. 11 (U.K.).

31 Frederick Jackson Turner, The Frontier in American History (Mineola, N.Y.: Dover, 1996).

32 See Albert Breton & Anthony Scott, The Economic Constitution of Federal States 37–39 (Toronto: U. of Toronto P., 1978).

33 Lincoln: Speeches and Writings 1832–1858 360, April 24, 1855 (New York: Library of America, 1989). Lincoln had perhaps forgotten a contemporaneous letter he wrote to Speed's wife in which he described the condition of the slaves in very different terms. *Id.* at 74. The Lincoln we admire was the later Lincoln.

34 Jeremy Waldron, The Dignity of Legislation (Cambridge: Cambridge U.P., 1999).

35 Charles Taylor, *Living with Difference*, in Debating Democracy's Discontent: Essays on American Politics, Law, and Public Philosophy 212, 216 (Anita L. Allen & Milton C. Reagan eds.) (New York: Oxford U.P., 1998).

Index